M.R. Haberfeld • Curtis A. Clarke
Dale L. Sheehan

Editors

Police Organization and Training

Innovations in Research and Practice

 Springer

D0310224

Editors
M.R. Haberfeld
John Jay College of Criminal Justice
New York, NY, USA
mhaberfeld@jjay.cuny.edu

Curtis A. Clarke
Alberta Solicitor General Staff College
Edmonton, AB, Canada
curtis.clarke@gov.ab.ca

Dale L. Sheehan
INTERPOL
Police Training and Development
Lyon, France
D.Sheehan@interpol.int

ISBN 978-1-4614-0744-7   e-ISBN 978-1-4614-0745-4
DOI 10.1007/978-1-4614-0745-4
Springer New York Dordrecht Heidelberg London

Library of Congress Control Number: 2011936013

© Springer Science+Business Media, LLC 2012
All rights reserved. This work may not be translated or copied in whole or in part without the written permission of the publisher (Springer Science+Business Media, LLC, 233 Spring Street, New York, NY 10013, USA), except for brief excerpts in connection with reviews or scholarly analysis. Use in connection with any form of information storage and retrieval, electronic adaptation, computer software, or by similar or dissimilar methodology now known or hereafter developed is forbidden.
The use in this publication of trade names, trademarks, service marks, and similar terms, even if they are not identified as such, is not to be taken as an expression of opinion as to whether or not they are subject to proprietary rights.

Printed on acid-free paper

Springer is part of Springer Science+Business Media (www.springer.com)

To my daughters, Nellie and Mia and
all those cops who make this world
a safer place.

Maria (Maki) Haberfeld

To Lois, Noah and Alec who make me
smile and to the SGPS Staff College team
who continue to inspire me.

Curtis A. Clarke

To my mother Marilyn and father Doug
for their unconditional love and support.

Dale L. Sheehan

Foreword

Until late in the twentieth century, policing was regarded primarily as a local domestic issue. Today, policing is thought of as embracing an entire nation's security. The terrorist attacks of September 11, 2001 will forever be credited for making the twenty-first century one where policing would visibly link the security of localities to that of nations and vice versa. As a result of this and subsequent terrorist attacks, now police, law enforcement investigators and prosecutors routinely work together to prevent and investigate transnational crimes with local targets. They launch collaborative international operations using joint investigation teams in order to keep both local communities and nations safe from transnational criminals. As law enforcement's need to work, to share information and to cooperate internationally has increased, the importance of the world's largest international police organization, INTERPOL, has taken on greater importance to bring together best practices of member countries' police forces.

Policing in the twenty-first century is an extraordinary challenge. Front line police officers who had been trained on domestic law are now routinely confronting situations where they encounter individuals who are non-nationals, who are under investigation in more than one country, who conduct criminal activities in multiple countries and who carry identity and other documents issued by several countries. To confront these challenges, the police officer of the twenty-first century needs not only to be equipped differently; they must be thought of differently in terms of their needed education, training and support. They also need to be provided with a solid understanding of the "new" world in which they find themselves. Put another way, a new standard operating procedure must be created for how we develop what we call the "new international police officer."

A not so subtle strength of INTERPOL is its ability to recognize the inextricable link between what it takes for citizens to be safe in their local communities and in their countries as a whole. That link is the new international police officer whose training, development and certification will come about through a process that draws on the experience and expertise of police training professionals from INTERPOL's almost 200 member countries. The success of nations and the international community at keeping their citizens safe from crime in the twenty-first century will depend on the new international police officer being able to discharge his or her duties more effectively at the local and international level as a result of the concepts, approaches and practices that will be highlighted in the following chapters.

This book explores both theory and practice in an effort to determine how best to meet the challenges facing the new international police officer. It analyzes current training standards, research, professional development and specialized programs in police academies and academic institutions around the world. The knowledge and breadth of operational expertise highlighted throughout the following chapters will assist others in implementing successful approaches. The imperative is straightforward: If we want a safer world, we must invest in the training and development of the new international police officer whose responsibility it is and will be to protect us all from threats near and far alike.

Lyon, France   Ronald K. Noble
                                                                                     Secretary General
                                                                                     INTERPOL

Acknowledgments

Our acknowledgment for this book goes, first, to Welmoed Spahr who provided, as usual, the much needed support and conceptual recognition of the importance of the topics discussed by our contributors. To Katherine Chabalko, who replaced Welmoed as the editor responsible for this project and delivered the greatest administrative and much needed concrete guidance and finally, to all the additional employees of the Springer House, who continue to exemplify the best of the publishing world.

New York, NY   M.R. Haberfeld
Edmonton, AB   Curtis A. Clarke
Lyon, France   Dale L. Sheehan

Contents

Contributors

Otto Adang Politieacademie, Appeldoorn, Netherlands

Kim Armstrong Alberta Justice, Edmonton, AB, Canada

Valerie Atkins Federal Law Enforcement Training Center, Glynco, GA, USA

Andrew Carpenter Department of Peacekeeping Operations, Office of Rule of Law and Security Institutions, New York, NY, USA

K.C. Cheung Hong Kong Police College, Hong Kong, People's Republic of China

Curtis A. Clarke Alberta Solicitor General Staff College, Edmonton, AB, Canada

Carol Glasgow Edmonton Police Service, Edmonton, AB, Canada

M.R. Haberfeld John Jay College of Criminal Justice, New York, NY, USA

Christine Hudy Royal Canadian Mounted Police, Regina, SK, Canada

Gregory P. Krätzig Royal Canadian Mounted Police, Regina, SK, Canada

Cheryl Lepatski Edmonton Police Service, Edmonton, AB, Canada

Dan McGrory National Police Improvement Agency (NPIA), London, UK

William A. Norris Federal Law Enforcement Training Center, Glynco, GA, USA

Chris Sharwood-Smith UNAMID Police Training, New York, NY, USA

Dale L. Sheehan INTERPOL, Police Training and Development, Lyon, France

Pat Treacy National Police Improvement Agency (NPIA), London, UK

Norbert Unger Bundeskriminalamt (BKA), Wiesbaden, Hesse, Germany

Robert F. Vodde School of Criminal Justice and Legal Studies, Fairleigh Dickinson University, Madison, NJ, USA

Agostino von Hassell The Repton Group LLC, New York, NY, USA

Chapter 1
Introduction

M.R. Haberfeld

Police Organization and Training

Given the changing realm of policing and public security, training should be understood as both a strategic mechanism by which to pursue organizational performance and a core business tool for the delivery of efficient and effective public security. Officers who retain knowledge or skills and bring them back to their jobs can use them to enhance their performance, provide better service to the community, and do it in a safe and efficient manner.

The objective of this book is to provide a resource/forum for students, training practitioners, policymakers, and scholars where they can examine the latest concepts and practices in adult learning, program delivery, and curriculum development. The corresponding chapters highlight the insights, efforts, and experiences of training practitioners, academics, and policymakers from the United Kingdom, The Netherlands, USA, Canada, and other international experts. Key themes that are explored and touched upon are the investigative training and standards, competency-based curriculum, recruit training models, training governance, training related liability, academic/police collaboration, adult learning, leadership, and the alignment of training to performance measures. The goal behind this volume is to introduce the students and practitioners of policing to the newest trends in the profession from the standpoint of both organizational structure and the training innovations that are supported by proactive thinking.

The genesis of this book was derived from feedback obtained during the 17th International Police Organization (INTERPOL) training symposium held in Edmonton, AB, June 2009. Delegates (200) from 35 countries over a 3-day period addressed the need for greater research to be conducted regarding, problem-based

M.R. Haberfeld (✉)
John Jay College of Criminal Justice, New York, NY, USA
e-mail: mhaberfeld@jjay.cuny.edu

M.R. Haberfeld et al. (eds.), *Police Organization and Training: Innovations in Research and Practice*, DOI 10.1007/978-1-4614-0745-4_1,
© Springer Science+Business Media, LLC 2012

learning, adult learning approaches, specialized program development, and policy consistent with law enforcement training. In recognition of this identified need, this book highlights best practices associated with effective law enforcement training. Training that would be beneficial for all layers of policing ensures more equitable and effective service to the communities as well.

To understand why police organizations and police officers do what they do, one must take a very careful look at the ways these organizations are structured and how they prepare, or do not prepare, their personnel to conduct and perform as members of the profession.

Policing is a pillar of democracy and effective policing will make this pillar stronger and more resistant to the changes and challenges facing law enforcement in the twenty-first century. Decades have passed since lack of skills or education was not seen as an impediment to becoming a police officer. Various accountability mechanisms have been put in place to assure that the organizational charts reflect the needs and the operational necessities of effective policing.

However, these have not been universal trends, and as this volume illustrates, despite decades of research on democratic policing that produced some valuable templates for what and how needs to be done in order to further this profession, not each and every country attained this level of desired professionalism.

Empirical research did not always move police profession toward progress. Police organizations, be it on a local or more global level, were and still are resistant to changes and innovations, and the political influence, on each and every aspect of the organizational development, from the appointment of its chief or commissioner to the ways officers are recruited, selected, and trained, leaves its imprint on the way changes are introduced and adopted – or not – by various law enforcement organizations around the world.

Finally, the omnipresent threat of lack of resources, which plaques police professions since its early beginnings, leaves much to be desired, as far as linear progress is concerned.

This been said, we would be remiss not to acknowledge that many good things are actually happening in the field of policing, both from the organizational and training standpoints. As the authors of various chapters in this volume point to, changes have been contemplated and implemented, starting with the conceptual thinking about the most appropriate methodology in which certain skills need to be delivered, through the use of technological and scientific innovations to the creation of new units, or at least acknowledgment that change needs to take place. Policing as a profession is moving forward and much can be done and actually is done to further its stand not only as a metaphor but also as a very much real pillar of a democratic society.

This volume represents a compilation of empirical research into various areas of police training and organizational structures. From the accounts of first-hand research conducted by some of the contributors, through secondary analysis of previously conducted studies to predictive policing approach which mandates proactive vision based on the lessons learned from the past, the analysis of the present, and prediction for the future, these chapters will afford the reader with knowledge and ideas that represent the cutting edge approach to police administration and training around the world. This approach should be used as a model for present and future thinking about police profession.

Organization of the Book

In Chap. 2, Clarke and Armstrong examine the function of training in reducing the risk of civil litigation and its more proactive role in broader risk mitigation. While each is linked via the shared concept of training, the expected outcomes are distinctly different. With respect to reducing the risk of litigation, the risk tends to be associated with a failure to train or negligence in adapting training needs to meet operational and legal requirements of policing. The authors argue that training should be woven into the operational model of the organization and garner the same strategic attention as any other facet of policing. It is not, as some would suggest, a necessary evil. While it does require strategic alignment with organizational outcomes, resources, logistical planning, and a cultural shift, there is little doubt of the long-term benefit. No agency can afford to sit back and ignore the risk of litigation and diminished public support due to ineffective training. If an agency is to be successful, it must attune the training needs to the changing realities and practicalities of police work. Training represents the mandatory first step in legitimization of police profession and as such validates the investment in police organization from the societal standpoint.

In Chap. 3, Vodde opens the discourse on how to deliver police training in a democratic society. While the traditional, pedagogical, military model of basic police training may have at one time served the needs and interests of police and society, its applicability and efficacy has been called into question. An adult-based, andragogical instructional methodology has been viewed as a more effective means for training police recruits. It features a holistic, integrative, and collaborative approach to training with a strong emphasis on experiential learning. Andragogy is based on critical distinctions between how adults learn differently from children (pedagogy) and bases its practices on the needs, interests, readiness, orientation, experience, and motivation of the adult learner. Vodde's study outlines six thematic and categorical constructs for organizing, facilitating, and assessing the process of basic police training.

Chapter 4, written by Atkins and Norris, describes the transformation that the Federal Law Enforcement Training Center (FLETC) in United States has undergone in its effort to incorporate emergent training theories and technologies. The reengineering, which began in 2004 with the creation of a new Directorate and Division, was tasked with guiding "innovative" training. This new Division oversees and implements a process of continuous review and an ongoing analysis of training techniques. The chapter explores how the integration of technology and simulation has both been a response to the research findings and transformed training at FLETC and highlights the importance of research and an evidence-based response to training.

Krätzig and Hudy, in Chap. 5, describe simulation research technology approach used by the Royal Canadian Mounted Police (RCMP), coupled with the educational design considerations, that has resulted in the successful integration of driving simulators into a police driver training program. Although the RCMP's philosophy to simulator-based technology is not to replace one training tool with another, simulators will be incorporated into the training program to augment and enhance existing training practices. As evidenced through the new program, the authors argue that cadets are graduating from the training academy better equipped to do their jobs. Using the resulting data from the current research phase of the simulator course-of-fire, the firearms program will be completely redesigned and simulators are expected to be a significant and integral part of the training program.

Chapter 6, written by Unger, provides an introduction to the process used in a joint Federation/Federal state initiative tasked with the redesign of specialized/advanced criminal investigation training in Germany. Guided by a working group representing 13 federal states, the Federal Police and the Federal Criminal Police Office (*Bundeskriminalamt*), the project's objective was to devise an advanced training model that would take into account the professional needs of police services, the requirement for uniform standards covering various criminal investigation working areas and phenomenal domains. The project provided a framework of agreed contents that had an impact on advanced training measures and standards. Additional benefit of the project created guidelines that were set within the modular structure that enabled similar configurations to be applied to tasks in other domains of police training.

Glasgow and Lepatski, in Chap. 7, examine recent challenges for police organizations in Alberta, Canada, and the educational response of the Investigative Skills Education Program (ISEP). ISEP program is discussed from multiple angels: adult learning theory and methodologies for both classroom and online education as well as the structure, content, research, validation, and pilot phases of the program. The future of competency-based educational program is analyzed based on the structure of ISEP which provides a responsive curriculum framework that is able to adapt and evolve to meet any needed changes.

Chapter 8, written by McGrory and Treacy, evaluate the British Association of Chief Police Officers (ACPO) and the Home Office initiative to create the Professionalising Investigation Programme (PIP) in 2004. The aim of PIP was to improve the professional competence of all police officers and staff whose roles involved conducting supervising or managing investigations. The intention was to embed a national process, which integrated underpinning knowledge and published guidance on the best practice and principles governing investigation, which included investigative interviewing. It has established a body of knowledge for investigative practice, adopted standards for investigation and interviewing as the benchmarks of competence, and aligned learning and development programs to the knowledge and standards and thus established a recognizable framework to professionalize investigation, which had been absent previously.

Cheung, in Chap. 9, discusses the ethical dimension of culture building in the Hong Kong Police Force. The Hong Kong Police Force has addressed the issues implicit in having three distinct generations represented in the same organization in an attempt to close generational gaps and prevent conflict. The Force's Values underpin the framework for addressing these issues. Police training now places new emphasis on attitudes and values in at least equal weight to the more traditional knowledge and skills. Through foundation and in-service training, integrated with career development strategies and other support structures, the Hong Kong Police Force attempts to influence the views and values of its officers. The strategy to draw together the generations into a common culture is built around the Force Values, producing a common culture in support of the police's core missions. This strategy of forging a unifying culture around its values provided a new impetus for impressing organizational norms.

In Chap. 10, Adang introduces a novel approach to deal with potentially dangerous situations and the vision for police education and training in The Netherlands. The author analyzes the specific ways in which officers approached potentially dangerous situations, followed by educational vision about situation-oriented use-of-force training with emphasis on the training tools that contribute to an effective transfer to professional practice. The need for a more practice and situation-oriented approach to testing was identified by the Dutch police, and competencies were formulated for officers dealing with (potentially) violent situations. These competences involve: problem-analytical, communication, operational effectiveness, motivational, and cooperative skills. In addition, the research program "managing dangerous situations" has been created with the specific purpose to study the interaction between police and civilians in a variety of potentially dangerous conflict situations.

Dale, in Chap. 11, examines the evolution of the INTERPOL and its strategic implementation of an international police training and development model. In 2010, Secretary General Noble was elected to serve a third term. With a new mandate, INTERPOL has entered an era of ambitious growth and support for the development of an INTERPOL Global Complex (IGC), to be constructed in Singapore and opened in 2014–2015. The center's mandate will focus upon capacity building, training, cyber crime, and advanced innovative methods for identification of crimes and criminals. In taking on this initiative, INTERPOL placed itself in a strategic and tactical position to enhance the delivery of its services. With an even stronger and enhanced organizational direction in the field of training and capacity building, INTERPOL extended its ability to form private and public sector partners and has made significant advances in the delivery of police training to member countries, partners, and its staff at the General Secretariat and regional offices. Dale posits that INTERPOL growth in the recent years renders it perfectly situated as a global hub for international police cooperation in police training.

Chapter 12, written by Carpenter and Sharwood-Smith, overviews international police keeping initiative and the ways they expanded dramatically in both function and responsibility as rapidly growing aspect of the United Nations peacekeeping operations; its role has become complex and essential to the UN mandate. To respond effectively to these changes and associated expectations, the Department of Peacekeeping Operations (DPO) continues to grapple with the importance of articulating and implementing a strategic training model. The authors highlight a number of the issues, objectives, and outcomes overseen by the UN Department of Peacekeeping Operations in its effort to address the need for standardized training and equitable program delivery and specialized skill development. Standardized UN FPU Pre-deployment Training Curriculum was created by the UN Police Division to be shared with all 192 UN Member States, the African Union, the European Union, as well as other regional or professional organizations. In addition to this initiative, the UN Police Division has further built upon the process used to develop the pre-deployment training courses and has established the concept of "Curriculum Development Groups" (CDGs), whereby, all UN Member States – as well as other regional organizations and professional bodies – are invited to nominate an expert and/or their existing training materials to contribute to the joint development of a specialized course designed especially to meet the requirements of the UN Police.

Finally, in Chap. 13, Haberfeld and von Hassell posit that maritime terrorism created a new law enforcement challenge that is yet to be met, and while addressing this hurdle, provides a natural transition from what has been done in the field of police administration and training into what needs to be done in the future. It is only natural to conclude this volume with a chapter dealing with the need for creation of a new organizational unit within local police departments around the world. Such unit, proposed to be called Joint Maritime Terrorism Task Force (JMTTF), would respond, on a local level, to the rapidly evolving terrorist tactic – maritime terrorism. Based on their research in a number of countries that battled the phenomenon of terrorism in urban environments for many decades, as well as other prior research on police trainings, the authors propose a more focused and specialized look at the state of police training in the counterterrorism area and address it from the perspective of police agencies facing yet another type of terrorist tactic, *maritime terrorism*, against which they need to prepare a pro-active response in the form of creation of new units, that need to be grounded in a legal response that will allow for new policies to either enhance the existing or create a new cooperation between the multitude of military and law enforcement agencies.

The Future of Police Training: Doing More with Less and Doing It Better

As the grim economic situation of 2009 and 2010 impacted upon many states and nation's budgets, police departments around the world are not immune from the dreadful concept of "doing more with less" as it permeates various governmental agencies. In the United States, similar to other countries hit by the recession problems, police departments experience the cuts almost on a daily basis. The budgets that are allocated by various municipalities and states look upon law enforcement organizations as fully capable of delivering the services they delivered routinely over the years, with the same effectiveness and professionalism albeit with less resources. Police training is usually the first one to be affected during financial duress, since it is somehow implied that police profession can continue to deliver the services in the most effective manner, regardless of the professional development, or lack of that its members receive.

This author identified in her previous writings, the concept of Pentagon of Police Leadership (Haberfeld, 2002, 2011). The term "Pentagon of Police Leadership" was introduced as a model to be emulated by police agencies in their attempt to maintain effective order within police organizations and outside in the community. The five prongs of the pentagon:

1. Recruitment
2. Selection
3. Training
4. Supervision
5. Discipline

Above represent the five approaches that police agencies need to look at, modify and customize in accordance with the principles of democratic policing. In order to ensure that an organization that derives its authority from the ability to use coercive force does not violate the rights and liberties of the citizens it polices, these five prongs need to be evaluated, re-evaluated, and adjusted on an ongoing basis in order to identify the errors, correct the deficiencies, and further democratic principles.

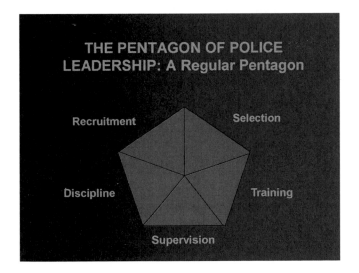

THE PENTAGON OF POLICE LEADERSHIP: A Regular Pentagon

Recruitment   Selection

Discipline   Training

Supervision

In the ideal world of police profession, the Pentagon of Police Leadership, would be composed of equal length prongs where each prong represents a substantial, and equally resource-loaded, approach to maintaining a professional organization.

However, in the case of political pressure to staff the academy class or to provide more officers on the street to give the public an impression that officers are present on the streets, the first two prongs are frequently shorthanded, thus the need to extend the prongs of supervision and discipline occurs (turning the supervision to more oppressive and the discipline to more severe) and a proper allocation to the prong representing training can mitigate the decline of a model democratic police organization. Turning the regular pentagon, in which all the prongs are even, to an irregular one where one or more prongs require more attention and, in police organizations, this could translate into a more oppressive work environment, is not something that law enforcement organization should strive for. Especially given the fact that the prongs that will be most extended will be the ones that deal with supervision and discipline.

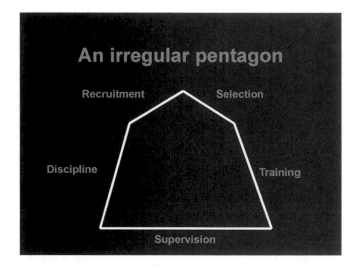

Given the traditional approach to training within police organizations, where under a financial duress, the first cuts are almost always directed at the training resources, it is imperative to find another way to maintain the level of training that is a necessary component of an effective and democratic policing and extend this prong far beyond the length of the ones that deal with supervision and discipline.

Such a solution can be possibly implemented by adopting the concept of "Meta-Leadership" that was originally developed by Marcus, Ashkenazi, Dorn, and Henderson (2009). The main concepts of Meta-Leadership refer to a style of leadership that challenges individuals to think and act cooperatively across organizations and sectors. Followers of this leadership theory develop ways to engage in interactions outside the scope of their traditional professional boundaries, providing inspiration, guidance, and momentum for a course of action that spans organizational lines.

Operating outside the traditional professional boundaries in providing adequate training for police organizations will indeed require a commitment from leaders across many sectors to contribute and guide the process but, at the same time, it will provide the collaborative activity that will improve the functioning and performance of any police department.

Following are some possible suggestions of "doing more with less and doing it better":

- Mandatory subscription to professional publications and journals will provide training tips perfectly suited for roll-call training sessions that can be delivered basically by any first line supervisor or any line officer – by taking turns.
- Join professional law enforcement training associations with periodical publications.
- Join local professional academic associations.
- "Adopt" a college – where collaboration with different departments can produce valuable new trends for police training and education.
- "Adopt" a professor/s – who will consider it their patriotic duty to share their academic knowledge with the local police forces in an attempt to enhance delivery of various police services.
- Provide the right environment: create a new concept "every officer – a training officer."

It is yet another challenge for police leaders to create a sound philosophical basis for the allocation of rewards and recognitions that will identify the officers who are leading the way in self-tutoring and sharing their knowledge with the colleague. Such creativity can be achieved by looking at the ideas inherent in the stewardship approach to leadership. Bowen (2000) identifies a number of concepts that might provide much guidance for police leaders buying into the idea of creating "each officer – a training officer" theme. The most important ones are treating employees as if they were partners with the leaders and a resource "on-loan" to the police organization.

If one of these valued employees will read this volume and share the knowledge gleaned from the pages with his/her colleagues and organizational leaders, then this act will truly exemplify the motto of "doing more with less and doing it better."

References

Bowen, R. B. (2000). *Recognizing and rewarding employees*. New York, NY: McGraw Hill.

Haberfeld, M. R. (2002, 2011). *Critical issues in police training*. Upper Saddle River, NJ: Prentice Hall.

Marcus, L. J., Ashkenazi, I., Dorn, B. C., & Henderson, J. M. (2009). The five dimensions of meta-leadership: National preparedness and the five dimensions on meta-leadership. Retrieved February 2, 2010, from http://www.metaleadershipsummit.org/leadership/practice/dimensions.aspx.

Chapter 2
Beyond Reproach: The Need for Effective and Responsive Training

Curtis A. Clarke and Kim Armstrong

Introduction

> The complex nature of the police occupation and dynamic changes that move through our society frequently make the job of policing extremely difficult and perhaps prone to civil litigation (Ross, 2000, p. 169).

In recent years there have been few professions or industries in which training and development have not been mentioned. Timely, relevant and effective training is a fundamental mechanism to prepare those involved in law enforcement to deal with the operational complexities of the modern world (HM Inspectorate of Constabulary, 1999). Marenin (2004) expanded upon the issue of occupational complexity by suggesting that police officers must continuously balance:

> every day, in every decision – legitimate yet conflicting values and rights: demands for effectiveness while still protecting individual rights, the maintenance of public order without unduly restricting liberty, the need to threaten or use force without deviating into abuse, being guided by law and professional expertise simultaneously (p. 108).

This occupational dynamic, coupled with organizational pressures to address stakeholder expectations of accountability, leadership, effectiveness, proactive service, morale, and liability, requires law enforcement organizations to be creative and engaged in continual reassessment. In order to do so, they can no longer rely on antiquated structural and philosophical approaches. One such shift places a greater onus upon training as a strategic mechanism by which to pursue organizational performance, effective service delivery, and risk mitigation. Here, training is no

C. Clarke (✉)
Alberta Solicitor General Staff College, Edmonton, AB, Canada
e-mail: curtis.clarke@gov.ab.ca

K. Armstrong
Alberta Justice, Edmonton, AB, Canada
e-mail: kim.armstrong@gov.ab.ca

M.R. Haberfeld et al. (eds.), *Police Organization and Training: Innovations in Research and Practice*, DOI 10.1007/978-1-4614-0745-4_2,
© Springer Science+Business Media, LLC 2012

longer considered in isolation to organizational change, but is inexorably tied to strategic and operational development. A further functional role associated with training is that of risk mitigation, more specifically, with respect to the risk of civil litigation. Scott (2005) aptly argues that any agency concerned with quality, productivity, liability, and morale must consider this training function as a critical and significant function.

In this changing, social, legal, and operational environment, training should be a strategic tool by which to address risk. Unfortunately, many agencies have been slow to embrace training in relation to risk management. As Scott (2005) argues, "too many wait to be sued or to be threatened with other court action before instituting preventive measures" (p. 2). Countering this trend will require those tasked with directing the development and delivery of training to view themselves as risk managers. They will also need to regard training as a means to an end and not, as has often been the case in the past, as an end in itself.

This chapter examines both the function of training in reducing the risk of civil litigation and its more proactive role in broader risk mitigation. While each is linked via the shared concept of training, the expected outcomes are distinctly different. With respect to reducing the risk of litigation, the risk tends to be associated with a failure to train or negligence in adapting training needs to meet operational and legal requirements of policing. Where training is viewed and understood as a critical aspect of risk management, it is considered a fundamental managerial responsibility and not simply a luxury or a knee jerk reaction to pending litigation (Ross, 2000).

Placing Training and Civil Litigation in Context

The question of whether there is a tie between policing and civil litigation is not an issue; in fact, increasing litigation is a reality confronting most police agencies (Archbold & Maguire, 2002; Ceyssens, 2004; Hughes, 2001; Ransley, Anderson, & Prenzier, 2007; Scott, 2005). What is of interest here is how training is aligned to the issue of civil litigation. Training and risk management are concepts that should be top of mind for today's police leaders. As Archbold and Maguire (2002) note, "police managers in some of the largest law enforcement agencies have begun to hire in-house risk managers and police legal advisors to help them review department training … in an effort to manage and prevent police officer exposure to liability" (p. 228).

Training's alignment to risk mitigation is further noted in an analysis of U.S. Chiefs of Police perceptions regarding civil liability: "participants reported that better training was the second most important strategy for preventing lawsuits" (Vaughn, Cooper, & Carmen, 2001, p. 20).

The value of training is additionally substantiated in a 2007 International Association of Chiefs of Police (IACP) survey that found training to be the top priority issue facing police organizations. It was also the issue with the most relative importance to organizational effectiveness and risk (Wellford, 2007). This is not to suggest that all civil litigation has its roots within the realm of training.[1] What it does highlight is that training is a realm that occupies both a point of concern and a potential solution with respect to the risk of litigation.

Civil litigation against police is often viewed as an important element of police accountability and stimulus for change. A cogent example of the interplay between litigation, training, renewed accountability, and managerial action can be noted in the analysis of training post *City of Canton v. Harris* (1989) decision. As noted by Alpert and Smith (1991) and Ross (2000), there was a dramatic increase in operational training and the strategic focus on training employed by police organizations post *Canton*. Although there is comparably less civil litigation against police officers and police chiefs in Canada than in the United States, it is unquestionably a growth area, and police executives need to be proactively involved in understanding risks and mitigating them where possible (Ceyssens, 2004).

The Landscape of Liability

On a daily basis, hundreds upon thousands of decisions are made by police officers on the front-line (whether to use force, when to use it, what force to use, and whether to charge, detain, or arrest) and within headquarters (how to train, equip, discipline, and supervise officers). Given the complex and dynamic nature of policing, combined with the frequent application of force and deprivation of liberties against citizens, and the highly visible nature of police work, there is little wonder why policing is a fertile environment for civil litigation. Ross (2000) aptly lays out this landscape of litigation in the following manner:

> First, the individual officer may be at risk of civil litigation for decisions he or she is frequently forced to make. Most civil suits arise when officers intentionally abuse their authority and, or, perform their duties in a negligent manner. The second level of exposure exists with police supervisors based on the notion that supervisors of the errant officer could have done something to prevent the misconduct (p. 169).

This awareness and recognition allow us to articulate points of departure for potential legal action. Ross (2000) goes on to suggest there are also central themes upon which litigation is based: policy, training, and supervision. In the specific context of impugned conduct and its relationship to training, Ryan (2007) argues that:

> Failure to train cases can be established in two ways. The first involves a lack of training in an area where there is a patently obvious need for training, for example an officer who is untrained in deadly force unreasonably shoots someone. The second method of establishing a failure to train by an agency is to establish a pattern of conduct by officers that would put the final policy maker on notice and the policymaker failed to respond with training (p. 2).

---

[1] The first Canadian case where the issue of negligent training was raised was *Johnson v. Adamson* (1981) 34 O.R. (2d) 236. In the United States, *the City of Canton v. Harris*, 489 U.S. 378 (1989) was the watershed case. Here the U.S. Supreme Court held that failing to train police officers may be the basis for managerial liability under Title 42 United States Code Section 1983.

The Issue of Supervision

Within the realm of liability, the torts of negligent supervision and negligent training are closely linked. The cause of action of negligent supervision stems from the principle that police officers owe a duty of care to people under their control. Supervisors do not have to actively participate in instances of officer negligence in order to be held liable. If the supervisor knew, or should have known, about a police officer's incompetence or lack of fitness for duty, they can be held liable. Here the notion of liability is based on the belief that a supervisor could and should have done something to prevent the misconduct. With increasing frequency, plaintiffs frame complaints against the police alleging the misconduct or resulting harm was a result of a failure to supervise and or a failure to train officers. To succeed, the plaintiff requires evidence that the supervisor (or agency) knew of a need to train or supervise an officer in a particular area and that the supervisor/agency made a deliberate or negligent choice not to take action (Grossman, 2003). A clear guideline as to when training is required is drawn from *Walker v. City of New York*, 974 F.2d 293(2d Cir., 1992):

> When policymakers and supervisors know to a moral certainty that officers will confront a particular situation and where the situation presents a difficult choice or there is a history of mishandling by employees and where the wrong choice frequently results in a deprivation of constitutional right (as cited in Ryan, 2007).

It is important to note that supervisors need not take an active role in the specific misconduct. If they were aware of or should have been aware of an officer's lack of training or incompetence and that these contributed to the officer's misconduct, then they may be held liable for abdicating/neglecting their supervisory responsibility. An example of this can be noted in *Clark v. Canada* (1994) 3 FC 323, where several RCMP supervisors were found negligent for failing to prevent inappropriate conduct by other officers toward a female constable. Often, in cases of sexual harassment, as was the situation in this particular case, employers are also criticized for having failed to provide adequate training to their employees on sexual harassment.

While the above section helps to guide a generic understanding of what might be the stimulus and or circumstances that underlie civil proceedings against an officer, a more accurate and detailed navigation of the legal landscape of police training requires an analysis of related case law, inquiry findings, and public commissions. Through analysis of current and developing case law that emanates from the courts and administrative tribunals that adjudicate on police misconduct, we refine and develop our understanding of expectations of service, responsibility, authority, and negligence.

Judicial Decisions and Commentary (Setting a Framework)

In Canada, there have been very few cases where the tort of negligent training proceeded to trial. In *Berntt v. Vancouver (City)* (1997) 4 WWR 505, the Court determined that the test as to the appropriate standard of care is what would be expected of a reasonable police force training a constable. The trial Judge in this case provided a useful example of the scrutiny with which the courts might examine an allegation of negligent training (Ceyssens, 2003). Justice Cohen stated:

> The allegation of negligence in relation to training and supervision requires the establishment of a duty of care, and a comparison of the defendants' conduct measured against the appropriate standard. The onus is on the plaintiff to establish all elements of the negligence alleged against the defendants. ... To succeed then against these defendants, the plaintiff must establish a duty of care, a breach of a standard of care, and he must prove that the negligence was the cause of his injuries (*Berntt v. Vancouver*, 1997, p. 140, 141).

In the United States, by contrast, this area of law is much more developed. In 1989, the United States Supreme Court decided *City of Canton v. Harris* (1989) and concluded that the failure to train officers could form the basis of managerial liability. In this case, the federal court concluded that liability should be predicated on a "deliberate indifference standard" (Grossman, 2003, p. 4). The standard requires evidence that an agency knew of a need to train or supervise in a particular topic but made a deliberate choice not to take action with respect to the identified need (Grossman, 2003). In summary, the *Harris* case set clear criteria by which a failure to train claim might proceed: (a) violation of a federally protected right, (b) inadequate training of employees, and (c) causation between the inadequate training and the plaintiffs injury. "It is only when these three factors converge that the governmental entity can be held liable for constitutional harm caused a citizen" (Savrin, 1999, p. 3).

Within the context of the above decisions, failure to train liability requires evidence that the police service was, or should have been, conscious of the need for a certain level of training and made a choice not to provide that level of training, or to provide inadequate training. Police services must pay particular attention to training officers in skills and competencies in high-risk functionalities that they engage in: criminal law, firearms, use of force, and emergency vehicle operation. Training should correspond directly with the tasks that officers routinely perform. The training does not have to be "perfect," but it should be consistent with the training offered by other police services of a similar size.

It should also be noted that the failure to train must be directly linked to the harm that the Plaintiff suffered. In the case *Johnson v. Adamson* (1981) 128 DLR (3d) 470, the Ontario Court of Appeal allowed a claim against the Toronto Police Service for negligent supervision and training of police officers. The issue focused on the fatal shooting of A. Johnson by a constable. One allegation was that the Chief knew or should have known of racist attitudes and racial provocations by Toronto police officers, leading to racial violence, and that he was negligent for failing to take steps through training and discipline to deal with the situation.

While the issue of training is not always the crux of a claim, it may feature prominently in the resolution of the issue or be considered a contributing factor in the inadequate service. In *Hill v. Hamilton-Wentworth Regional Police Services Board* (2007) 3 S.C.R. 129, the Supreme Court of Canada affirmed that the tort of negligent investigation exists in Canada. The majority held that police officers owe a duty of care to suspects and that their conduct during an investigation should be measured against the standard of how an officer in similar circumstances would have acted.

The Court further stated that the standard of care that is applied must recognize the existence of discretion in police investigations and that minor errors or errors of judgment will not breach the standard. Finally, the Plaintiff must show that they suffered damages that are causally connected to the breached standard of care. While this case does not relate directly to an issue of training, it highlighted the need for consistent and standardized practices. Moreover, it emphasized the reality that the complex investigative knowledge required by police officers continues to increase. Failure to provide adequate education continuously throughout the span of an officer's career may result in significant costs, both financial and otherwise, associated with inadequate investigations. Outcomes in these cases include the withdrawal or dismissal of charges, civil litigation, and complaints against the involved police officers.

In *Regina v. Clayton and Farmer* (2004) 194 C.C.C. (3d) 289, while not the focal aspect of the particular claim, the lack of training was highlighted as either a contributing factor or direct cause of concern and as such contributed to an acquittal. In the rendered Judgment, Chief Justice McMurtry, stated:

> The testimony of these officers strongly suggests that their police force has made no effort to embed the approach to the ancillary power doctrine adopted by the courts into police training. This systemic failure would suggest that the court must deliver its message in a more emphatic way. The exclusion of evidence may provide that added emphasis … The systematic failings that underlie the conduct of Officers Robson and Dickson make the infringement of the rights of Farmer and Clayton serious. Police training that leaves officers in the field unequipped to engage in the balancing process required by the ancillary power doctrine invites police officers to ignore individual rights whenever those rights get in the way of the execution of police duties. If the rights guaranteed by the Charter are to have real meaning and shape the interaction between the police and individuals, police forces must take those rights seriously. Officers must be trained to perform their duties in a manner that is consistent with those rights (*Regina v. Clayton and Farmer* (2004), p. 89, 90).

It is clear from Justice McMurtry's decision that the failure to educate officers in important legal developments poses significant risk. It has the potential to undermine the quality of service delivery, negatively affect individual rights, as well as damage the reputation of the constabulary generally. Taking a similar tone, in *R. v. Dornan* (2008), Justice Forestell, noted:

> In the case before me, the officers were properly asked about their source of a clearly mistaken belief in the state of the law. This is a critical area of inquiry in assessing the good faith of the officers on an individual level and on an institutional level. The inquiry in this case has disclosed improper training as a source for the mistake. Abella J. did not say, in *Clayton and Farmer*, that such evidence would never be relevant. In fact she said that police training is important (*R. v. Dornan* (2008) ON SC 40).

Justice Forestell went on to state:

> In the instant case, there is not a 'single misguided police officer' but three police officers and their supervisor who all believe, based on their training, that they have authority for an act that violates the constitutional rights of the Applicant. … On an institutional level, the improper training of the officers raises greater concerns for the administration of justice (*R. v. Dornan* (2008) on SC 40, p. 41, 43).

Similar concerns regarding improper or inadequate training had been drawn out in *R. v. D. (J.)* et al. (2007) ON CJ 154 and *R. v. N.M* (2007) CanLII 31570 ON SC. The outcome of these cases was the exclusion of evidence and dismissal of charges due to *Charter* infringement.

The concern in respect of ongoing training, exposure to changing legal principles, and the failure to prepare police officers for a changing law enforcement environment are also highly relevant to police governance boards and oversight agencies. For example, the issue of training and the need to effectively respond to a changing legal environment is succinctly noted in the following RCMP Public Complaints Commission excerpt:

> RCMP officers need to keep up to date on developments in criminal law, especially those that affect the use of police powers, acceptable methods of gathering evidence, and the rights of accused persons. In reviewing complaints, the Commission frequently concludes that the police officer in question was unaware of an important element of the law he or she was attempting to enforce. This shortcoming is not confined to junior officers of the Force; some supervisors have given unsound advice to police under their command because they failed to consider all relevant provisions of a law. The commission notes that policing is becoming more complex as case law increases the detail of the legal regime that governs the rights of the accused and the admissibility of evidence. The Commission is concerned that resources be committed so that RCMP officers may be provided with regular opportunities to train and, thus, keep pace with the growth in complexity (R.C.M.P. Public Complaints Commission, Annual Report, 1997–1998, p. 21).

Further guidance about the importance of training and more specifically, the recklessness of undercutting funding for police training, is aptly noted in recommendations forwarded in the 1996 *Bernardo Investigation Review*:

> The bottom line in any discussion about training be it for new recruits, senior officers or specialty squads is that you can never have enough. Uniform officers, criminal investigators and case managers cannot be skilled if they are not properly trained. Initial training, specialized training and ongoing training must be available. The tendency to cut training when restrictions are placed on the police budget must be re–examined, for it is often a question of pay now or pay later when it comes to the education and training of police officers. It is, to repeat, a form of institutional recklessness to reduce police training budgets below the essential requirements for good police work (Justice Archie Campbell, *Bernardo Investigation Review*, 1996, p. 315).

These are but a few examples of how and where training has been flagged. The concerns that continue to arise, either through case law or other mechanisms of oversight, suggest that the legal environment of policing is constantly changing and in order to mitigate the associated risk of inadequate training, agencies must provide a thorough regimen of training responsive to operational reviews, identified trends within professional standards, and other external pressures. Critics argue that there are vast areas of law (ones which continue to pose risks of litigation or other operational consequences) that are not adequately taught or absent from law enforcement curriculum. Ceyssens (2003) argues:

> Police are regularly criticized by the judiciary and oversight bodies for their failure to provide adequate legal training on an ongoing basis, and police require annual 'refresher' courses that address legislative and judicial developments that have occurred since the

previous such course, not only in criminal law but in other areas of the legal regulation of the police as well (p. 6).

Echoing Ceyssens (2003) argument, Kinnaird (2007) suggests "being constantly aware of new laws and legal procedures is of integral importance in the training process" (p. 205).

Exploring the Training Function

The breadth of knowledge an officer must draw upon in his/her career trajectory is neither static nor a matter of a simple data dump. It is much more than a shopping list of information to be drawn upon at a later date. Effective training is strategic, applied, evidence based, and aligned to the reality of the policing function. It should build an officer's capacity to address operational, social, and procedural changes, to assist them in knowing how to act and react to situations, to continuously learn and relearn. Training must be comprehensive and aligned to the particular function of policing; it should incorporate the individual and organizational competencies of policing. "Police training needs to address not only procedural rules and substantive laws, but also how to use them, when and how to avoid their use, and when and how to use force when force is appropriate" (Marenin, 2004, p. 109).

Development of the skill and knowledge that Marenin (2004) and others refer to requires a comprehensive framework, one that not only responds to the needs of various stakeholders but ensures that specific standards and competencies are connected. In 1999, the HM Inspectorate of Constabulary suggested that a comprehensive framework of training encompass the following components:

- Training needs of individuals, teams, and the organization are all effectively linked to one another
- All assessed training needs have relevance to the overall development of the organization in the short, medium, and long term
- Training needs have a direct relationship to improved police performance

Drawing from this framework, but expanding its strategic alignment, the UK Home Office set in motion, a national review of current and required competencies for policing. At the forefront of the Home Office's effort was the recognition that an organizational training strategy required a set of core principles by which police training/education would be guided. The Home Office (2003) principles included the following:

- The purpose of training is to help develop individuals for the purpose of improving performance, both individually and across organizations.
- Learning opportunities should be available continuously throughout a member's career.
- Competence should be the criterion by which people are assessed, not the length of time spent training.

- Appropriate learning opportunities should be properly resourced and available to all staff.
- Training/education programs should be delivered using a variety of methods, including distance learning, team and group learning, case studies, and scenarios as well as residential training.
- The organization has a responsibility for ensuring that staff are adequately trained to do their job and their performance assessed on a regular basis. Individuals also have responsibility for pursuing learning opportunities in order to maintain competence and improve performance.

A supplementary example of an organization's alignment between operating principles and strategic focus of training can be noted in the Ontario Provincial Police 2001 Education Development Initiative.

Operating Principles for Our Learning Organization

1. We will always ensure that our colleagues and partners understand the philosophy that learning is a personal, team, and organizational responsibility shared by all. It is not a course or program but a state-of-mind, a culture in which members of the organization carry out their daily activities.
2. We will focus our evaluation, assessment, and review on learning outcomes and not merely on the way programs, courses, and development are delivered. Quality learning outcomes will be our major business.
3. We will build teams in order to achieve our mandate and create our culture of learning. We will promote the problem-solving leadership model within our bureau and throughout the OPP.
4. We will continually listen to all of our constituents, both internal and external, in meeting our obligations as the service center for quality learning and innovation within the OPP.

While there is little contestation among policymakers, administrators, and police executive as to the value of articulating educational principles, sadly, the converse exists with respect to the operationalization of these sentiments. So often there is a disconnect between mission, the organization, and the training (Birzer, 2003, p. 34). The challenge for an organization exists in the translation of these broad principles into an applied model, one that coordinates functional needs with an effective learning pathway. In order to make this translation successful, police organizations have recognized the importance of the following concepts:

- Development of individuals and teams should be based upon job function and performance
- Ensure appropriate timeliness and access to training so as to develop an individual's KSA (knowledge, skill, and attitude) for the job at hand
- Learning opportunities are based upon identified needs. This is guided through the analysis of national and international policing and community trends (i.e., policy, procedure, law, and technology)

Additionally, organizations have become cognizant that training must occur at all levels, from the probationary constable to the Chief. These activities are foundational to all officers, but the degree of development varies as officers assume different roles and ranks (e.g., detectives will develop greater mastery of investigative skills; community liaison officers may develop mastery in community service). Similarly, leadership skills are developed progressively as officers move through supervisory, to executive positions.

The concept of a learning path must also be framed within the context of career paths. As the skills and knowledge required for policing become more complex and specialized, the development of competencies and career paths for officers is thus more critical. To make informed choices in their learning options, personnel must understand their goals and how to achieve them. Knowledge development must be tailored to the needs of each employee and each job within the organization. Marenin (2004) argues:

> From the perspective of the organization, formal training in all its forms (basic, field, in-service, specialized, managerial, etc) is not the beginning or the end of learning how to be a good police officer .... Learning is a career-long reality for all officers and officers learn how to do their job by a variety of means and practices (p. 110).

By providing a defined learning path and the associated just-in-time training, personnel can access information at the time they need it. A cogent example of this pertains to the timely training/knowledge transfer associated with the realm of law. The criminal law and civil law in relation to policing are developing at a rapid rate. As a result, it is critically important that every police service has the capacity – either through internal counsel, or external counsel – to immediately adjust its training, policies, and procedures in the face of court judgments that alter the law. An effective example can be drawn from the Supreme Court of Canada decision *R. v. Feeney,* which fundamentally shifted how officers can enter private residences. Here it was imperative that Police Services were aware of the decision and thus began modification of their existing processes and training to account for the new legal landscape.

Linking Principles and Functions to Learning

While information access may be fast, *learning* takes time. An emphasis on learner-centered learning is that adult learning principles, active learning, and problem solving have increased our attention on how learning occurs and the ways in which learning opportunities can and should be delivered within a law enforcement organization. This, of course, has implications for curriculum design, program delivery, training resources, and the importance of on-the-job learning. Moreover, it has an impact on whether or not we can meet particular strategic training objectives, such as:

- *Just-enough*: present the correct, relevant, needed information, without "padding" courses with extraneous details

- *Just-for-me*: offer a variety of learning techniques, ranging from group based classrooms to on-the-job individual assignments
- *Just-in-time*: set appropriate time for training as it relates to specific job functions being performed (short term) and the development of a talent pool capable of moving into strategic positions (long term)

The question this leaves us with is whether or not the current training approaches support the complex strategic, operational, and structural needs. For years, the police science literature has acknowledged that police training appears to be inconsistent with the police role (Birzer & Tannehill, 2001; Bradford & Pynes, 1999; Bumgarner, 2001; Kelling, 1999). "While traditional law enforcement education and training programs do a good job of developing technical and procedural skills, police training does little to promote the acquisition of essential non-technical competencies such as problem solving, judgment and leadership" (McCoy, 2006, p. 79). The issue of content is not the only point of concern, so too is the manner in which we teach law enforcement personnel. It is as important for a learning organization to understand how officers learn as it is to understand what to teach and how to teach.

Lecture is the dominant instructional method used in traditional law enforcement education; it is a well-known and acceptable method with which most adults and law enforcement instructors are familiar and comfortable. Lecture is, in most cases, a one-way transmittal of information from the teacher to the student. Lecture is used to identify concepts and present content in an organized way in a short period of time. The advantages of the lecture technique include being able to be used with large groups and being efficient in both energy and expenditure of time. However, lecture is not an appropriate method to modify attitudes or teach motor skills (Farrah, n.d., as cited in Galbraith, 2006). Research has also identified that retention rates from lecture only instruction is 5%. Without application of the information learned, the amount retained (5%) is reduced by 50% within a month and nearly 0% by 2 months (Madore, 2006, p. 5). Within a 16–20-week recruit training program, a great deal of disseminated information could potentially be lost using strictly lecture style instruction. As a point of caution regarding lecture as the only means of training, Ryan (2007) references the *Zuchel v. Denver* case (1993):

> Following a civil case against the City of Denver, a jury came back with a verdict against the city for $330,000 based upon a failure to adequately train. The City of Denver appealed. In upholding the verdict, the court cited testimony by a Denver police detective as well as testimony from the plaintiff's expert on police training. The detective testified that the only shoot-don't-shoot training that existed at the time of Zuchel's death consisted of a lecture and a movie. The plaintiffs police practices expert testified that if the only shoot-don't-shoot training officers received was a lecture and a movie, then the training was grossly inadequate (p. 3).

To effectively train today's law enforcement officers, there must be a move away from the traditional philosophy of education in which the teacher feeds knowledge to a dependent learner and then the learner is expected to reproduce the knowledge in some clearly observable behavioral outcome. In order to accept, remember, and use new information, adults need to be able to integrate it with what they already know, to place it on their own "reality map" (United States Department of Justice, 2004).

Adult learning experts advise that adult education should incorporate six learning principles:

- Adults learn throughout their lives.
- Adults exhibit diverse learning styles and learn in different ways, at different times, for different purposes.
- Adults prefer learning activities to be problem centered and to be meaningful to their life situation.
- Adult learners want their learning outcomes to have some immediacy of application.
- The past experiences of adults affect their current learning, sometimes as an enhancement, sometimes a hindrance.
- Adults exhibit a tendency toward self-directedness in their learning (United States Department of Justice, 2004).

Problem-Based Learning

Problem-based learning (PBL) is an andragogical model of teaching adults, "the science or art of teaching adults": "Adults are aware of specific learning needs generated by real life tasks or problems. Adult education programs, therefore, should be organized around 'life application' categories and sequences according to learners' readiness to learn" (Croal, 2006, p. 27).

PBL orientates students toward meaning-making over fact-collecting. They learn via contextualized problem sets and situations (Rhem, 1998). PBL places students in the active role of problem solvers who are confronted with complex problems similar to those confronted in workplace situations. It is an instructional strategy in which students confront contextualized, ill-structured problems and strive to find meaningful solutions.

Properly conducted, problem-based, learning-promoted collaboration builds teamwork skills and develops leadership abilities though cooperative work group experiences. Researchers believe that learning new knowledge in the context of problems may foster its transfer and use when needed for the solution of similar problems (Bradford & Pynes, 1999). This training will bridge the gap between problem-based learning in real-world environments in the classroom and on the street for the success of community service, leadership, and personal development. Introducing PBL concepts prior to entering into street training will make the transition realistic and more valuable for the recruit, trainers, and organizations.

Teaching Style

Adults differ from each other in experience, ability, background, and in preferred styles of learning. Different people will process information more effectively using different stimulus. Common learning styles are: tactile, visual, social, auditory, and repetition (Madore, 2006). Police trainers must be able to identify the learning strategies of recruit and in-service police officers to more appropriately accommodate for effective teaching and learning in the police training environment. Accordingly, effective delivery should attempt a blend of all the learning styles and lesson plans need to be designed to accommodate these differences (United States Department of Justice, 2004, p. 4).

The new generation of police applicants, who grew up with interactive video games, reality television programming, and electronic technology that allows for instant video replays, are not aware of the true issues surrounding today's police organizations. However, this new officer entering the workforce is highly educated, highly motivated, and particularly unwilling to appreciate blind authority (Croal, 2006, p. 4).

In the learner-centered classroom, it is the learner and the learner's needs that are most important. Training conducted in the police academy should highlight self-directed learning, which goes hand in hand with community policing. For community policing to succeed, police officers must be self-directed; when they discover a problem, they must solve it. The manner in which police trainers deliver training can have a significant impact on indoctrinating recruits with problem solving and self-direction (Birzer & Tannehill, 2001). The police use skills such as problem solving, communication, resource identification, conceptual, and mediation on a frequent basis. The learner-centered approach assumes that learners are proactive, are self-directed and self-motivated, and have unlimited potential to develop:

> The teacher is a facilitator who tries to meet individual needs as perceived by the student, acts as a resource, and trusts learners to pursue their own educational goals. Curriculum is based on problems and actual situations within a student's own life and not on a predetermined course with specific information to be absorbed. Evaluation is not as formal as with the teacher-centered style but is accomplished more through self-evaluation and constructive, informal feedback from the teacher. The adult education literature supports the collaborative approach to teaching as the most effective means of teaching adults (Conti, n.d., as cited in McCoy, 2006, p. 79).

Training Facilities

The facility requirements of a PBL environment are significantly more demanding than within the traditional law enforcement education. In order for students to learn effectively in a problem-based/scenario training environment, a number of elements must be incorporated into the learning process. The learner must: understand the information given, see it demonstrated, have opportunities to practice, apply the learning, and be coached on their performance (Oregon DPPST, 2004). To be successful in this process, facility design must support each of these learning elements. This can be achieved, in part, by the following:

- Ensuring the academic building incorporates traditional classrooms and smaller break-out rooms so as to facilitate interactive work sessions.
- The design of skill's centers, firearms ranges, and EVOC courses must enable learners to practice skills and problem solving in controlled and flexible settings.

- City street venues, scenario rooms, tactical training facilities, and EVOC courses must support the incorporation of real life exercises that test proficiency, decision making, and problem solving (Oregon DPPST, 2004).

The benefit of this design approach is that it provides learners with an opportunity to incorporate all elements of training (problem-based decision making, tactical skills, ethics, communications, law, etc.) in realistic scenarios. Furthermore, it offers learners an opportunity to learn from their mistakes in a safe environment. An effectively designed scenario-based facility supports an environment wherein the four components of the Learning Cycle – experience, reflection, generalization, and application – are woven throughout an officer's development.

Conclusion

As Scott (2005) aptly notes: "inadequate training can have a negative impact on delivery of services, officer safety, police resources and the ability of police Executives to lead their agencies" (p. 1). Given this potential outcome, training cannot be taken for granted nor considered a simple band-aide that can be applied as needed. We argue that training should be woven into the operational model of the organization and garner the same strategic attention as any other facet of policing. It is not, as some would suggest, a necessary evil. While it does require strategic alignment with organizational outcomes, resources, logistical planning, and a cultural shift, there is little doubt of the long-term benefit. No agency can afford to sit back and ignore the risk of litigation and diminished public support due to ineffective training. If an agency is to be successful, it must attune the training needs to the changing realities and practicalities of police work. It must adapt to not only the changing social and legal environment but also the pedagogical realm of training. Kelling (1999) suggests that:

> In order to achieve a meaningful impact on the attitudes and actions of officers, we must design training courses that focus on the substantive content of police work; find and delineate the means to conduct police work morally, legally, skillfully and effectively (p. 2).

References

Alpert, G., & Smith, W. (1991). Beyond city limits and into the wood(s): A brief look at the policy impact of City of Canton v Harris and Wood v Ostrander. *The American Journal of Police, 10,* 19–40.

Archbold, C., & Maguire, E. (2002). Studying civil suits against the police: A serendipitous finding of sample selection bias. *Police Quarterly, 5*(2), 222–249.

Bernardo Investigation Review. (1996). Justice Archie Campbell. Ontario Attorney General, Toronto, Ontario.

Berntt v. Vancouver (City). (1997). 4 WWR 505.

Birzer, M. L., & Tannehill, R. A. (2001). More effective training approach for contemporary policing. *Police Quarterly, 4*(2), 233–255.

Birzer, M. L. (2003). The theory of andragogy applied to police training, in Policing: *An International Journal of Police Strategies and Management, 26*, p. 1.

Bradford, D., & Pynes, J. (1999). Police academy training: Why hasn't it kept up with practice? *Police Quarterly, 2*(3), 283–301.

Bumgarner, J. (2001). Evaluating law enforcement training. *The Police Chief, 68*, 32–50.

Ceyssens, P. (2003, October). The police discipline process: What have we achieved and where do we go from here. *Presentation to CACOLE annual professional development conference.* Toronto, Canada.

Ceyssens, P. (2004). *Legal aspects of policing.* Salt Spring Island, BC: Earlscourt Legal Press.

City of Canton v. Harris. (1989). 489 U.S 378.

Clark v. Canada. (1994). 3 FC 323.

Croal, L. (2006). *Problem-based learning in basic police recruit training.* Master's thesis, Royal Roads University, Victoria, BC.

Galbraith, M. W. (2006). *Adult learning methods.* Malabar, FL: Krieger Publishing.

Grossman, R. (2003). *Law enforcement liability risk, loss control best practices.* Tampa, FL: Florida Partnership for Safety and Health.

Hill v. Hamilton-Wentworth Regional Police Services Board. (2007). 3 S.C.R. 129.

HM Inspectorate of Constabulary. (1999). *Managing learning: A study of police training.* London, England: HMSO.

Home Office. (2003). National Police Strategy, London.UK.

Hughes, T. (2001). Police officers and civil liability: "The ties that bind". *Policing: An International Journal of Police Strategies and Management, 24*(2), 240–262.

Johnson v. Adamson. (1981). 128 DLR (3d) 470.

Kelling, G. L. (1999). *Broken windows and police discretion.* Washington, DC: National Institute of Justice.

Kinnaird, B. (2007). Exploring liability profilers: A proximate cause analysis of police misconduct. *The International Journal of Police Science and Management, 9*(3), 210–213.

Madore, M. (2006). *Computer learning centre – New horizons, 'Just In Time Learning.'* Retrieved May 7, 2007, from http://www.tucsonspin.org/Archive/260.

Marenin, O. (2004). Police training for democracy. *Police Practice and Research, 5*(2), 107–123.

McCoy, M. (2006). Teaching style and the application of adult learning principles by police instructors. *Policing: An International Journal of Police Strategies and Management, 29*(1), 77–91.

Ontario Provincial Police. (2001). *Education and development Services Bureau, Building our future on a proud past.* Retrieved from http://www.opp.ca/ecms/index.php?id=285.

Oregon Department of Public Safety Standards and Training. Retrieved January 24, 2004 from http://www.orednet.org/-bpsst/misc/certchart.htm.

R. v. D. (J.), et al. (2007). ON CJ 154.

R. v. Dornan. (2008). ON SC 40.

R. v. N.M. (2007). CanLII 31570 ON SC.

R.C.M.P. Public Complaints Commission. (1997–1998). Annual Report, Ottawa.

Ransley, J., Anderson, J., & Prenzier, T. (2007). Civil litigation against police in Australia: Exploring its extent, nature and implications for accountability. *The Australian and New Zealand Journal of Criminology, 40*(2), 143–160.

Regina v. Clayton and Farmer. (2004). 194 C.C.C. (3d) 289.

Rhem, J. (1998). Problem-based learning: An introduction. *The National Teaching and Learning Forum, 8*(1), 1–4.

Ross, D. (2000). Emerging trends in police failure to train liability. *Policing: An International Journal of Police Strategies and Management, 23*(2), 169–193.

Ryan, J. (2007). *Training liability in the use of deadly force.* Indianapolis, IN: Legal and Liability Risk Management Institute.

Savrin, P. (1999). *Failure to train as a theory of section 1983 liability in the 11th circuit, FindLaw for legal professionals.* Retrieved from http://library.findlaw.com/1999/Jan/1/128567.html.

Scott, E. (2005). Managing municipal police training programs with limited resources. *The Police Chief, 72*(10), 1–5.

United States Department of Justice, National Institute of Corrections. (2004). *Designing learner centered instruction*. Longmont, CO: United States Department of Justice, National Institute of Corrections.

Vaughn, M., Cooper, T., & Carmen, D. E. (2001). Assessing legal liabilities in law enforcement: Police chiefs' views. *Crime and Delinquency, 47*(1), 3–27.

Walker v. City of New York, 974 F. 2d 293 (2d Cir. 1992).

Wellford, C. (2007). IACP launches new committee to guide law enforcement policy research. *The Police Chief, 74*(10), 1–6.

Zuchel v. City and County of Denver, Col., 997 F. 2d 730 (10th Cir. 1993).

Chapter 3
Changing Paradigms in Police Training: Transitioning from a Traditional to an Andragogical Model[*]

Robert F. Vodde

Introduction

Basic police training within the United States, ostensibly a nonexistent function until the early twentieth century, has been underrated and unrepresented in its importance as a critical function and component in the police mission. It was not until the Wickersham Commission Report of 1929 that the conspicuous absence of training was cited as a systemic problem within American policing. Appalled by the lack of substance and design, August Vollmer, a prominent author of the Commission's report, described the lack of training and education for police officers as "deplorable," declaring that "no one apparently cares to heed the lesson they should teach...where untrained persons are permitted to function as policemen," and consequently, "no person's life or liberty is safe" (Vollmer, 1936, p. 231).

While strides have been made since Vollmer's indictment, the philosophical methodology subscribed to at many of America's police academies has not kept current of changes within society (Birzer & Tannehill, 2001; Conser & Russell, 2000; Gaines & Kappeler, 2005; Holden, 1994; Vodde, 2009; Walker & Katz, 2008). To understand the reasons, it is important to recognize that America's police have undergone four eras of change in what historians have described as the Colonial, Political, Reform, and the current Community Policing Era. While the Colonial Era reflected a rudimentary and fragmented approach to policing in which basic training was nonexistent, the corrupt and ill effects of the Political Era yielded cries for wide-spread reform within society and government, to include reorganizing its

[*]Further information on this topic is available by going to Cambria Press at: http://www.cambriapress.com/index.cfm.

R.F. Vodde (✉)
School of Criminal Justice and Legal Studies, Fairleigh Dickinson University,
Madison, NJ, USA
e-mail: rvodde@fdu.edu

M.R. Haberfeld et al. (eds.), *Police Organization and Training: Innovations in Research and Practice*, DOI 10.1007/978-1-4614-0745-4_3,
© Springer Science+Business Media, LLC 2012

police. Consequently, in the pursuit for restoring social order and control, early twentieth century society endorsed the reform and professionalization of its police, to include adapting many quasi-militaristic characteristics. Despite many of the benefits associated with a hierarchal structure, a fervent chain of command, and military bearing, the ill effects of an autocratic culture continue to resonate within many of today's police departments and training academies despite societal changes that ushered in the era of community policing.

Consistent with influences that spurred the philosophy of community policing, unprecedented social, cultural, legal, political, economic, and technological changes within today's society call for a host of new proficiencies and competencies beyond those associated with technology. Skill sets and competencies in critical thinking, problem solving, decision making, effective communication, emotional intelligence, and the ability to recognize and understand the multidimensional dynamics of a diverse society are but a few of the demands made upon today's police. Yet many of the principles and practices employed within many of America's police academies are reminiscent of a traditional, pedagogical, military model of training (hereafter referred to as the traditional model). While aspects of such a training methodology still hold value, the philosophy and practices influenced by the Reform Era continue to resonate despite the needs and expectations of an ever-changing, sophisticated, and fast-paced society; consequently, its applicability and efficacy has been called into question (Birzer & Tannehill, 2001; Conser & Russell, 2000; Gaines & Kappeler, 2005; Holden, 1994; Vodde, 2009; Walker & Katz, 2008).

Increasingly, it is recognized that the training of new police officers has broad implications in their ability to meet changing duties and responsibilities. Notwithstanding some of the positive attributes of a traditional model, many argue that its linear, prescriptive, and autocratic nature inhibits recruits and its overall efficacy, while an adult-based, andragogical methodology by contrast, is viewed as a more holistic, integrative, collegial, collaborative, and responsive approach to training – one that serves the needs and interests of the recruit, the police organization, and that of a changing and sophisticated society. While popular in Canada and many parts of Europe, only recently has it begun to be recognized within the United States. Despite anecdotal inferences advocating its many advantages, little, if any, evidence existed, until a recent 2-year study provided empirical data supporting its efficacy – the subject of this chapter.

Changes in Training Methodologies: Traditional vs. Andragogical

Many advocates for exploring change within police training argue that traditional methodologies are predicated on an outdated military model that emphasizes structure, regimen, discipline, and curricular content, with little, if any, deliberation on the transactional processes associated with learning. Addressing this concern,

Dwyer and Laufersweiler-Dwyer (2004) contend that "for years, academicians and police trainers have suggested changes not only in academy content but also [the] methods of educating officers to meet changes in society, technology, law, and crime" (pp. 18–24). Similarly, Birzer (2003) suggests that "one area of police-training that has remained fairly uniform is the manner in which academy training is conducted (p. 31)." He contends that "many police training programs are conducted in a very behavioral and militaristic environment," which "has paralleled police officer selection strategies over the past 50 years," that is, one in which police officers "were hired for their good physical condition, their interest in crime control, and their ability to follow command decisions without hesitation" (Birzer, pp. 29–42). He argues that "the paramilitary model of policing has created myriad problems not only in the training environment, but also in the general culture of the organization" (Lorinskas & Kulis, 1986; Weisburd, 1989, as cited in Birzer, pp. 29–42). Referencing the work by McNeill (1992), Birzer (2003) suggests that "theoretical scholarship has pointed out that the behavioral and paramilitary training environment has created a warrior-like mentality on the part of the police," which not only inhibits learning, but may paradoxically condition a recruit in a manner that is contrary to the philosophy of community policing (p. 31).

Addressing the disparate styles that characterize police training programs in the United States, Holden (1994) contends that there exist two schools (1) academies that subscribe to a traditional, military, pedagogical model and (2) academies that subscribe to a collegiate model – one that is consistent with the philosophy and principles of adult-based, andragogical learning. He posits that because America's "police organization is built along military lines …there has been a tendency to structure police training academies similarly" (Holden, pp. 282–286). Consequently, because "the police boot camp style of the academy is still the salient feature of the traditional police organization…the curriculum suffers" (Holden, pp. 282–286). Rather than focusing on the skills needed to "accomplish their jobs, they are trained in accordance with the myth that they are soldiers in a war against crime" – a mindset that is reminiscent of the Reform era (Holden, pp. 282–286). Arguing against the traditional model, he writes that "police academies that are designed along military lines are archaic and dysfunctional … [that] they teach the wrong lessons for the wrong reasons" (Holden, pp. 282–286). Pointing out that a subscription to a militaristic, "boot camp" philosophy is counterproductive and outdated, he writes that "even the military has altered its approach to training over the past 20 years," suggesting that today's police "should be taught utilizing adult education methodologies rather than behavioral techniques which are currently utilized in a fair number of police academies" (Holden, p. 286). Birzer (2003) contends that "the paradox here readily comes to light: the police work in a democratic society but are trained and learn their jobs in a very paramilitary, punitive, and authoritarian environment;" hence, there is a discernable disconnect between society's expectations of today's police and the training mentality of the traditional model of training, thus opening the door to explore more viable and pragmatic alternatives (p. 5).

Andragogy: An Alternative Methodology

Addressing the importance of basic police training, Birzer and Tannehill (2001) wrote that "if the police are to stay current with the trends taking shape in society, then so too must police training" (p. 238). Underscoring the significance of a police officer's formative years, Birzer (2003) strongly advocates the philosophy and practice of andragogy as what he describes as "a more dynamic approach to learning" (p. 238). While the assumption upon which the andragogical model is based does not radically deviate from existing principles and practices within the field of adult-based learning, it is the assembly and integration of its principles that serve to distinguish andragogy as a resilient and adaptable methodology. It is this flexibility and holistic approach that makes it especially applicable to basic police training.

In espousing andragogical principles, Knowles, Holton, and Swanson (1998), considered by many as *the father of andragogy*, contrasts how adult learning needs and interests significantly differ from those of children. Emphasizing critical distinctions between how adults learn differently from children (upon which the pedagogical model is based), Knowles et al. (1998) itemizes them into six categories, explaining that adult learners possess a uniqueness as it relates to their (1) need to know (2) self-concept, (3) life experience, (4) readiness to learn, (5) orientation to learning, and (6) motivation. Given the modality and climate of the traditional model of basic police training, and considering that police recruits are adult learners, it becomes evident that Knowles' et al. tenets have direct applicability to recruits and the process of basic police training.

Andragogical Assumption 1: The Need to Know

In his first tenet, Knowles et al. (1998) writes that "adults need to know why they need to learn something before undertaking to learn it," pointing to the research of Tough (1971), who found that "when adults undertake to learn something on their own, they will invest considerable energy in probing into the benefits they will gain from learning it and the negative consequences of not learning it" (pp. 64–65). He emphasizes that the *need to know* incorporates three dimensions (1) *how* learning will be conducted, (2) *what* learning will be conducted, and (3) *why* learning is important – all of which are directly applicable to a police recruit (Tough 1971 1979, p. 65).

Andragogical Assumption 2: The Learner's Self-concept

Knowles' et al. (1998) second principle contends that "adults have a *self-concept* of being responsible for their own decision and their own lives".

Once they have arrived at that *self-concept* they develop a deep psychological need to be seen by others and treated by others as being capable of self-direction.

They resent and resist situations in which they feel others are imposing their wills on them (pp. 64–65).

Which by all measures is antithetical to the philosophy and modality of a traditional model of basic police training.

Andragogical Assumption 3: The Role of the Learner's Experience

In his third tenet, Knowles et al. (1998) explains that "adults come into an educational activity with a greater volume and a different quality of experience than youths," and that "by virtue of simply having lived longer, they have accumulated more experience than they had as youths. But they also have had a different kind of experience," which collectively translates into a greater frame of reference that enhances the learning process (Knowles et al., p. 67). He suggests that the heterogeneity of an adult's experiences in terms of their background, learning style, motivation, needs, interests, and goals has broad implications in their learning (Knowles et al.). He explains that adults, consistent with their age and maturity, enter a learning encounter with a greater volume and variety of experiences, which enhances not only their self-concept but the value and meaning of their learning as well (Knowles et al.). In this regard, Knowles et al. suggests that the use of experiential learning techniques involving hands-on, problem-based learning activities serve to capitalize on the experiences of the learner, thus enhancing the learning process.

Andragogical Assumption 4: Readiness to Learn

In his fourth tenet, Knowles et al. (1998) explain that "adults become ready to learn those things they need to know and be able to do in order to cope effectively with their real-life situations" (p. 67). The critical implication of this assumption is the importance of "timing learning experiences to coincide with those developmental tasks," assuming of course that the facilitator (instructor) has instituted mechanisms to appraise any such changes or needs on the part of the learner (Knowles et al., p. 67). While the implications of a recruit's *readiness* to learn may appear obvious, that is, a recruit is ready to learn all s/he needs in order to perform effectively as a police officer, the degree of *readiness* changes relative to one's progress, thereby, underscoring the importance of feedback and the instructor's role as a facilitator (Knowles et al.).

Andragogical Assumption 5: Orientation to Learning

Knowles' et al. (1998) fifth tenet explains that "adults are life-centered (task-centered or problem-centered) in their orientation to learning," and "are motivated to learn to the extent that they perceive that learning will help them perform tasks or deal with problems that they confront in their life situations" (p. 67). He states that as adults, "they learn new knowledge, understandings, skills, values, and attitudes most effectively when they are presented in the context of application to real-life situations," thus underscoring the emphasis he places on hands-on, experiential learning exercises that involve case scenarios, a hallmark of andragogy (Knowles et al., p. 67). The *need to know* on the part of the recruit, therefore, when coupled with the use of experiential, hands-on learning, serve to enhance, as well as affirm, the purpose and efficacy of the training process.

When the context of learning is directly related to discernable outcomes, such as acquiring specific knowledge, skills, and competencies, the value of the content and the techniques used to convey it are validated. In the case of basic police training, therefore, not only is a recruit *ready to learn* what s/he needs to know in order to effectively serve as a police officer but are "motivated to learn to the extent that they perceive that learning will help them perform tasks or deal with problems" (Knowles et al., 1998, p. 67).

Andragogical Assumption 6: The Adult Learner's Motivation

Knowles' et al. (1998) last tenet recognizes the work of Herzberg (1966), Maslow (1970, 1972), McClelland (1953), Vroom (1995), and other motivational theorists, acknowledging that while extrinsic motivators such as job, promotions, salary, policies, and working conditions are important, it is the intrinsic variables such as self-esteem, achievement, recognition, advancement, and personal growth that are more important (p. 68). Given the nature of policing and the sense of duty and service that police officers possess, their motivation serves to drive and reinforce their need for learning.

Andragogy: A Process Model

In consideration of Knowles' et al. (1998) six principles, it is important to emphasize that the means toward facilitating effective learning does not necessarily rest with any single instructional method, practice, or procedure; rather, it embodies a holistic approach embedded in a philosophy that focuses on the overall needs and disposition of the adult learner. Knowles et al. emphasize that while the pedagogical model places primacy on *content*, the andragogical model is based on a *process design* so that the emphasis is placed on the *process* of the learning transaction and not necessarily on the goals and aims of that transaction. This is not to suggest, however, that the goals and objectives that inform and direct adult learning are not important. Rather, it is based on the premise that if an adult is comfortable learning, the goals and objectives sought will be more readily achieved. Acquiring this *comfort level*, that is one that serves to recognize, understand, and attend to the needs and disposition of the adult learner, underscores the importance of the *process* and *facilitation* of learning. Incorporating these principles so as to realize true efficacy within the process of basic police training, six thematic and categorical constructs serve to provide a framework for structuring and facilitating the training process:

1. Institutional and instructional philosophy
2. Affective orientation: climate, tone, and environment
3. Self-concept and self-directedness
4. Integration and facilitation of curriculum
5. Application and integration of experiential learning
6. Stress and discipline

Institutional and Instructional Philosophy

One of the most important components for identifying, understanding, and assessing a police academy's overall operations is its mission statement, which, in principle, should reflect its institutional and instructional philosophy. While the implications of a mission statement may be obvious, its mere existence, or absence, reflects the essence of an academy's operations. A mission statement, when conscientiously designed, has a profound impact on the nature, design, direction, methodological practices, and outcomes of an academy's training program. When properly researched and institutionalized, a philosophy represents the product of a deliberate and reflective process that represents the values, beliefs, ideologies, expectations, and desired outcomes of all the stakeholders impacted by an academy's training program.

Roberg, Kuykendall, and Novak (2002), discussing training philosophies, posit that andragogical oriented training programs place a greater emphasis on learning and education, which ostensibly represents the core of basic police training. They point out that basic police training "is broader in scope and is concerned with theories, concepts, issues, and alternatives," as opposed to traditional training programs that focus on rote learning which are "heavily oriented toward teaching facts and procedures to the exclusion of theories, concepts, and analytical reasoning," arguing that "so much of police work requires analysis and reasoning" (Roberg et al., 2005 p. 149). Given the needs, demands, and expectations that the public, as well as police organizations place on new recruits in areas such as critical thinking, problem solving, decision making, and effective communication skills, underscores the importance of an andragogical approach and for police academies to identify and articulate their philosophy. Inherent to andragogy is the belief that recruits need to be apprised of an academy's institutional and instructional philosophy in order for them to understand, not just *how* the training is to proceed but *why* particular instructional methodologies and practices are being used. This study revealed that when recruits from the onset were appraised of the nature, design, purpose, and reasoning behind the training process and its many activities, they came to understand and appreciate what awaited them, despite the anticipatory challenges and anxiety typically associated with the first day of training.

Affective Orientation: Climate, Tone, and Environment

Bloom (1969), renown for developing a *Taxonomy of Educational Objectives*, explains that learning occurs within three domains: the cognitive, affective, and psychomotor. While emphasis on the cognitive (knowledge and understanding) and psychomotor (hands-on practicums) are readily apparent within basic police training, consideration of the affective variables (feelings and emotions) has been, retrospectively, conspicuously absent. While a growing understanding has been directed toward the emotional impact associated with policing (e.g., critical incident stress syndrome), traditionally, the notion of considering a police officer's "feelings" has been readily dismissed under the guise that "cops had to be tough and macho."

Addressing the affective domain, Bloom (1969) writes a "question posed by modern behavioral science research is whether a human being ever does thinking without feeling, acting without thinking, etc.," adding that "it seems very clear that each person responds as a "total organism" or "whole being" whenever he does respond" (p. 7). Underscoring the idea that learning does not occur without human emotions, Bloom describes the affective domain as encompassing "objectives which emphasize a feeling tone, an emotion, or a degree of acceptance or rejection" (p.7). He explains that affective variables are often expressed in terms of "interests, attitudes, appreciations, values, and emotional sets or biases" (Bloom, p. 7).

Emphasizing the importance that affective factors have on learning, Knowles (1984) argues that setting the right climate is critical to learning and is influenced by both the physical environment and psychological atmosphere. He explains that the right psychological climate creates a setting where mutual respect, collaboration, trustworthiness, support, openness and authenticity, humanness, and pleasure can flourish, emphasizing that "people are open to learning when they feel respected," as opposed to "being talked down to, ignored, or regarded as dumb, and that their experience is not valued" (Knowles, 1984, p. 15).

Conser and Russell (2000), discussing these factors in context to police training, concur that the *affective* components of learning "impacts one's values, emotions, and/or attitudes" and is central to recruits "keeping an open, acceptive mind to new knowledge" (pp. 325–326). An instructor's attitude, therefore, plays a critical role in setting the right tone and climate, and consequently, directly influences a recruit's disposition and receptivity toward learning. While not to suggest that there needs be a pre-occupation with a recruit's feelings, it is nevertheless important to recognize that emotions play an instrumental role in the overall training and learning process (Bennett & Hess, 2004, p. 230; Birzer & Roberson, 2007, p. 226). While in the past such variables were stereotypically considered superfluous and/or irrelevant to police training, Holden (1994) acknowledges that one of the most important tools for enhancing training of police is to provide an environment that is conducive to learning, arguing that "common sense suggests that officers will learn better in a comfortable setting" (pp. 286–287).

Furthermore, given the implications of Bandura's theory of social learning and modeling, which propounds that learning occurs most often through observation and imitation, Ormrod (1995) explains that modeling is a process that "focuses on the ways in which individuals learn from observing one another" (p. 131). Morgan (2002) argues that social learning accounts "for a much greater amount of learned behavior in humans than do basic learning principles," which underscores the importance of a police instructor's attitude and affective orientation toward recruits (pp. 178–179). He emphasizes "that some of life's most important lessons are learned simply by observing others" (Morgan, 2002, p. 170). This is true not only from a cognitive perspective in terms of *what* is learned but also from a social learning perspective in terms of *how* it is presented by the instructor and received by the recruit. Thus, if recruits are constantly exposed to an autocratic, prescriptive, and discipline-oriented instructor, as opposed to one that is benevolent, fair-minded, and mentoring, such behaviors will inevitably be modeled, the latter of which lends itself to expectations of today's society and the philosophy of community-oriented policing (Bandura, 1997; Knowles et al., 1998).

Conversely, this is not to suggest that recruits need to be coddled or overindulged; certainly, given the nature of basic police training and its curriculum, there may be times when a strict, no-nonsense, disciplined, and behavioral approach may be appropriate. However, considering the affective influence that climate, tone, and environment play in the learning process and its potential effect on an officer's attitude and performance, every consideration should be given toward creating a challenging, yet comfortable, benevolent, inviting, and collaborative environment for learning – concerns that were the consistently expressed by recruits during the study.

Self-concept and Self-directedness

Knowles et al. (1998), addressing his second andragogical tenet, suggest that adults have a self-concept presupposing that they are responsible for their own lives and their own decisions, explaining that "once they have arrived at that self-concept they develop a deep psychological need to be seen by others and treated by others as being capable of self-direction" (p. 65). They emphasize, moreover, that adult learners "resent and resist situations in which they feel others are imposing their wills on them" (Knowles et al., p. 65).

Inherent to the importance of an adult learners' self-concept is their sense of personal autonomy, which speaks to the importance of "taking control of the goals and purposes of learning and assuming ownership," which, in turn, "leads to an internal change of consciousness in which the learner sees knowledge as contextual and freely questions what is learned" (Knowles et al, 1998, p. 135). Activities such as participating in small breakout groups and brainstorming sessions, working on collaborative group projects and, in particular, actively researching, planning, and developing problem-based learning simulations and case scenarios, underscore the notion of self-concept and self-directedness.

Considering the philosophical mindset necessary for advancing self-directed learning, it is apparent why any such initiatives are limited within a traditional model of training, where the curriculum is prescriptive, and instructors assume full control of its recruits and the learning process. The notion of autonomous, self-directed learning is fundamentally antithetical to its principles and practices, and consequently, recruits feel disenfranchised. To this point, Knowles et al. (1998) argue that when self-directed initiatives are nonexistent or even worst, discouraged, it leads to an environment that produces tension, resistance, and resentment (p. 65; pp. 135–139). Despite the comprehensive and prescriptive nature of the basic police training curriculum, ample opportunities exist to recognize a recruit's need for self-concept, autonomy, and self-directedness. Recognizing its importance not only attends to the intrinsic need for acquiring personal autonomy and empowerment but fosters an environment that encourages collaboration and uninhibited learning.

Integration and Facilitation of Curriculum

Despite an oversimplification in definition and misleading perceptions on the part of the general public as to what basic police training encompasses, police instructors understand that it represents a comprehensive and complex process of learning that involves the attainment of outcomes measured in the form of discernable knowledge, understanding, skills, attitudes, behaviors, and competencies. Not only does achieving these outcomes involve various sequential steps identified by Bloom,[1] but requires the planning of deliberate strategies for integrating, facilitating, and presenting the outcomes dictated by the curriculum. While logistically the training curriculum can be achieved by presenting the respective subjects as independent disciplinary constructs in a linear and sequential manner – as is often the case in a traditional model – the curriculum of an andragogical model, by contrast,

---

[1] Bloom's (1969) taxonomy identified three domains of learning that are directly applicable to basic police training: the cognitive, affective, and psychomotor. The cognitive domain addressed cognitive behaviors such as remembering, reasoning, problem solving, concept formation, and creative thinking. Within this domain, six major classes of educational behaviors were identified and arranged in a hierarchy by level of complexity so that "the objectives in one class are likely to make use of and be built on the behaviors found in the preceding classes on the list." These consisted of: knowledge, comprehension, application, analysis, synthesis, and evaluation. The affective domain addresses what Bloom described as "objectives which emphasize a feeling tone, an emotion, or a degree of acceptance or rejection." The affective domain comprises five categories: receiving, responding, valuing, organizing, and characterizing. The *Psychomotor Domain addresses* muscular or motor skill, some manipulation of material and objects, or some act which requires neuromuscular co-ordination. These include imitation, manipulation, precision, articulation, and naturalization.

is facilitated with an eye toward the logical integration of unifying concepts and themes. This holistic approach recognizes that most of the topics within basic police training are interrelated and serve as conceptual foundations for other subjects. For example, when addressing the importance of effective communications skills – whether in the form of verbal, nonverbal, or written transactions – rather than addressing it as a stand-alone topic, it is emphasized that communication lies at the heart of effective police work and is integrated throughout the curriculum as it relates to report writing, electronic transmissions, building dialogue within the community, making public presentations, providing testimony, assuming a command voice, taking charge of investigations, effecting arrests, etc. Robbins (2000) describes this process as a systems approach, that is, one in which all its parts are arranged in a manner that produces a unified whole.

Stark and Lattuca (1997), addressing the importance of curricular integration, espouse a comprehensive model where a curriculum can best be understood as an *academic plan* – one that represents "a deliberate planning process that focuses on important educational considerations," yet acknowledging that any number of internal, external, and organizational factors can influence the planning process (pp. 9–16). Given the dynamic nature of a curriculum, the authors suggest that an *academic plan* takes into consideration (1) purpose, (2) content, (3) sequence, (4) learners, (5) instructional processes, (6) instructional resources, (7) evaluation, and (8) adjustment.[2] These elements are important, not only because they set forth the institution's understanding of the purpose of the curriculum and methodology, but that it takes into consideration the needs and interests of the learner, an element that is central to andragogy. Given that basic police training represents an ever-changing learning and educative process, Stark and Lattuca's *academic plan* provides an operational and pragmatic template that aligns with Knowles' (1984) recommended

---

[2] *Purpose*: The general goals that guide the knowledge, understanding, skills, attitudes, behaviors, and competencies to be learned, i.e., it focuses on the intended learning outcomes. *Content*: The subject matter or content within which the learning experiences are embedded; here, the authors note that "the separation of the first and second elements of the plan emphasizes that the purpose (or desired learning outcomes) and the subject matter are not synonymous." *Sequence*: The arrangement of the subject matters so that it leads to specific outcomes for the learners. Stark and Lattuca explain that it "means the ways in which the subject matter is arranged to facilitate the learner's contact with it', i.e., "is the material presented chronologically or thematically?" *Learners*: This addresses information about the learners for whom the plan is derived, which speaks directly to Knowles' concerns and considerations. *Instructional Processes*: The instructional activities used to facilitate the learning process. Learning processes, Stark and Lattuca explained, "are often discussed separately from the curriculum, but, realistically, [the choice of] the teaching and learning mode ... dictate the learning outcomes." *Instructional Resources*: Collectively encompasses materials and settings to be used in the learning process, including the use of experiential learning activities, the setting and environment, and other auxiliary support that affect climate and tone. *Evaluation*: Strategies used to determine whether skills, knowledge, attitudes, and behavior change as a result of the learning process. *Adjustment*: Making changes in the plan to increase learning, based on experience and evaluation. Stark suggests that based on the evaluative process, improvements are made to the academic plan and, in effect, the planning process (Stark and Lattuca, 1997, pp. 9–16).

principles of practice for providing a flexible and integrative process. By carefully and deliberately planning, coordinating, and integrating the curriculum, a climate is created that encourages critical and analytical thinking in its broadest form.

While significance of developing such an *academic plan* is a critical component toward improving police training, it would be remiss not to acknowledge the critical role that an academy's faculty and staff plays in the success of the training process. While doing so warrants a separate and dedicated discussion, it is suffice to say that their role and success bears upon their interest, attitude, dedication, training, experience, and education in a wide range of areas apart from their respective areas of specialization. In this regard, recognizing the idiosyncratic nature of learning, along with a familiarization of learning theory, such as the behavioral, cognitive, humanistic, experiential, and social process schools of thought, provides an instructor the ability to recognize and apply different modalities of instruction relative the subject matter being taught and the receptivity of the learner. Summarily, the integration and facilitation of the curriculum is presupposed on the notion that all components of the curriculum are interrelated and interdependent and recognizes that the whole is greater than the sum of its parts.

Use and Integration of Experiential Learning

Addressing the importance of experiential learning, Knowles et al. (1998) explain that adults enter into a learning activity with a greater volume and variety of life experiences, which enhance not only the value and meaning of learning, but the importance of a learner's self-concept (Knowles et al., 1998, Brookfield, 1986). He posits that the implications of an adult learners' life experience are threefold (1) adults have more to contribute to the learning of others; (2) adults have a richer foundation of experience with which to relate new experiences; and (3) adults possess a greater number of fixed habits and patterns of thought for which new learning techniques can be introduced (Knowles et al., 1998). Given these three factors, Knowles et al. (1998), suggest that when adults engage in experiential learning activities, that is, the process of making meaning from direct experience, there exists a greater degree of heterogeneity in terms of their "background, learning style, motivation, needs, interests, and goals" (p. 66). As such, he underscores the importance for the use and integration of experiential learning activities such as group discussions, hands-on simulation exercises, problem-solving activities, and the case method. Also, because the use of experiential learning typically is multi-sensory in nature and involve visual, auditory, verbal, and kinesthetic functions, they advance learning on multiple experiential, perceptual, cognitive, and behavioral dimensions (Kolb, 1984, pp. 20–38).

Underscoring the importance of experiential learning, Hughes, Ginnett, and Curphy (1996) explain that practical, hands-on exercises not only serve to provide the requisite training opportunities but provide for a process of constant monitoring, feedback, and evaluation. Similarly, Bennett and Hess (2004), praising the importance of experiential learning, point to the increased rate of retention learners acquire when using as many of their senses as possible, citing Confucius' edict, "what I hear, I forget; what I see, I remember; what I do, I understand" (p. 236), which centuries latter was echoed by Aristotle addressing his adult students saying, "what we have to learn to do, we learn by doing."

While experiential learning entails a host of activities, its design and purpose provides recruits the opportunity to synthesize all that they have learned into discernable competencies, most notably, critical thinking, problem solving, decision making, good judgment and discretion, and effective communication skills. Robbins (2000), advocating its use, explains that such activities serve to "sharpen [one's] logic, reasoning, and problem-defining skills, as well as [one's] abilities to assess causation, develop alternatives, analyze alternatives, and select solutions" (p. 284). In summary, experiential learning represents an approach that builds a curriculum around authentic, intriguing, real-life problems and asks students to work cooperatively to develop and demonstrate their solutions. Its strengths revolve around building student cooperation and collaboration, higher-order thinking, cross-disciplinary work, utilizing artifacts and exhibits, and represent authentic, real-life learning (Sadker & Sadker, 2005, pp. 99–101). Notwithstanding the distinct advantages of experiential learning, Bennett and Hess (2004) acknowledge that from a planning and logistical perspective, it is labor intensive, consumes valuable resources, "and requires a greater degree of teaching skill, creativity, and a greater depth of instructor knowledge" than other styles of instruction (p. 230). Despite, however, the challenges associated with developing, integrating, and institutionalizing such activities, they are popular among recruits and serve as an integral component to realizing the outcomes and success of basic police training.

Stress and Discipline

The nature of policing requires an atmosphere of structure, control, and discipline on an organizational, as well as on an individual level (Roberg et al., 2002, pp. 17–19). Despite the need for operating within hierarchal structure in order to ensure accountability and provide for the efficient and effective operation of a police department, changes within society and the police organization itself call for a less bureaucratic and autocratic approach (Roberg, Novak, & Cordner, 2005). Doing so, however, is not to the exclusion of working within an atmosphere of mutual trust, respect, collaboration, and a certain degree of autonomy.

As such, the importance for ensuring organizational structure, control, and discipline is equally important on the individual level. This is especially so, given the wide range of duties and responsibilities incumbent upon today's police officers, not the least of which include ensuring their own safety and security, and those they are sworn to protect and serve. Given the unpredictable and volatile nature of policing, an officer's day can range from being mundane and routine, to being hostile, violent, and life-threatening – factors that warrant serious consideration when training and preparing police recruits. Unarguably, the paradoxical nature of policing is such that officers will bear witness to the best and worst of human nature – the ultimate dichotomy being when they bear witness to or are instrumental in life's beginning or end, the latter sometimes under the most tragic of circumstances. For these reasons, basic police training, in realizing its mission, needs to infuse relevant aspects of stress and discipline throughout the training process, however, not at the expense of compromising the learning process that takes place, nor creating what has been characterized as a "us against them mentality." As such, an effective police training program should present a balanced and pragmatic approach – one which empha- sizes the importance of an officer's role and responsibilities within the community, "while at the same time attuning them to the importance of maintaining a high degree of situational awareness and tactical vigilance" (Vodde, 2009, p. 309).

Abrams, Puglisi and Balla (1988), discussing the importance for infusing stress as part of basic police training, explain that the process of *conditioning* recruits for the physical and emotional stress related to real and potential threats endemic to police work is referred to as *stress inoculation* (pp. 334–340). The rationale behind this process, which Celeste (1996) characterizes as *engineered stress*, is not only intended to condition recruits for a wide range of unpredictable physical and emo- tional situations but also to serve as an indicator in how one will react under stress. For example, a response to a physical confrontation can result in over-reacting – using an excessive amount of force that can lead to complaints of police brutality or, conversely, under-reacting – freezing or failing to act under stress, which could lead to injury or death (and claims of misfeasance, malfeasance, or nonfeasance). Abrams et al. (1988) explain that:

> Although many organizations, particularly in the military, rely heavily on stress training… there are several arguments against [it]. First, research into cognitive processes has shown that under conditions of high stress, learning is hampered. If new skills are introduced under high stress conditions, the cognitive interference of stress reduces the chances of learning. The more complex the behavior, the less likely the individual will learn (pp. 334–340).

The second point that they make against the use of excessive stress and discipline is that "if an environment is set where failure due to stress is obviously inevitable, the fear of failure itself may create an additional decrement in individual perfor- mance" (Abrams et al., 1988, pp. 334–340). Their third point is that the use of "indiscriminate stress during training may not resemble the stress of the actual event" (Abrams et al., pp. 334–340). Indiscriminate yelling, screaming, demeaning, and derogatory name calling conducted under the guise of "toughing them up for the real-world" – a practice often associated with the traditional model of basic police training – is counter-productive; that is, "it is difficult to equate the practice of *name-calling* with actual stress in the field" (Abrams et al., pp. 334–340). However, by infusing real-life, practical case scenarios that require self-control and discipline – one which induces real-life physical and emotional stress – recruits not only acquire valuable experience but are able to collaboratively assess and critique their performance, thus making for a more meaningful learning experience. Abrams et al. argue that "the more closely the situation which requires a particular response resembles the training environment, the greater the probability of the successful transfer of skills" (pp. 334).

Speaking to the point of stress and discipline, Earle (1973), who specifically examined the effects of stress at two contrasting style police academies, discovered that "graduates of the training program which was not run like boot camp performed significantly better, reported greater job satisfaction and were rated higher in terms of living up to organizational expectations" – findings that were consistent with this author's 2-year study (Vodde, 2009; Earle 1973). Similarly, Birzer and Roberson (2007), addressing the need for recruits to understand the breadth of their roles and responsibilities, argue that police academies "should increasingly deviate from the mechanical, militaristic, and behavioral aspects of training to programs that inform police recruits how to identify, respond to, and solve problems" (p. 226). They emphasize that "it is essential that training be conducted in such a way as to be as meaningful as possible to adult participants;" not one where "there is a disconnect between the mission, the organization, and training" (Birzer & Roberson, 2007, p. 226). They further report that "some contemporary scholarship has reported a disturbing growth of military tactics and ideology within U.S. law enforcement agencies" and, consequently, "when police organizations train officers to act and think like soldiers, these organizations alienate them from communities of which they are supposed to be a part" (Birzer & Roberson, 2007, p. 218).

Consistent with these findings, Holden (1994), addressing the changing landscape in police training, writes that "even the military has altered its approach to training over the past 20 years," explaining that "the purpose of the academy is to provide knowledge and skills necessary for the recruit to perform competently in an independent manner (p. 287). It cannot be stressed strongly enough" he argues, "that academies stressing high discipline crush the initiative and creativity out of recruits," adding that "police work is an occupation requiring motivation, imagination, and initiative" – traits "not found in organizations obsessed with military like discipline" (Holden, p. 287). While acknowledging that "boot camp training does a good job of teaching chain of command, saluting, and personal appearance, when such behaviors preoccupy officers, it can unwittingly result in recruits not questioning incompetence or blindly following orders they know may be wrong" (Holden, p. 287). Consequently, "the boot camp approach to police training literally pushes the recruit into the arms of the subculture. It does this by stressing group loyalty over duty, form over substance, and adherence to command over respect for constitutional values" (Holden, p. 287). He argues that "much of what is wrong in law enforcement starts with academy systems that are dysfunctional" (Holden, p. 287).

While not to suggest that indoctrinating recruits to the importance of stress and discipline does not have its place, it is the means, however, by which these factors are incorporated within the curriculum that determine whether its effects are desirable. Certainly, there are times when the police must assume an autocratic posture, take charge and command, and respond with physical force; however, when such a disposition is the norm, it undermines not only public trust and confidence, but, in effect, the efficiency and effectiveness of the police mission (Conser & Russell, 2000, pp. 324–325). In summary, the nature and unpredictability of police work imposes a high degree of stress on officers, which requires a high degree of self-control and discipline. When carefully engineered and integrated as part of basic police training, stress and discipline can serve to inform and prepare recruits for the challenges and rewards of a professional career in law enforcement.

Conclusion

The mission of policing in the United States, as in most democratic societies, is to maintain social order and control. As society has grown, matured, and evolved, so too has the complexity of fulfilling that mission. Because today's fast-paced, ever-changing society continues to experience unprecedented social, cultural, legal, political, economic, and technological change, the expectations of its police have grown exponentially. Next to recruitment, the training of new police officers has become a high-priority issue, as have the methods employed for preparing them for a professional police career. While not to suggest that basic police training is the panacea for the innumerable challenges that face today's police, it nevertheless plays a significant role in the formative years of a police officer's career. In many respects, basic police training leaves an indelible imprint that influences an officer's values, attitudes, understanding, and abilities (Bandura, 1977, 1995, 1997).

While a traditional, pedagogical, military model of training may have at one time served the needs and interests of society and the police organization, its applicability and efficacy have come under question. Andragogy, predicated on the belief that adults learn differently than children (pedagogy), bases its practices on the predisposed needs, interests, readiness, orientation, experience, and motivation of the adult learner. When subscribed and applied to basic police training, andragogy provides for a holistic, integrative, and collaborative approach to learning, which, when compared to a traditional model of training, proved empirically more effective as revealed in a 2-year study – the subject of this chapter.

Operationally, when subscribing to an andragogical philosophy and methodology, recruits at the commencement of their training are provided with a detailed and insightful explanation of the training program's purpose, processes, and rationale, which serve as a compass and barometer throughout the training process. It creates a physical and psychological climate that takes into consideration the affective needs of the recruit, thus providing for a healthy, engaging, challenging, and collaborative atmosphere in which recruits may develop a clear understanding and perspective of their role within the greater context of society. Underscoring the significance of these factors, the training program represents a well-planned and skillfully orchestrated process that thematically integrates all aspects of the curriculum, to include the infusion of comprehensive multi-sensory experiential learning activities that allow recruits to apply what they have learned. Lastly, given the physical and psychological challenges associated with police work, stress and discipline are skillfully integrated and engineered throughout all components of the curriculum as a means for assessing, preparing, and conditioning a recruit's tolerance for stress and their capacity for appropriate response. While stress is also infused into self-directed activities that require self-discipline and control, the focus of these activities is on developing a positive attitude toward and accepting the responsibilities that accompany the specific activities and their real-life analogues. Stress and discipline, while demanding in their own right, are not perceived as punitively oriented or used in a derogatory context, but rather as an important and necessary element in the process toward reaching a clear and well defined goal.

In summary, this chapter highlighted the empirical results of a 2-year study that revealed the efficacy of employing an andragogical instructional philosophy and methodology within basic police training. Compared with a traditional, pedagogical, military model, its findings indicated is an effective means for training police officers in serving the mutual needs and interests of the police recruit, the police organization, and society at-large. In comparison to a traditional model, not only did it lead to a greater degree of achieving the intended outcomes needed to meet the changing needs of a sophisticated, fast-paced, and ever-changing constituency, but is one that serves to challenge and engage recruits which translates into a positive, productive, and respectful context. While limited in its scope, its findings have wide reaching implications considering that many police departments throughout the United States continue to subscribe to traditional model of training (Birzer & Roberson, 2007, p. 99). Former NYPD Deputy Police Commissioner James O'Keefe (2004, p. 250), addressing the future of police training and education, and reviewer of this study, wrote that "what still remains to be developed . . . is an integrated, sustained commitment to the philosophical, intellectual, and spiritual education and training of the human resources involved in law enforcement;" the use of an andragogical instructional methodology in basic police training may be one of many avenues toward that realization.

References

Abrams, J., Puglisi, D., & Balla, J. (Eds.). (1988). *Leadership in organizations*. Garden City Park, NY: Avery Publishing Group.

Bandura, A. (1995). *Self-efficacy in changing societies*. Cambridge: Cambridge University Press.

Bandura, A. (1997). *Self-efficacy: The exercise of control*. New York, NY: W.H. Freeman and Company.

Bandura, A. (1977). *Social learning theory*. Englewood Cliffs, NJ: Prentice-Hall.

Bennett, W. W., & Hess, K. M. (2004). *Management and supervision in law enforcement* (4th ed.). Belmont, CA: Wadsworth/Thomson Learning.

Birzer, M. L., & Roberson, C. (2007). *Policing today and tomorrow*. Upper Saddle River, NJ: Pearson Prentice Hall.

Birzer, M. L., & Tannehill, R. (2001). A more effective training approach for contemporary policing. *Police Quarterly, 4*(2), 233–252.

Birzer, M. L. (2003). The theory of andragogy applied to police training. *Policing: An International Journal of Police Strategies and Management, 26*(1), 29–32.

Bloom, B. S. (Ed.). (1969). *Taxonomy of educational objectives*. New York: David McKay Company.

Celeste, R. (1996). *Development of a police academy administrator's handbook outlining a comprehensive curriculum model of a police recruit training program.* Doctorial dissertation, Nova Southeastern University.

Conser, J. A., & Russell, G. A. (2000). *Law enforcement in the United States.* Gaitherburg, Maryland: Aspen Publishing.

Dwyer, R. G. and Laufersweiler-Dwyer, D. L. (2004, November). The need for change: A call for action in community-oriented police training. *FBI Law Enforcement Bulletin,* 73(11), 18–24.

Earle, H. H. (1973). *Police recruit training: Stress vs. non-stress.* Springfield, IL: C.C. Thomas.

Gaines, L. K., & Kappeler, V. E. (2005). *Policing in America* (5th ed.). Cincinnati, OH: Anderson Publishing.

Herzberg, F. (1966). *Work and the Nature of Man.* Cleveland: The World Publishing Company.

Holden, R. N. (1994). *Modern police management* (2nd ed.). Upper Saddle River, NJ: Prentice-Hall.

Hughes, R. L., Ginnett, R. C., & Curphy, G. J. (1996). *Leadership, enhancing the lessons of experience.* Chicago, IL: Times Mirror Higher Education Group.

Knowles, M. S. (1984). *Andragogy in action.* San Francisco, CA: Jossey-Bass Publishing.

Knowles, M. S., Holton, E. F., & Swanson, R. A. (1998). *The adult learners: The definitive classic in adult education and human resource development* (5th ed.). Woburn, MA: Butterworth-Heinemann.

Kolb, D. A. (1984). *Experiential learning: Experience as the source of learning and development.* London: Prentice Hall.

Lorinskas, R.A. and Kulis, J.C. (1986), "The military model and policing: a misunderstood Ideology." *Police Studies,* Vol. 7 No. 2, pp. 184–93.

Maslow, A. H. (1970). *Motivation and Personality.* New York: Harper and Row.

Maslow, A. H. (1972). "Defense and Growth." *The Psychology of Open Teaching and Learning.* M. L. Silberman, et al. (eds.). Boston: Little, Brown, 1972, pp. 43–51.

McNeill, W.H. (1992). *The Pursuit of Power: Technology, Armed Forces, and Society since AD1000,* University of Chicago Press, Chicago, IL.

McClelland, D. C., Atkinson, J. W., Clark, R. A., and Lowell, E. I. (1953). The Achievement Motivation. New York: Appleton-Century-Crofts.

Morgan, D. L. (2002). *Essentials of learning and cognition.* Boston, MA: McGraw Hill.

O'Keefe, J. (2004). *Protecting the republic: the education and training of American police officers.* Upper Saddle River, NJ: Pearson Prentice Hall.

Ormrod, J. E. (1995). *Human learning.* Englewood Cliffs, NJ: Prentice-Hall.

Roberg, R. R., Kuykendall, J., & Novak, K. (2002). *Police management* (3rd ed.). Los Angeles, CA: Roxbury Publishing.

Roberg, R., Novak, K., & Cordner, G. (2005). *Police and society* (3rd ed.). Los Angeles, CA: Roxbury Publishing.

Robbins, S. P. (2000). *Managing today* (2nd ed.). Upper Saddle River, NJ: Prentice Hall.

Sadker, M. P., & Sadker, D. M. (2005). *Teachers, schools, and society* (7th ed.). Boston, MA: McGraw Hill.

Stark, J. S., & Lattuca, L. R. (1997). *Shaping the college curriculum: Academic plans in action.* Boston, MA: Allyn and Bacon.

Tough, A. (1971). The adults learning project: Episodes and learning. In P. Jarvis & C. Griffin (Eds.), *Adult and Continuing Education: Major Themes in Education* (2nd ed., Vol. II, pp. 35–44). Toronto: Ontario Institute for Studies in Education (London: Routledge, 2003).

Vollmer, A. (1936). *The Police and Modern Society.* Berkeley: University of California Press.

Vroom, V. H. (1995). *Work and Motivation (class reprint).* San Francisco: Jossey-Bass.

Vodde, R. F. (2009). *Andragogical instruction for effective police training.* Amherst, NY: Cambria Press.

Walker, S., & Katz, C. M. (2008). *The police in America* (8th ed.). New York: McGraw-Hill.

Weisburd, D., McElroy, J., and Hardyman, P. (1989), "Maintaining control in community-oriented policing", in Kenney, Dj. (Ed.), *Police and Policing. Contemporary Issues,* Praeger, NY.

Chapter 4
Innovative Law Enforcement Training: Blended Theory, Technology, and Research

Valerie Atkins and William A. Norris

Introduction

This chapter describes the transformation that the Federal Law Enforcement Training Center (FLETC) has undergone in its effort to incorporate emergent training theories and technologies. The reengineering began in 2004 with the creation of a new Directorate and Division tasked with guiding "innovative" training. Correspondingly, this new Division would oversee and implement a process of continuous review and an ongoing analysis of training techniques. The chapter begins with an overview of two of FLETC's major research studies. The objective of these studies was to evaluate law enforcement performance under stressful conditions. Findings from these studies were then utilized as a starting point from which to discuss changes in the areas of learning and training. Following on this discussion, the chapter explores how the integration of technology and simulation has both been a response to the research findings and transformed training at FLETC. The chapter highlights the importance of research and an evidence-based response to training. Several aspects of the FLETC training process have been revised based upon the cited studies and a supporting body of literature dealing with learning and training transformation.

The Survival Scores Research Project

The Survival Scores Research Project was conceived and conducted in 2000 with the ultimate goal of saving lives through improved training strategies for high-stress encounters. The project took its name from a concept paper that proposed placing

V. Atkins (✉) • W.A. Norris
Federal Law Enforcement Training Center, Glynco, GA 31524, USA
e-mail: Valerie.Atkins@dhs.gov

M.R. Haberfeld et al. (eds.), *Police Organization and Training: Innovations in Research and Practice*, DOI 10.1007/978-1-4614-0745-4_4,
© Springer Science+Business Media, LLC 2012

students in realistic, highly stressful scenarios and grading them with a "survival score" rather than a written or practical skills exam. The score would reflect the student's ability to respond (and survive) in a highly stressful confrontation. A high-stress law enforcement scenario was developed by subject-matter experts and used existing training objectives to comprise the 97 performance elements that were used for scenario scoring. The scenario incorporated escalating stress, clear transition points, and a minimal amount of physical exertion in order for the physiological measures of cognitive stress to not be impacted by physical movement or stress. There were 1,268 students given the initial screening tests and from that group 105 volunteers were selected to be in the study.

There are numerous definitions that describe stress, but for the purposes of this chapter, stress occurs when the "perceived demand exceeds the individual resources" (Salas, Driskell, & Hughes, 1996). Additionally, the study examined the effects of *acute stress* on performance rather than *chronic stress*. Acute stress is "sudden, novel, intense, and of relatively short duration, disrupts goal-oriented behavior, and requires a proximate response" (Salas et al.). Chronic stress occurs when there are repeated exposures to low-stress situations and frequently lead to alterations or breakdowns in any number of body functions.

Basic training students from both the Criminal Investigator Training Program (CITP) and Mixed Basic Police Training Program (MBPTP) volunteered to be subjects for the study. The factors of heart rate, blood pressure, cortisol, and State and Trait Personality indicators were used to detect relationships between these factors and their performance. Demographic data, previous training and experience, and basic training scores were all used in the analysis. After reviewing current research and training methodologies, the scenario was structured to provide answers to the five following questions:

- Can we validate training scenarios as being realistic/highly stressful?
- Can specific psychological factors be identified that predict performance in a highly stressful law enforcement encounter?
- Can specific physiological factors be identified that predict performance in a highly stressful law enforcement encounter?
- Can specific physiological factors be used to identify an "optimum stress level for optimum performance" as suggested by various authors?
- What effect does high stress have on decision making (cognitive processing)?

Existing Research in this Area

Previously, a great deal of information has been written on the physiological (heart rate, blood pressure, and cortisol) response to stress (Driskell & Salas, 1996; Hancock & Desmond, 2001; Hockey, 1997; Lazarus & Folkman, 1984). Limited research, however, has focused on the impact of short-term, emotionally strong (acute) stress on performing specific job functions and decision-making skills. Additionally, most of the training literature has theorized on the precise control these systems have in determining performance levels without actually testing the theory to verify its accuracy. Simply stated, most writings predict how the body should respond under stress rather than testing the theory using a research study with subjects. It was also rare to find research that compared the psychological characteristics (traits) of the subjects to their performance levels in a high-stress scenario. Few research institutions allow scientists to intentionally expose subjects to high levels of psychological stress. This, however, is the type of training environment the FLETC creates for trainees in order to replicate the dangerous and stressful situations they may experience on the job.

This research was conducted with oversight and approval of the Human Factors Research Review Board at Walter Reed Army Institute of Research. Additionally, the Chief of Neuroendocrinology and Neurochemistry at Walter Reed provided technical assistance and chemical analyses of cortisol. FLETC researchers also teamed with The Director of Center for Research in Behavioral Psychology of the University of South Florida for the detailed study of psychological behavioral indicators linked to performance (Spielberger & Reheiser, 2003). These distinguished research colleagues assisted with the development of the research protocol and project evaluation.

Research Design

Scenario testing was done just prior to graduation from training. The 105 students were evaluated for both State and Trait Personality indicators for psychological assessments. The physiological indicators of heart rate and blood pressure were collected using mobile units concealed under protective clothing. Cortisol, which is released during the "fight-or-flight" response, was used to measure the stress response and was collected from the students' saliva. Background demographics and basic training scores were documented to explore the impact of previous experiences and training on performance levels. The data set thus included 368 variables available for analysis and comparison. The seven segments of the scenario were as follows:

1. Call in service
2. NEVO (NonEmergency Vehicle Operation) as driver
3. ER (Emergency Response) as driver
4. Spin out and response to scene
5. Enter shoot-house to take a report
6. Gun take-away and shooting
7. Interview

Subject-matter experts designed the scenario with the intent of invoking maximum stress in a realistic law enforcement environment. The scenario was captured on film for post-event scoring and was designed to be "winnable" for the tested subject. The research study verified several of the anticipated effects of stress on performance.

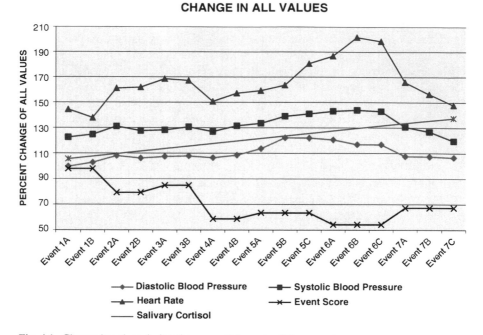

Fig. 4.1 Change in values during the sequential events of the scenario

A general statement could be made that as the stress levels increased, the cognitive ability decreased. Not only did judgment skills decline, but also performance skills, as shown by the average event score in Fig. 4.1. As the indicators of heart rate, systolic blood pressure, and cortisol increased, performance and decision-making ability decreased. More specifically, the study provided answers to the five original research questions.

Findings

The results of the study indicate that law enforcement training scenarios of this nature are indeed realistic and highly stressful. The response of the various body systems is comparable to those observed in other studies using acute stress on inactive subjects. Law enforcement encounters are particularly mentally and emotionally demanding, and require training that addresses these unique demands. High-stress training is required to expose trainees to these conditions in order to prepare officers for making decisions under stressful conditions. The decrease in cognitive ability (which in turn impairs performance) was demonstrated throughout the research study. It is the belief of the research team that performance levels can be improved through a greater exposure to high-stress training.

The relationship of psychological factors to performance in a high-stress encounter will require further examination. The trait of anger showed a significant correlation in more than one area, but all of the relationships were minimal. These relationships require closer review to explore their significance to responding in a stressful environment as well as how this information would be used to improve training. In this study, there were no psychological factors that demonstrated strong predictive power in identifying the successful performer from the unsuccessful performer.

One of the more notable findings of this study was that physiological factors do indeed respond to this type of stressful encounter, but not precisely in the manner that was anticipated. Although heart rate does elevate with emotional stress, it did not increase to the extent we had believed it would. Not only was the general range of heart rate response lower than projected, but also the range of increase had no relationship to satisfactory and unsatisfactory performance. The degree of increase in heart rate was unique to each individual and was not a limiting factor for mental or physical performance. Heart rate guided training has been promoted by several programs as the preferred method of choice for replicating high emotional stress. This study did not support that premise and showed that the stress zone (as measured by heart rate) is much lower, at least for an inactive subject. Additionally, even when heart rate is monitored, it provided no indication/predictability of successful performance. Low heart rates had the same pass/fail rate as high heart rates. Systolic blood pressure values more closely resembled the magnitude of increase previously reported in literature. Systolic values, nevertheless, had no predictive capacity in differentiating between the successful and unsuccessful students in the scenario.

Based upon the results of this study, there appeared to be no optimum zone of performance. When measured by heart rate, there was no difference in success rates for trainees who had heart rates in the low, middle, or upper portions of their heart rate zones. Identifying a "zone of optimum performance" as a zone where individuals perform at their best may possibly be identified through some other assessment, but were not identified from a specific heart rate, blood pressure, or cortisol level in this study. It was the mental/emotional stress that created the decision-making errors, but there was little relationship to the physiological indicators recorded in this project. Due to these results, trainers should not believe that they can identify a high-stress or low-stress individual based upon a specific heart rate or blood pressure value.

The physical exertion level of the students was intentionally minimized so that the changes observed in the physiological factors would be caused by emotional stress rather than physical stress or movement. It is commonly known how physical activity elevates heart rate and blood pressure levels. What is often overlooked is that the movement portion of the brain is separate from the emotional area, thereby exerting little control over mental operations. When an individual is performing a 2-mile run, the role of the brain is far different in handling the stress (physical versus emotional stress). The acute-stress scenario used in the study requires the cerebrum to analyze thousands of pieces of information in order to respond to numerous unknown situations. It is the brain's perception of a potential threat and activation to the "fight-or-flight stress response" that triggers the increased heart rate and blood pressure. In exercise-induced stress, the "perceived" threat is known – it is the challenge of lifting a certain weight or running at a specific pace. When individuals run, heart rate and blood pressure respond automatically. It is the exercise dictating the cardiovascular response, as opposed to the emotions triggering the cardiovascular response as observed in the research scenario. It would be erroneous to use physical activity solely as a stimulus to elevate heart rate and blood pressure in order to simulate a highly stressful "psychological" encounter. Training under psychological/emotional stress will better prepare the brain to perform under those conditions when the need arises versus having trainees exercise. The focus should be in the *process* of how the stress is created (the stimulus), rather than in the *product* of how the stress is measured (the response).

Finally, there indeed are situations when physical techniques and tactics are required in making an arrest. In this situation, the officer must utilize the motor areas of the upper brain as well as the thinking areas of the upper brain. In order for these multiple, complex operations to be performed by the brain, it is essential that the upper regions are allowed to operate efficiently and not be shut down by stress. When highly stressed, the brain preferentially seals off the upper (thinking) brain and only allows the lower (nonthinking, fight or flight) brain to operate as part of man's primitive, self-preservation instinct. Although this natural reaction is intended to streamline the response time, it inhibits an effective response by public safety or military personnel who are called upon to react in a specific manner that is oftentimes different from what the natural response would be. Training under stressful situations (stress exposure training) can correct how the brain interprets stressful factors and allow the upper brain (with complex thinking and motor skills) to be used. Several training strategies such as Information Training, Intensity Training, Overlearning, and Stress Exposure Training have been shown to improve performance under stressful situations.

This project provided repeated and measured examples of perceptual narrowing, poor decision-making skills, low cognitive scores, the reduced ability to perform sequential motor skills, and diminished recall of events during high stress. Decisions to not use the radio or verbal commands, maintain position of advantage while under fire, and to shoot at inappropriate times were cognitive decisions that produced notably poor performance. Manual skills such as reload failures, improper clearing of the weapon, and operation of the radio were physical skills negatively impacted by the cognitive process. These findings support previous research as to the negative effects of stress on decision making and on performance.

Outcomes and Implications

As identified in the research design, one of the objectives of this project was to identify a "survival score index" that would assist trainers in evaluating performance in a stressful training environment. This project has made significant contributions toward achieving that goal. The practice of incorporating physical exercise into an arrest techniques class to imitate psychological stress is no longer being done. Trainers have a clearer understanding of the difference between physical stress and psychological stress. Identifiable law enforcement skills were isolated and evaluated within the data set. While no survival scoring system was developed from this study, the work did serve as a foundation for knowledge of the stress response, and demonstrated the need for further research which is described in Phase II of the SSRP.

The Survival Scores Research Project: Phase II

In 2006, a new research team was formed with the goal of building on the previous findings and expanding its application to training. Subject-matter experts (SMEs) from the various training divisions at FLETC were used to review the previous study and the 97 performance elements. During the review, the research team realized that most of the skills were actually universal skills that could be found in many of the training disciplines (i.e., behavioral science, tactics, counterterrorism, vehicle operations, firearms, intermediate weapons, etc.). Additionally, the team conducted an extensive review of literature from law enforcement publications, Office of Personnel Management (OPM) competency statements, lessons learned from assaults on officers, reality-based training, and research on decision making under stress. Using the information from these multiple sources combined with the universal nature of the 97 performance elements, the SMEs restructured the elements into eight areas for use in measuring scenario performance. The SMEs believed that the eight factors more accurately represented "survival factors" associated with the ability to survive a confrontation. The new assessment model, termed the "STAR" for Scenario Training Assessment and Review (Fig. 4.2), are:

1. Situation Awareness (involves being aware of what is happening around you to understand how information, events, and your own actions will impact your goals and objectives, both now and in the near future)
2. Threat Identification (threats and nonthreats are accounted for, properly prioritized, effectively communicated, and appropriate response is efficiently planned)
3. Initial Response (strategy to counter threat or emergency situations including position of advantage, tactics, or other corrective actions)
4. Scene Control after the Initial Response (strategy to maintain control of the situation including evidence, crime scene, threats, victims, and witnesses)
5. Application of Force (application of appropriate/timely force options and articulation consistent with Constitutional Standard)
6. Arrest/Processing Techniques (initiation of correct procedures during an arrest including position of disadvantage, handcuffing, and search)
7. Communication (information exchange between entities through correct/timely verbal commands, nonverbal behaviors, and written accounts)
8. Articulation/After Action Review (AAR) (providing factual/accurate information during a scenario debriefing session)

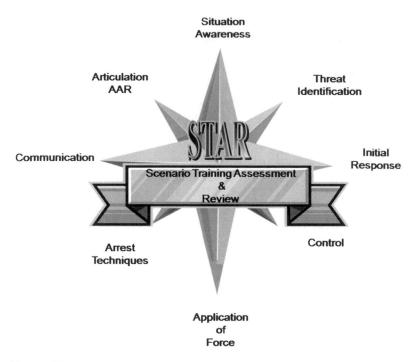

Fig. 4.2 The STAR

After reviewing the scoring process used in Phase 1, the research team sought to have a universal scale that would not only reflect the student's likelihood of winning a threat encounter, but also provide a more accurate and objective basis for feedback and mentoring of students following each scenario. A new "survival index" was created to more accurately capture the spectrum of student performance ranging from unacceptable to desirable. The survival index was based upon the comparison of risks associated with the performance and how the student's actions reduced the likelihood and severity of harm. Establishing an objective scale for risk assessment is a formidable task due to the fact that risk levels are interpreted differently by each individual. A general definition of risk assessment for this study was "the determination of quantitative or qualitative value of risk related to a concrete situation and a recognized threat." Clearly defined actions and responses were used as indicators of decision making, perception of the level of threat, individual vulnerabilities, potential consequences, and the resulting degree of anxiety.

In developing a risk-assessment scale, subject-matter experts thoroughly reviewed each scenario and identified those objects, situations, individuals, etc. that could cause harm, particularly to the officer/agent. After identifying each risk, the team determined how likely and severe the risk was, and then weighted the measures appropriately. In this manner, a more precise system of scoring was created that also provided more complete and detailed feedback to the student, and rendered a more realistic "survival score." The resulting risk-based scale can now award points for

Table 4.1 Scenario performance assessment scale

Rating	Description
0. Not applicable	Does not apply or is not observable
1. Not acceptable	Actions are not consistent with legal standard, creates serious risk, or did not perform
2. Least desirable	Actions generally acceptable but create identifiable risks
3. Acceptable	Actions are consistent with training but not most effective method or tactic
4. Desirable	Actions demonstrate sound and effective tactics

less-than-perfect performance as well as differentiate between the various levels of risk-based performance. The assessment scale for scoring student performance used a "0–4" Likert scale. Table 4.1 identifies each rating and provides a brief description of applicable student actions.

An example of this type of rating would award the student with a "4" (Desirable) if they successfully and timely performed a "Tap, Rack" during a weapon malfunction requiring a primary immediate action procedure. They would receive a "3" (Acceptable) if they cleared the malfunction in a timely manner but failed to "Tap" before raking the slide. They would receive a "2" (Least Desirable) if they failed to recognize the weapon malfunction in a timely manner or took an extended amount of time to clear the malfunction. They would receive a "1" (Not Acceptable) if they required multiple attempts or failed to clear the weapon.

The Research Objectives for Phase II of the SSRP

1. Refine "survival score assessment" scale to measure a student's ability to survive a threat encounter as well as to evaluate the training program itself and identify areas where training requires modification.
2. Refine measurement of psychological indicators of stress in a training environment simulating real-life, high-risk, highly stressful situations.
3. Develop and evaluate a feedback process that will enhance subsequent performance above that which is currently being used for trainees.
4. Evaluate the process of stress exposure. As students transition through four novel scenarios, how does that impact their level of stress and performance?

Research Design

Four research scenarios were developed in order to measure student performance in a realistic environment. Law enforcement students who satisfactorily completed all coursework and training at the FLETC volunteered as participants for the study.

There were 49 male and 9 female students who ranged in age from 23 to 56 years with a mean age of 29.8. In order to compare performance scores to the lethality of the scenario, the 58 students performed two lethal force scenarios (Active Shooter and Armed Robbery) and two nonlethal force scenarios (Trespasser and Attorney). The four scenarios were administered over a consecutive two-day period.

Prior to the first scenario (Response to Active Shooter), students received a pre-brief from an instructor. Immediately following each scenario, students were seated in an interview room and asked to complete a questionnaire that recorded the self-reported anger and anxiety levels they experienced during the scenario. Upon completion of the questionnaire, an instructor provided feedback to students regarding their performance during the scenario. Prior to the start of the second scenario (Noncompliant/Trespassing Protestor), students received the scenario pre-brief. Following the second scenario, students again completed the anger and anxiety questionnaire, received feedback on their performance, and received a situational awareness (SA) interview conducted by an FLETC instructor. During the SA interview, students were asked to recall details from the shoot scenario in order to determine their ability to articulate facts, the accuracy and detail of their recall, and understand their perception and thought process during the scenario. Based upon the level of detail students provided, the instructor would ask more specific questions in order to collect additional details. The instructors typically used follow-up questions such as "How many people were present? How many threats?" and additional questions about scenario details that were missed. On the following day, two new scenarios were used. Scenario three was a Noncompliant/ Attorney and scenario four was an Armed Robbery in Progress scenario. All four scenarios reflected similar fact patterns and required execution of basic law enforcement skills.

Results

Figure 4.3 provides an illustration summarizing the average ratings for each scenario. Each color reflects the range of performance ratings and provides a visual reference to the risk level associated with the rating. Blue (rating 4) indicates the "most desirable" performance level, green (rating 3) indicates performance that is rated "acceptable," gold (rating 2) reflects performance scored as "least desirable," and brown (rating 1) represents performance levels that were rated "not acceptable." The Active Shooter scenario had the highest average score with an average rating of 2.41. The Armed Robbery scenario had the second highest score, followed by the two nonlethal scenarios of Trespasser and Attorney. The Active Shooter and Trespasser scenarios contained several elements typically experienced during training. While the Armed Robbery scenario had fact patterns similar to the Active Shooter scenario, it included the additional challenge of a second armed suspect. The Attorney scenario presented the most novel experience and included multiple threats, one of which was a noncompliant authority figure.

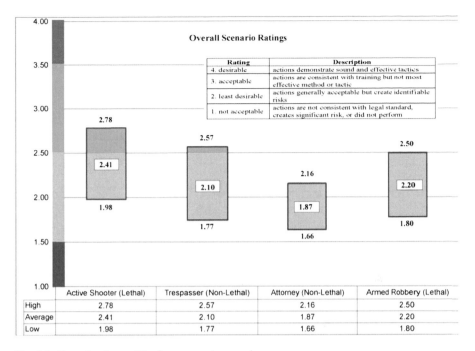

Fig. 4.3 Overall ratings of the four research scenarios

Findings

The stressful scenarios were created to realistically model lethal and nonlethal force situations typical for law enforcement officers and agents. The SSRP Phase II research team developed a new scale, the STAR, to identify the essential elements required to evaluate a student's ability to make decisions under threat conditions and implement those decisions to control the situation. The new scale made scoring more rapid and consistent between evaluators. The STAR factors provide a unique perspective by identifying eight skills that blend together to make a scenario that replicates a real-world confrontation. It is because the law enforcement skills become blurred in a dynamic encounter that such a scoring tool such as the STAR becomes most useful.

Similar to Phase I, a customized Spielberger State Trait Personality Inventory (STPI) and State Trait Anger Expression Inventory (STAXI) were used. The Spielberger instrument was selected due to the reliability and validity, and can be easily administered in a limited time period. Several performance elements were significantly correlated to STPI/STAXI personality traits and emotional states during the "Lethal" scenarios and one significant relationship was identified during the "NonLethal" scenario. During the "Active Shooter" scenario, both State Anxiety and State Anger negatively influenced scenario performance. The most significant state emotion variable related to lower scenario performance scores was State Anger.

With multiple STPI/STAXI scores correlating to the scenario performance scores, the Spielberger STPI/STAXI instrument provided an excellent tool to determine the relationship between emotions and performance.

The student-centered feedback model appears promising as a student training technique for highly dynamic training environments. The data, however, are not conclusive in identifying a superior method of feedback for law enforcement scenarios. The body of literature in this area, combined with feedback from the participant and general performance trends, supports further research to determine the level of effectiveness.

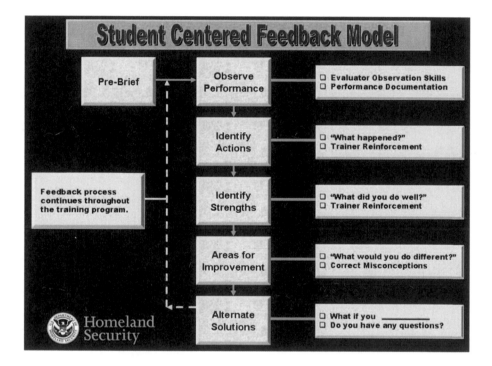

Although a significant drop in student anxiety was observed between the first and second scenario, no further reduction in anxiety or anger was observed between the remaining scenarios. It was also observed that students generally performed best in situations that most closely replicated the training they received. It is hypothesized that, because more training time is focused on lethal encounters, this facilitates higher scores in the lethal scenarios. Students performed better with the more familiar situation of a single (nonlethal) "Trespasser," and a single (lethal) "Active Shooter" where it was somewhat easier to identify and focus on the threat. This is in contrast to the crowded (nonlethal) "Attorney" and crowded/multiple threat (lethal) "Armed Robbery" scenarios where threat identification was more complex, and, hence, produced slower response times. Based upon the results of this study and a review of literature, trainers should not be of the false assumption that training with single suspects will prepare students for dealing with multiple suspects, or that training for lethal situations will prepare students for nonlethal situations – they do not. Students need to participate in diverse situations that are performed to completion in order for memories to be established that may be of invaluable use at a critical time in the future.

Outcomes and Implications

Several significant events took place while video recordings were shown to viewers. Students were very passive when feedback was provided from a clipboard checklist. When video was used along with the checklist, students were truly amazed that they indeed had committed several critical errors, overlooked several items, and, basically, had a totally incorrect assessment of their performance. During the review of their videotaped performance, *every* student realized that their memories were distorted by stress, and that more stress-exposure training would benefit their future performance. For the various training divisions, the use of video replay provides an objective, non-confrontational way to evaluate training effectiveness. Rather than using subjective terms such as slow, out of position, ineffective, etc., to describe student performance in a scenario, a video provides objective information (video) to trainers and they quickly view (or review multiple times) what is/is not working for their students without any other issues clouding the central focus of student performance.

Rather than providing evaluative information back to students on their recent performance without specific guidelines as to "how" the information is given back, several instructor-training programs have incorporated the guidelines for "student-centered" feedback. Based upon extensive research, the student-centered process provides structure and consistency for new instructors, and structured opportunities for experienced trainers to dig deeper and determine what students fully comprehend and can apply to novel situations.

The SSRP has provided a self-assessment of our training process as it prepares officers for real-world encounters. The research has provided a scenario scoring process that is more accurate and consistent, with a better process for determining if the appropriate amount of stress and complexity are in a specific scenario or training program. One of the major benefits of this type of applied research is that it has indeed allowed us to test many traditional and novel training methodologies to scientifically determine if proficiency in law enforcement knowledge, performance, and application has increased, decreased, or remained the same.

Corresponding Lessons (Derivatives of Research)

While the above sections highlight outcomes specific to two research initiatives undertaken by FLETC, there are a number of corresponding lessons gleaned from the research process. Each on their own adds a valuable dimension to the process of program development and delivery.

Learning: As part of the FLETC's research on stress and performance, an extensive review of literature was performed in order to apply those methodologies that would increase learning transference. Beyond traditional learning theory models, recent studies on the "science of learning" and memory "chunking" became an integral part of the FLETC strategy to increase learning transfer. During this internal assessment, it became clear that more attention needed to be focused on what the student does with the content (outcomes), rather than the delivery process for the content. While the learner bears a significant responsibility in the learning process, the training institution, which controls the content and the delivery process, has a greater role in determining whether the student will "get it" and not "forget it." By understanding how students learn, instructors can more effectively design both their content and delivery to take advantage of current research. The FLETC also focused on a complex component of learning: information recall, and how recall takes place in the big filing cabinet between the ears (a.k.a. "the brain"). The storage and retrieval of information are key to effective learning. While it is not difficult to cram "stuff" into the filing cabinet, it is often difficult to find specific information when the law enforcement officer needs it. Good instructional design can have a huge impact on how well information is stored and retrieved. In order to comprehend what takes place during the learning process, it is essential to understand how the brain stores and retrieves information.

Short-term memory: The first stage of memory is short-term memory. This is probably the most essential goal of instruction. What takes place in short-term memory has the greatest impact on what is learned. Short-term memory lasts for minutes or hours, but is temporary unless it is committed to long-term memory. Short-term memory is also known as "working" memory and more readily defines the fact that short-term memory is the information that one is thinking about at the moment. The content of this page is entering into your short-term memory, while the traffic route used daily to get to work is not in short-term memory. The content of this page is floating around in your short-term memory, and may or may not become permanent. Things that prevent short-term memory from converting into long-term memory include interruptions, lack of reinforcement, and lack of motivation. One thing is certain. This paragraph has written out the term "short-term memory" enough times in this one paragraph to reinforce the concept. If you were interrupted or lack the motivation to understand the term, this concept could be gone by tomorrow.

Long-term memory: How exactly are things remembered? What a person knows, their body of knowledge, perceptions, interpretations, emotions, and experiences are stored in long-term memory. Long-term memory is a lot like a hard drive, or for the older reader, a filing cabinet. Information only gets stored in long-term memory when the learner is attentive during the short-term or working memory phase. This means the learner considered the information meaningful, focused on it, and was motivated to retain the information. The time it takes for the information to transfer from short-term into long-term memory is not known, but research suggests that the transfer typically takes place during sleep. There are a number of studies demonstrating that sleep is critical for the conversion of short-term information into long-term memory (Stickgold, Hobson, Fosse, & Fosse, 2001). Knowing this "window of opportunity" helps trainers in developing blocks of instruction that follow these biological guidelines. Learning can indeed be improved when the old adage of "sleeping on it" is applied. Consider the potential impact on instructional planning. Next is an understanding of how memories are formed.

Experiences count: Memories are truly a reflection of one's experiences. For example, someone who has survived a direct hit by a tornado will probably seek cover when hearing the tornado warning sirens. For those who have not yet experienced this force of nature, curiosity may provoke them to wander outside to get a closer look. Using a law enforcement example of instructing students on the use of deadly force provides some framework for the challenges confronted by trainers. What does the student already know about deadly force?

Students pull their "experiences" out of long-term memory and try to add the new deadly force instruction on top of their experiences or thoughts on the topic. Once the existing memory is modified with the new information, it goes back into long-term memory. There is no telling, however, what the newly modified memory of deadly force looks like. It becomes the instructor's responsibility to properly shape and redefine what the student knows about deadly force. Remember several paragraphs ago the term "short-term memory" was described and then reinforced? So too should important memories be reviewed, practiced, and refined. Deadly force may be presented in the lecture, and, then three days later, the student might be asked to review some decision-making scenarios on a firearms simulator. The memory of deadly force is retrieved from the file cabinet, modified, clarified, and reinforced with the simulation scenarios, and, once again, tucked away. Each time the deadly force topic is reviewed; the knowledge is reinforced, and becomes a stronger, clearer memory and experience for the student. Remember the list of items (religion, shooting to wound, etc.) different students might think about when the topic was first introduced? The original experiences or memories prior to the law enforcement instruction are weakened as the newly molded knowledge is reinforced and becomes dominant in the mind of the learner. Thus, training has effected change. Trainers can use this process to constantly build, reinforce, and refine learning by steering the learner with clear goals and objectives of the law enforcement task.

Rule of 7: While long-term memory appears to have an endless storage capacity, short-term memory (the inbox) is considerably small. In fact, research has shown that short-term memory can handle an average of only seven things (plus or minus two) at a time (Hays, 2006). Tests have shown that when one is given a list of words to read and remember, the average person can recall about seven words on the list. However, one can remember more words if they are "chunked" into groups. For example, if the list contains ten words and three of them are trout, bass, and catfish, learners can group the fish as one chunk of information, facilitating the recall of the entire list. Later, the various groupings are retrieved from long-term memory as chunks. The phone company used this research as the basis for seven-digit phone numbers (LeDoux, 2002). People can generally recall the seven individual numbers in short-term memory long enough to allow it to enter long-term memory as a chunk of information.

An area of concern, however, is trying to learn very similar chunks of information before they have a chance to gravitate to long-term memory. An example would be learning to tie a Windsor knot, a half-Windsor knot, and a four-in-hand knot. While each technique represents a "chunk" of information, learning them all at the same time would not permit each technique to stand alone as a chunk of information. The three techniques would first transfer to short-term memory, and later to long-term memory as one chunk. When retrieved from memory, it would take considerable time for the thought process to sort through the entire chunk of knot-tying techniques in order to separate them into three different techniques. In fact, the memory may be so convoluted that the person cannot actually tie the knot until some re-learning (and thus re-wiring and reinforcement of the technique) occurs. In the law enforcement context, this could be an issue for weapons loading, reloading and unloading procedures, hard and soft hand controls, verbal commands, and, yes, even tying knots on police boats. When considering training delivery, trainers should try to keep the chunks of information within the magic number of seven items, and dissimilar enough to ensure the information transitions properly to the long-term memory internal hard drive.

Order of training: A simple, yet important, rule to follow when conducting training is to ensure that the most important information in the lesson should be conveyed first. Students will generally retain more of what is presented early in the lesson as opposed to what is presented late in the lesson. Factors influencing this phenomenon include attention levels, motivation, and the rule of seven. Instructional design becomes a little more complicated for lessons where the instructional points build on each other, with the "crescendo" of the learning often coming at the end of the lesson. Topics that fall in this area should be presented through part-task training, and breaking up the lesson into mini-lessons so there are multiple lesson "start" points.

Motor skill learning: The learning of skills and improving motor performance has been the subject of numerous studies. For law enforcement trainers, it is important to understand the differences between motor learning (performance) and cognitive learning (knowledge). Performance is an observable behavior, whereas, learning, knowing or knowledge are not observable and must be either inferred or evaluated through an observable process (a test). Motor learning begins the same way all learning begins – with the knowledge stage. In this stage, information is learned about the skill and, similar to other areas, a file is created in the brain incorporating the skill requirements. Next is the skill stage where the technique is practiced, thereby connecting the motor domain to the cognitive domain. As practice continues, the performance is evaluated and mistakes are corrected. This step allows the memory to be updated with refined data of what a good performance truly looks and feels like. Finally, practice should lead the learner to the automatic or habitual phase. In this phase, the student does not concentrate on the motor performance itself, but rather on the aspects of the performance that may vary the outcome. For example, when learning to shoot, students first learn the grip and draw as a set of rules about hand placement on the grip, the movements required to break free of the holster, and the smooth movement of the weapon to the supporting hand and the shooting position. Second, the student learns what this feels like. As the student repeats the "push–pull" action required to break free of the holster, they feel and refine what is needed for skillful execution. In the third and final phase, drawing the weapon is an automatic action or "habit" and not a series of steps that need to examined and considered each time. The student draws the weapon and concentrates instead on the delivery of the shot and the conditions and decisions made in delivering the shot.

There are some key points that trainers should consider when teaching motor skills topics:

1. Retention of a skill can be improved through repetition. "Proper practice makes perfect, and more practice makes more perfect" is certainly true. A caveat to practice and retention, however, is the law of diminishing returns. There is definitely a threshold for skill improvement from practice, and it is the instructor/ trainer's job to figure out where the threshold of diminishing returns is. Tremendous variations influence the "practice factor" and how much is enough to achieve optimum efficiency without hitting the performance peak and wasting precious training time.

2. Skills are better retained if the practice is spaced. There is significant research pointing to distributed practice as superior to massed practice when it comes to performance. The skill and the learning stages for students will dictate the instruction time required for them to learn the skill. In the early stages of learning, the mind can reach a point where little additional information can be retained. Once a level of mental fatigue is reached, performance can actually diminish due to the mental effort involved in processing the new information (before you get to automatic learning). Depending on the skill and repetitions, physical fatigue may also kick in and impact performance. The experienced trainer should be alert to these changes and consider smaller blocks of instruction in order to optimize performance improvement.

As a result of a high level of failure to follow proper procedures while clearing a weapons malfunction under stress, an examination of FLETC instructional methodology was scrutinized. The training involved providing two hours of detailed classroom instruction consisting of lecture and hands-on walk-thru of five loading, reloading, unloading, and weapons clearing skills. This was followed with reinforcing practice during live-fire training. However, during the stress research, the FLETC research team found that fully 95% of the students failed to properly (as trained) clear the weapon. Later, the same instruction was broken down into separate lessons delivered on different days. By providing smaller chunks of information on weapons handling to the students, it was easier to store and retrieve the information from long-term memory. The change in the delivery process made the information more accessible. Students no longer had to sort through a large chunk of information to rapidly uncover the proper skill to perform. After changes to the delivery, 86% demonstrated the ability to properly clear the weapon.

Motivation: One final consideration that can have a dramatic impact on learning is motivation. Motivation is a critical component of learning. Research tells us that motivation is both value-based and emotion-based. If students see value in the information, they will be motivated to learn the material. The higher the value placed on the information, the greater the effort applied to paying attention to all aspects of the instruction. The emotional nexus also impacts learning and retention. Training that is highly enjoyable or stressful adds an emotional component that serves to provide additional cement to imbed the information into memory.

Conclusion

While it would seem that much "space" has been devoted to the discussion of applied learning, the understanding of learning and its application to training is an important outcome for FLETC. The study of learning theory and learning science reveals a tremendous pool of considerations for the law enforcement trainer. The ability to test and evaluate outcomes of various instructional methodologies for law enforcement officers is unusual in the law enforcement profession. The opportunity to apply this body of knowledge toward improving the training outcome is imperative to improving the knowledge, skills, and abilities of law enforcement officers worldwide. Though research takes considerable time and effort, the FLETC recognizes the unique opportunities to apply theory to practice, and measure those outcomes through evaluation in an applied law enforcement setting. The study of learning is one facet of the FLETC's efforts to create effective strategies that will facilitate improved outcomes.

References

Driskell, J. E., & Salas, E. (Eds.). (1996). *Stress and human performance*. Hillsdale, NJ: Erlbaum.

Hancock, P. A., & Desmond, P. A. (Eds.). (2001). *Stress, workload and fatigue*. Mahwah, NJ: Erlbaum.

Hays, R. T. (2006). *The science of learning: A systems theory perspective*. Boca Raton, FL: Brown Walker Press.

Hockey, G. R. J. (1997). Compensatory control in the regulation of human performance under stress and high workload: A cognitive-energetical framework. *Biological Psychology, 45*, 73–93.

Lazarus, R. S., & Folkman, S. (1984). *Stress, appraisal, and coping*. New York: Springer.

LeDoux, J. E. (2002). *Synaptic self: How our brains become who we are*. New York: Viking Penguin.

Salas, E., Driskell, J. E., & Hughes, S. (1996). The study of stress and human performance. In J. E. Driskell & E. Salas (Eds.), *Stress and human performance*. Hillsdale, NJ: Erlbaum.

Spielberger, C. D., & Reheiser, E. C. (2003). Measuring anxiety, anger, depression, and curiosity as emotional states and personality traits with stai, staxi, and stpi. In M. J. H. M. Herson & D. L. Segal (Eds.), *Comprehensive handbook of psychological assessment* (Vol. 2, pp. 70–86). Hoboken: Wiley.

Stickgold, R., Hobson, J., Fosse, R., & Fosse, M. (2001). Sleep, learning and dreams: Off-line memory reprocessing. *Science, 294*, 1052–1057.

Chapter 5
From Theory to Practice: Simulation Technology as a Training Tool in Law Enforcement

Gregory P. Krätzig and Christine Hudy

Introduction

What is simulation? While most people can articulate a basic definition, Merriam-Webster (1991) defines simulation as "the imitative representation of the functioning of one system or process by means of the functioning of another," whereas simulator is defined as "a device that enables the operator to reproduce or represent under test conditions phenomena likely to occur in actual performance" (Merriam-Webster). Apart from dictionary definitions, the term simulator may conjure up images of a pilot surrounded by instruments with computer screens in place of windows, or arcade games in which you and a friend are racing along in a car at over 300 kph through the streets of San Francisco.

A Brief History of Simulation

When you consider the advances of simulation technology, it is hard to imagine that simulation as an instructional tool can be traced back to the sixteenth century where military commanders used games of chess to reproduce the battlefield (Perkins, 2007). It was not until the early 1900s that simulation really began to take root in other areas of instruction. Seven years after the Wright brothers first took to the skies, simulators such as the Saunders Teacher or the Billings Trainer allowed novice pilots the opportunity to understand how an airplane works in the air, without personal risk (Haward, 1910; Page, 2000). However, the Antoinette "Apprenticeship Barrel" Trainer was one of the first and probably best-known flight simulators

G.P. Krätzig (✉) • C. Hudy
Royal Canadian Mounted Police, Regina, SK, Canada
e-mail: gregory.kratzig@rcmp-grc.gc.ca

M.R. Haberfeld et al. (eds.), *Police Organization and Training: Innovations in Research and Practice*, DOI 10.1007/978-1-4614-0745-4_5,
© Springer Science+Business Media, LLC 2012

(Koonce & Bramble, 1998, p. 2000). Using two halves of a barrel mounted one on top of each other, the pilot, who sat in the uppermost barrel, experienced the pitch and roll of an airplane created by workers who independently moved the barrels based on what the pilot was doing with the landing gear. While these simulators were viewed as effective training tools, it was not until the Link Trainer, developed just before World War II, that flight simulators gained widespread acceptance (Koonce & Bramble, p. 2000). Today, flight simulation has been so readily ingrained as a training tool that some multi-engine fixed-wing commercial pilots may have up to 40% of their total logged flight hours occur in a simulator, all of which go toward their accreditation (Federal Aviation Administration, Part 142).

The popularity of the Link Trainer led to other professions looking for ways simulations could be developed for their specific needs. For example, the National Aeronautics and Space Administration (NASA) used simulations to repair not only Skylab, but also used it as a training tool for the Apollo program (Rosen, 2008). Examples of other professions that use simulations for training are Air traffic controllers and the military, while the National Highway Safety Administration (NHSA) is working on protocols for a national driving simulator program (Rosen; Sanderson, Mooij, & Neal, 2007; Smith, 2010). The medical profession has incorporated simulation into many training programs, and as of 2005, more than 35% of medical schools in the United States have medical-based simulation centers (Ahlberg et al., 2007; McGaghie, Issenberg, Petrusa, & Scalese, 2010). In fact, students can practice such things as cardiac resuscitation, delivery of babies, or attending to a severe trauma victim, all without touching a human patient (Issenberg, McGaghie, Petrusa, Gordon, & Scalese, 2005; Rosen, 2008). Currently, medical simulation training has proven to be so valuable and effective that the Risk Management Foundation of Harvard Medical Institutions offers lower insurance rates for employees who train, at least some of their time, using an anesthesia simulator (Friedrich, 2002). Whether it is a pilot transporting 700 people on an Airbus 380, or a surgeon performing laparoscopic surgery, many professionals have received a significant amount of training in a simulated environment. While most current heavy users (e.g., medicine) of simulation as a training tool were not early adopters of this technology, the newness of this technology in the area of law enforcement training has seen skepticism and resistance, a curious observation considering that its acceptance in life-or-death professions such as surgery or air travel.

Although the military is the main driver of the multi-billion-dollar simulation industry, many companies have identified business opportunities in the area of law enforcement. As a result, simulators are available that allow a police officer to navigate a vehicle through an intersection while responding to an emergency call, deal with a life-or-death situation in a video-based judgment simulator, or shoot at a simulated target using laser-based weapons. However, a review of the extant literature has revealed a paucity of empirical research using simulation technology in a law enforcement environment. While this equipment is readily available, many jurisdictions are hesitant to commit a significant portion of their budget toward the purchase of this largely untested technology. While the aforementioned example might be a reason why many police agencies do not have simulators in their training programs, this is not the entire reason. Also evident are the traditional biases which suggest that in order to learn how to shoot a pistol or navigate an intersection, you need to see "smoke come out of the barrel" or "feel the car move." While these may be possible environmental considerations, it should be pointed out by the time that many of our sensory systems (e.g., olfactory) have identified the smell of the gunpowder, the bullet has already passed through the target. This chapter will present how the Royal Canadian Mounted Police (RCMP) has integrated simulation technology into its Cadet Training Program (CTP).

Before graduating from the RCMP training academy, cadets (i.e., police students and recruits) must complete an intensive basic training program (i.e., CTP). The curriculum is designed using an integrated, problem-based learning (PBL) methodology, meaning that cadets acquire the fundamental competencies required for policing by solving representative problems they would typically face as police officers in the field. They begin by working through simple scenarios (e.g., a shoplifting offence) to obtain foundational and transferable knowledge and skills. As their training program progresses, cadets deal with increasingly complex scenarios (e.g., sudden death and sexual assault), which enable them to gain advanced knowledge and skills, and at the same time apply the material they have already learned. In essence, PBL teaches cadets how to transfer the concepts, and, more importantly, the processes for dealing with new and novel situations. Cadets thus develop their abilities to think critically and solve problems, which are widely recognized as critical competencies for police officers (Birzer, 2003; Bloss, 2004; Chappell, 2005; McCoy, 2006).

Training Gaps

Driving. While PBL is still the primary approach to training, simulation technology allows, for the first time, opportunities to expose cadets to situations that they will encounter in the field but are too dangerous to teach during basic training (e.g., intersection clearing). Consider for a moment the example of the "Miracle on the Hudson" in which a US Airways Airbus A320 struck a flock of birds resulting in both engines shutting down. While the pilot (Captain Sullenberger) successfully landed the jet on the Hudson River in New York, for obvious reasons this procedure cannot be practiced in situ. Although Captain Sullenberger is a seasoned pilot and his years of experience cannot be discounted, he does indicate that landing a passenger jet without engine power is practiced in a flight simulator during a pilot's recertification period (Sullenberger, personal communication, 2010). Although the previous statement demonstrates the value that simulation technology brings to the pilot training environment, for the first time this technology now provides law enforcement educators an opportunity to address serious training gaps.

Police training is extensive, intensive, and comprehensive; yet, there are areas in which police cadets cannot be adequately trained. For example, cadets are provided with instruction on how to drive in both urban and rural settings. However, teaching emergency vehicle response intersection clearing (EVRIC) procedures in situ, without considerable risk to both the public and student, is not possible. Most new police officers therefore, acquire their EVRIC skills in less-than-ideal conditions, and if they are fortunate, they have a seasoned officer sitting next to them.

Barrows (1996) and Dochy, Segers, Van en Bossche, and Gijbels (2003) argued that learning environments should be representative of real-life situations offering opportunities to learn through interaction. Although some high-risk skills are taught on a closed driving track, most EVRIC skills are taught "on the fly"; a process counter to what is prescribed by Barrows and Dochy et al. This last point is particularly salient as most emergency vehicle collisions occur during EVRIC situations (Hunt et al., 1995; Pipes & Paper, 2001). Therefore, equipping police officers with the skills they needed to respond safely and quickly will ultimately save lives and reduce injuries. The EVRIC training gap provided a research opportunity at the RCMP training academy and, during a 2-year period, this problem was investigated using recently acquired driving simulators (L-3 Communications, 2000).

Research

Emergency Vehicle Response Intersection Clearing

A series of studies was undertaken at the RCMP training academy, designed to provide the empirical evidence needed to integrate driving simulators into the driver-training program. Despite the scant research in this area, we did review some existing research which was conducted by Applied Simulations Technologies (AST) (2006). Their findings suggest that good performance can be attained over the course of 16 unique EVRIC simulations; however, there was little evidence that those skills transferred into the real world. Using AST's research protocol, the study was replicated using police cadets, and the resulting data verified AST's findings; however, when these data were examined in greater detail it was discovered that performance asymptotes approximately midway through the session (i.e., no performance improvement after the seventh of 16 scenarios), a finding that was also revealed with the RCMP data. By completing seven scenarios, cadets were able to achieve the same level of performance as those cadets who were exposed to 16 scenarios. Once satisfied that cadet performance had been maximized in the simulators, additional research studies were designed to investigate whether the skills learned transfer to a real-world setting. In an effort to collect this type of data, an intersection was constructed on a portion of driving track located on the grounds of the training academy (see Fig. 5.1 for intersection configuration).

The next line of studies was designed to measure skill transfer from a simulated environment to a real-world setting, to determine if skill transfer does take place, and, if so, to what extent does it occur. In order to answer this question, cadets first completed the seven simulation scenarios (i.e., SIC; simulation intersection clearing)

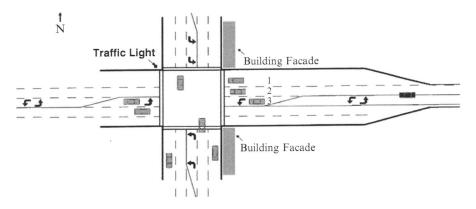

Fig. 5.1 Traffic and traffic light change depending on the scenario (e.g., Red light and *lane 1, 2, 3* blocked with eastbound traffic; Krätzig, Bell, Groff, & Ford, 2010)

before completing the three track exercises (i.e., LIC; live intersection clearing). Because only a single controlled intersection was constructed, scenario development was limited to three different configurations (e.g., green light, red light turn lane open, and red light turn lane closed). These scenarios were modeled after the first (SIC1), third (SIC2), and sixth (SIC3) simulated scenarios. Cadets completed the LIC scenarios in sequence (i.e., scenario LIC1, LIC2, and LIC3), the same order in which the SIC scenarios are presented. This approach allowed for a direct comparison between in situ performance and simulator performance.

These results revealed that skills acquired in a simulator transfer into a real-world setting. However, the LIC training occurred without the benefit of cars moving in the intersection (i.e., static), something that the cadets would have encountered in the simulated scenarios, and something that they will encounter as a police officer. This point is particularly important when research from the aviation and medical fields is considered. Following a review of the literature, a common theme emerged suggesting that in order to achieve the best training success, a simulated scenario must generalize in situ (Abrahamson, Denson, & Wolf, 2004; Bürke-Cohen, Go, & Longridge, 2001). The next LIC training session considered these recommendations, and a dynamic environment was created in which the north- and south-bound vehicles (i.e., actor vehicles) moved into the intersection as the cadet approached from the east in their police car.

Cadet performance between static and dynamic LIC scenarios was compared. These data revealed that performance in the dynamic environment was significantly better than performance in the static environment. However, this was not the only factor affecting performance improvement. When the data were examined within subjects, it revealed that performance during red light scenarios was significantly better than green light scenarios, regardless of whether actor vehicles are moving. Nonetheless, as evidenced with the static LIC exposures, performance in the dynamic environment also appeared to plateau after LIC2 (Fig. 5.2).

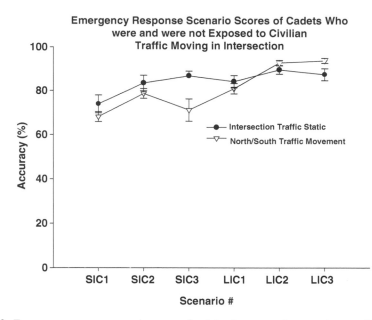

Fig. 5.2 Emergency response scenario scores of cadets who were and were not exposed to civilian traffic moving in intersection. *Note*: *SIC1* Simulator scenario straight through on green light; *SIC2* simulator scenario turn left on red light; *SIC3* simulator scenario straight through on red light; *LIC1* track scenario straight through on green light, *LIC2* track scenario turn left on red light; *LIC3* track scenario straight through on red light (Krätzig et al., 2010)

The goal of this research was to investigate whether skills acquired in a simulator were transferable to a real-world setting, and the results demonstrate that simulator training is an effective method in which to deliver this type of instruction (Krätzig et al., 2010). Traditional methods of driver training provide kinesthetic sensations that the simulators do not (e.g., physiological sensation of acceleration); however, the intent was not to teach cadets how to drive, but instead was to teach decision-making and hazard recognition skills. Just like landing an aircraft on the water, training in a simulated environment allows cadets to be exposed to potentially hazardous situations. If a cadet hits a car or pedestrian, it becomes a valuable teaching moment before the instructor resets the scenario and the cadet moves on to their next attempt.

Firearms Course-of-Fire

Simulation training is not limited to driver training, and research is also underway investigating the effectiveness of teaching cadets the pistol course-of-fire (COF) in a simulated environment, to determine whether those skills can be transferred in situ.

Although the intent is to teach cadets how to shoot the pistol COF in a virtual environment, it was decided that a pilot study comprising University of Regina undergraduate Police Studies students would be used. Using this pilot group was a way of collecting the empirical evidence needed before this technology could be used to train cadets. The university students were taught the entire COF in the virtual environment. In order to keep the testing conditions consistent between the virtual and live environments, and to measure the transferability of skills between these environments, the three evaluation sessions (i.e., benchmark 1, benchmark 2, and final qualification) were conducted on the live-fire range.

An analysis of the data from the pilot group revealed that the skill level at each of their evaluation sessions was comparable to a control group of live-fire-trained cadets. The results of the pilot study also indicate that the pass/fail rate between the pilot group and a control group of live-fire-trained cadets was not significantly different. These data provided, for the first time, the evidence needed to train a regular troop of cadets to shoot the pistol COF in a virtual environment.

Competency in firearms is one of the many skills where a cadet must demonstrate professionalism before being engaged into the field. With this in mind, steps were taken to address any potential problems that might result in moving from virtual to live-fire training.[1] Additionally, it is not uncommon to have some members of each cadet troop struggle with their pistol-training portion of the program. When this occurs, they are afforded additional opportunities, after hours, to practice shooting (i.e., learning assistance). Once the cadet has completed their learning assistance, they are given a second opportunity to pass their benchmark. Due to the success of the University of Regina pilot study, it was decided that a cadet troop would receive all their learning assistance in the simulated range. This was done in part because the University of Regina students received their learning assistance in this environment and they successfully passed their final qualification. Additionally, because the efficacy of pistol training in a simulated environment was being investigated, it was important to limit the number of live rounds fired.

The results of this research suggest that this skill can be taught in the absence of live fire. When performance was measured at benchmark 1 and benchmark 2, there were no pass/fail differences between the live-fire control group and the simulation training group. The most interesting part of the study was not realized until the final qualification session. Following this session, significantly more cadets failed their first attempt compared with the live-fire-trained control group. Although initially it was unclear why this group underperformed the live-fire-trained cadets, it was clear by the second learning assistance session that these cadets had the necessary skills to be successful with their pistol. In fact, each cadet increased their scores significantly, and, in some cases the improvement was by as much as 35%, a finding not evidenced by cadets taught strictly in a live-fire environment. If this session had been their second attempt at their final qualification, each cadet would have passed.

---

[1] If there was evidence that these skills were not being transferred to the cadets, arrangements were made to switch training to the live-fire range. Additionally, live-fire range time was scheduled following their final qualification session to give the cadets live-fire exposure.

Fig. 5.3 *BMK1* Benchmark
1; *BMK2* Benchmark 2;
FQ Final Qualification; *Extra*
Extra live shooting following
the completion of the Final
Qualification session

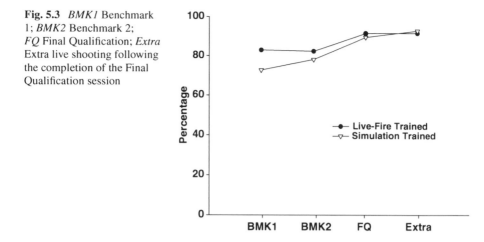

However, to maintain consistency and adhere to the research protocols established at the beginning of the study, it was important to give all cadets who failed their first final qualification the same amount of learning assistance as live-fire-trained cadets. When this group had completed their last learning assistance session, they attended their second attempt to pass their final qualification. In this instance, all of the cadets passed and successfully graduated from the training academy. Three observations emerged from this study. (1) Police cadets can be taught their entire pistol COF in a simulated environment, with no negative impact. (2) While there were a high number of cadets trained in the simulated environment who failed their final qualification, by their second session of learning assistance they were scoring markedly higher. These results suggest that there was not a deficit in skill level, but that the failure rate might be more attributable to test anxiety. (3) The simulation-trained cadets shot an average of eight points higher than an average live-fire-trained troop upon leaving the training academy (Fig. 5.3).

While the results of several years of research have provided sound empirical evidence that simulators are an effective training tool, it is important to note that this technology is not intended to replace some traditional training practices. Instead, they are intended to enhance and augment the CTP, filling training gaps that could not be previously addressed (e.g., EVRIC). Additionally, when it was found that the driving simulators could provide an effective teaching environment, it was important not to "bolt" them on to the program, but instead to integrate them directly into the CTP.

Redesign of Police Driving

The completion of the 2-year research study investigating the efficacy of the driving simulators coincided with the redesign of the Police Driving Unit (PDU) program.

Table 5.1 Systems Approach Model (SAM) (Dick & Carey, 1978)

Step	Step description
1	Identify instructional goals
2	Conduct instructional analysis
3	Analyze learners and contexts
4	Write performance objectives
5	Develop assessment instruments
6	Develop instructional strategy
7	Develop and select instructional materials
8	Design and conduct formative evaluation
9	Revise instruction
10	Design and conduct summative evaluation

Note: This table represents information from the SAM

This redesign needed to integrate the driving simulators into the program, while resolving several outstanding training issues. For example, the existing program focused on precision driving and perfecting civilian defensive driving techniques rather than refining knowledge and skills related specifically to police driving, such as critical thinking, task prioritization, radio communications, and emergency vehicle operation (EVO). In addition, training time during in-vehicle sessions was being used inefficiently. During these sessions, the troop ($n=32$) was divided into teams of three and, with the facilitator in the passenger seat, each cadet took a single turn as the driver and two turns in the backseat as a passive observer-learner. Summative evaluations of the sessions established that passive observer learning was nominal as it related to driver performance. This, in concert with the efficacy of the driving simulators and the desire to enhance police driving skills, provided the stimulus to undertake a comprehensive review and redesign of the PDU program, and integrate the driving simulators.

Several critical decisions were made early in the review and redesign process, with the most important being that the curriculum would be developed as if no driving program was in place. This was a radical departure from past program redesign practices at the RCMP training academy; however, a complete rewrite offered the best mechanism for fully integrating the driving simulators and ensuring that cadets were graduating with the required competencies in police driving. To achieve these targets, the Systems Approach Model (SAM) was adopted to guide the instructional design of the curriculum (see Table 5.1 for SAM detail) (Dick & Carey, 1978). The Model's detailed procedures for designing instruction provided a solid foundation upon which to construct the program. A multidisciplinary project team[2] began by identifying the project's scope, tasks, and timelines, setting a 1-year development phase and a 1-year implementation phase with three successive pilot troops. These critical decisions outlined the structure and parameters for the redesign of the PDU program.

---

[2] Instructional designers, subject-matter experts, multimedia designer.

Table 5.2 Police Driving Unit (PDU) before and after program redesign

Before			After		
Week	Session	Hours	Week	Session	Hours
2	Orientation	3	2	Orientation	4
3	Patrol Drive 1	4	3	D-Sim 1 and Introductory Radio Communications	2
7	Patrol Drive 2	4	4	D-Sim 2 and Intermediate Radio Communications/ Patrol Drive 1	4
9	Collision Investigation	10	7	D-Sim 3 and Intermediate Radio Communications/ Patrol Drive 2	4
11	Police Patrol Techniques Test	3	10	Patrol Drive 3	4
14	Patrol Drive 4 (BOLO)	3	11	D-Sim 4/Tire Deflation Device	2
15	Advanced Driving Theory	2	13	Collision Investigation	10
16	Highway and Gravel Road Drive	7	15	AEVOC Theory	1
18	Advanced Driving Practical	14	15	Highway and Gravel Road Drive	7
20	Re-testing	3	16	AEVOC Practical	14
21	EVO Theory	3	18	D-Sim 5/EVO Theory	4
22	EVO Scenarios/High-Risk Vehicle Extraction	6	19	D-Sim 6/EVO Exposure	4
23	EVO Exam	1	20	EVO Scenarios/High-Risk Vehicle Extraction	6
			21	EVO Exam	1
	Total hours	63		*Total hours*	67

Note: *D-Sim* Driving simulators; *EVO* Emergency Vehicle Operation; *AEVOC* Advanced Emergency Vehicle Operator's Course

In the first step of SAM, the instructional goals must state, in observable terms, what the cadets will be able to do upon the completion of the PDU program. Based on a needs assessment, four primary instructional goals were identified: (1) conduct a patrol drive; (2) engage in EVO (including emergency response, closing the distance and pursuit); (3) carry out a basic collision investigation; and (4) perform a high-risk vehicle extraction. As the design process unfolded, an unexpected opportunity for using the driving simulators arose. Although the RCMP's purpose for acquiring the driving simulators was for intersection clearing instruction, it became evident that this technology could be used to introduce and reinforce certain elements of patrol driving and emergency response. They could also be used to provide exposures to closing the distance and night driving. By dividing a troop into two relays (i.e., each relay $n = 16$), and switching the relays between a simulator and an in-vehicle session, the amount of time a cadet spends sitting in the backseat of a vehicle would be significantly reduced. Using this information, the next step in the design process involved developing the instructional strategies, resulting in the outline for the new PDU program (Table 5.2).

Driving Simulators in Patrol Driving and Emergency Response

The first three sets of driving simulator and radio communications sessions (Table 5.2) introduce and reinforce cadets' knowledge, skills in relation to specific patrol driving, and emergency response objectives. In the first session, the troop is divided into two relays. One relay proceeds to the driving simulators, while the other relay attends the classroom session. In the classroom, cadets form pairs and practice introductory radio communications, rotating between being the police officer and dispatch. Within the context of scenarios, they: log on; use basic ten codes and the phonetic alphabet; and conduct rolling and parked computer checks on a vehicle's registration and whether it has been linked to any criminal activity, then log off. The computer checks are done on a series of license plates which are projected at the front of the classroom.

For those training in the driving simulators, cadets are again paired up, with each taking turns completing a series of three drives that gradually increase in complexity. This is achieved by progressively introducing more hazards (e.g., pedestrians, vehicles, etc.). These drives enable cadets to apply the Search (i.e., environmental cue identification)–Identify (i.e., potential hazards)–Predict (i.e., anticipate effect of potential hazards)–Decide (i.e., choose course of action)–Execute (i.e., carry out action) method of driving (SIPDE); employ defensive driving techniques, talk out loud while driving, and prioritize tasks (i.e., focus cognitive resources on those tasks requiring immediate attention). The two relays switch locations at the conclusion of their respective sessions.

In the second session, the troop is again divided into two relays. This time, one relay attends Patrol Drive 1 (Table 5.2), the other relay is further divided into two groups ($n=8$). One group receives their instruction in the driving simulators, while the other group is taught in the classroom. Using the same method as in the first classroom session, cadets practice intermediate radio communications. They review previously acquired radio communications skills by applying the procedures to new scenarios. Cadets also build upon their skills by running computer checks on a vehicle that has been pulled over on the side of the road. Additionally, to emphasize the importance for a police officer to memorize a license plate quickly and accurately, cadets are required to complete certain checks on computer-generated license plates which are designed to fade away over a specified period of time. This simulates a suspect vehicle moving away from a police officer, and illustrates to the cadet how difficult it is to read a license plate at any significant distance while trying to drive safely in a public environment.

For those training in the driving simulators, cadets are again paired up with each taking turns completing a new series of three, increasingly complicated, scenario-based drives. These drives provide cadets the opportunity to reinforce the skills[3] they acquired in the first driving simulator and radio communications sessions.

---

[3] SIPDE, talk out loud while driving, prioritizing tasks, and employ defensive driving techniques.

They also advance their skills by applying a problem-solving process and risk assessment to the scenarios – using an advanced steering technique, and identifying driving infractions (e.g., a driver's failure to signal, illegal turn, etc.). The groups switch locations at the conclusion of their respective sessions, with the classroom group moving to the driving simulators and the driving simulator group to the classroom. Once each relay has completed their training session, the classroom relay begins the driving simulator training, and the relay that just completed the simulator training will begin the classroom training.

For the third session, the troop is again divided into two relays. One relay attends the Patrol Drive 2 in-vehicle session (Table 5.2). The other relay is again divided into two groups, with one going to the driving simulators and the other to the classroom. The cadets practice additional intermediate radio communications using the same method evidenced in the first two classroom sessions. The radio communication skills acquired in those sessions are transferred to novel scenarios. In addition, cadets are now tasked with building on their prior learning by requesting computer checks on a person's driver's license, prior involvement with police and criminal activity.

In the driving simulators, cadets form pairs and each takes turns completing another new series of three, scenario-based drives that become successively more difficult. These drives allow cadets to further strengthen the skills they learned in the first two driving simulator sessions. They build upon these skills by sending and receiving intermediate radio communications, and are also required to locate a suspect vehicle. These processes are designed to reinforce skills previously learned in both the simulator and classroom sessions, and are designed to provide the foundation for the acquisition of advanced skills in upcoming simulator sessions.

The driving simulators, in combination with the radio communications sessions, resolved several training issues with the PDU program. Formative and summative evaluations suggest that these sessions appear to be effective in improving cadets' overall performance in patrol driving and emergency response. For example, radio communications are developed to a level of automaticity in the classroom, and then combined and reinforced with other foundational driving skills in incremental layers on the simulators. By using this approach, cadets achieve basic proficiency in these skills before they drive a police vehicle in a dynamic, changing urban environment on Patrol Drives 1, 2, and 3 (see Table 5.2). The design of the old program did not have the capacity to teach cadets these skills before they participated in their Patrol Drives.

In addition, the driving simulators have significantly reduced the amount of downtime cadets' experience as they wait to take their turn during the patrol drive in-vehicle sessions. Because cadets now complete the in-vehicle sessions in pairs, the time they spend as passive observer-learners is reduced by more than 50%. Another benefit realized through the introduction of the driving simulators into the PDU program is the number of instructors required for the in-vehicle sessions decreased by approximately 30%, and the number of police vehicles involved in these sessions dropped from 11 to 8.

Driving Simulators in Closing the Distance and Night Driving

As previously discussed, driving simulator technology provides a means by which cadets can acquire advanced decision-making skills. During the fourth driving simulator session (Table 5.2), cadets take turns completing a closing the distance and a night drive. The closing the distance drive involves a Be-on-the-Look-Out-for (BOLO) scenario in which cadets must locate and accelerate up to a suspect vehicle in order to run computer checks. In teams of four, cadets participate in a simulated night drive in which they must respond to a collision. The closing the distance drive further enhances the cadets' skills by enabling them to utilize national policy regarding this component of EVO (e.g., RCMP officers do not have the legal authority to break the speed limit in order to close the distance unless their emergency lights are activated). They also demonstrate driving principles for closing the distance (e.g., keeping a safe distance between the suspect and police vehicles), and recognize the tendency to focus on the suspect vehicle and mitigating these effects by consciously scanning the external environment. On the night drive, cadets acquire additional skills in relation to implementing strategies for driving in the dark (e.g., not overdriving their headlights). In addition, they send and receive radio communications between multiple vehicles and plan a response as part of a team. This night drive replicates elements of a gravel-road scenario that cadets are dispatched to as part of the Highway and Gravel Road Drive (Table 5.2), thus assisting in preparing them for that in situ session. The driving simulators facilitate the delivery of training in closing the distance and night driving which could not be offered previously due to a number of safety concerns (i.e., the inability of practicing closing the distance on a public highway) and logistical barriers (i.e., scheduling night drives in the summer due to the extended daylight hours).

Driving Simulators in Emergency Vehicle Response Intersection Clearing

The research on EVRIC imparted clear, evidence-based direction for the design of this element of the PDU program (Krätzig et al., 2010). In the fifth driving simulator session, cadets complete the seven optimal SIC scenarios. The track-based intersection clearing exercises are done in the EVO exposure session. In this session, cadets are dispatched to two emergency response scenarios that require them to drive through the intersection with the red light turn lane open and the red light turn lane closed. As they proceed through the intersection, actor vehicles move slightly into the police vehicle's path to create a sense of reality. By responding to the scenarios, they execute the same maneuvers they learned on the driving simulators. The cadets' knowledge and skills in negotiating the intersection are then formally assessed in the EVO Scenarios session (Table 5.2). The training would not have been possible without the driving simulators and the extensive research which presented defensible strategies for the design of this high-risk curriculum.

Conclusion

Simulation technology has a relatively short history; however, the medical and aviation simulation fields have generated a rich body of empirical evidence supporting the efficacy of this technology as an irreplaceable training tool. In contrast, this type of research is lacking in many other areas including law enforcement training. Although the gap in the literature can be attributed in part to law enforcement's reluctance to adopt this type of technology, it is worth further exploration to determine why a surgeon can perform a delicate surgery on a person after being trained in part on a simulator; yet, firing a pistol at a computer-generated target is considered subpar.

The research approach used by the RCMP, coupled with the educational design considerations, has resulted in the successful integration of driving simulators into a police driver training program. Research revealed the capabilities and limitations of simulation technology, and allowed educational methodology to determine how simulators could be used to best achieve the objectives and goals of the PDU program.

Based on the experiences with the driving simulators, this approach will be used for the upcoming redesign of the firearms training program. An extensive research phase will precede any program redesign; however, as discussed earlier, initial evidence suggests that simulation technology can replace live-fire pistol training. Although the RCMP's philosophy to simulator-based technology is not to replace one training tool with another, simulators will be incorporated into the training program to augment and enhance existing training practices. As evidenced through the new PDU program, it can be argued that cadets are graduating from the training academy better equipped to do their jobs. Using the resulting data from the research phase of the simulator COF, the firearms program will be completely redesigned and simulators are expected to be a significant and integral part of the training program.

References

Abrahamson, S., Denson, J. S., & Wolf, R. M. (2004). Effectiveness of a simulator in training anesthesiology residents. *Quality Safe Health Care, 13*, 395–397. doi:10.1136/qhc.13. 5.395.

Ahlberg, G., Enochsson, L., Gallagher, A. G., Hedman, L., Hogman, C., McClusky, D. A., et al. (2007). Proficiency-based virtual reality training significantly reduces the error rate for residents during their first 10 laparoscopic cholecystectomies. *The American Journal of Surgery, 193*, 797–804. doi:10.1016/j.amjsurg.2006.06.050.

Applied Simulation Technologies (AST). (2006). *Statistical analysis of effectiveness in the second year of EVOC-101 training courses using UDPS driver training simulators in 2006* (Tech. Rep.).

Barrows, H. S. (1996). Problem-based learning in medicine and beyond: A brief overview. In L. Wilkerson & W. H. Gijselaers (Eds.), *New directions for teaching and learning* (Vol. 68, pp. 3–11). San Francisco: Jossey-Bass.

Birzer, M. L. (2003). The theory of andragogy applied to police training. *Policing: An International Journal of Police Strategies and Management, 26*(1), 29–42. doi:10.1108/13639510310460288.

Bloss, W. P. (2004). Creating critical thinkers: Interactional approaches to police instruction. *Law Enforcement Executive Forum, 4*(5), 147–162.

Bürke-Cohen, J., Go, T. H., & Longridge, T. (2001). Flight simulator fidelity considerations for total air line pilot training and evaluation. *Proceedings of the AIAA modeling and simulation technologies conference, Montreal, QC.* Retrieved June 2009 from http://www.raa.org/Portals/0/CommitteePages/FlightTraining/10-12_AIAA2001-4425final_header.pdf.

Chappell, A. T. (2005). *Learning in action: Training the community policing officer.* Doctoral dissertation. Retrieved April 2010 from http://etd.fcla.edu/UF/UFE0011615/chappell_a.pdf.

Dick, W., & Carey, L. (1978). *The systematic design of instruction.* Boston: Scott Foresman/Addison-Wesley.

Dochy, F., Segers, M., Van en Bossche, P., & Gijbels, D. (2003). Effects of problem-based learning: A meta-analysis. *Learning and Instruction, 13,* 533–568. doi:10.1016/S0959-4752(02)00025-7.

Federal Aviation Administration (FAA), Part 142. Retrieved April 2010 from http://www.faa.gov/about/initiatives/nsp/.

Friedrich, M. J. (2002). Practice makes perfect: Risk free medical training with patient simulators. *The Journal of the American Medical Association, 288,* 2808–2812. doi:10.1001/jama.288.22.2808.

Haward, D. M. (1910). The Sanders Teacher. *Flight, 2*(910), 1006–1007.

Hunt, R. C., Brown, L. H., Cabinum, E. S., Whidey, T. W., Prasad, H. N., Owena, C. F., et al. (1995). Is ambulance transport time faster with lights and siren than without? *Annals of Emergency Medicine, 25,* 506–510. doi:10.1016/S0196-0644(95)70267-9.

Issenberg, S. B., McGaghie, W. C., Petrusa, E. R., Gordon, D. L., & Scalese, R. J. (2005). Features and uses of high-fidelity medical simulations that lead to effective learning: A BEME systemic review. *Medical Teacher, 27,* 10–28. doi:10.1080/01421590500046924.

Koonce, J. M., & Bramble, W. J., Jr. (1998). Personal computer-based flight training devices. *The International Journal of Aviation Psychology, 8,* 277–292. doi:10.1207/s1532710 8ijap0803_7.

Krätzig, G. P., Bell, G., Groff, R., & Ford, C. (2010). Simulator emergency police vehicle operation: Efficiencies and skill transfer. *Interservice/industry training, simulation and education conference, Orlando.*

L-3 Communications. (2000). Murray Hill, Midtown Manhattan, NY.

McCoy, M. R. (2006). Teaching style and the application of adult learning principles by police instructors. *Policing: An International Journal of Police Strategies and Management, 29*(1), 77–91. doi:10.1108/13639510610648494.

McGaghie, W. C., Issenberg, S. B., Petrusa, E. R., & Scalese, R. J. (2010). A critical review of simulation-based medical education research: 2003–2009. *Medical Education, 44,* 50–63. doi:10.1111/j.1365-2923.2009.03547.x.

Page, R. L. (2000). Brief history of flight simulation. *SimTecT 2000 Proceedings,* 1–11. doi:10.1.1.132.5428.

Perkins, G. D. (2007). Simulation in resuscitation training. *Resuscitation, 73,* 202–211. doi:10.1016/j.resuscitation.2007.01.005.

Pipes, C., & Paper, P. (2001, July). Police pursuits and civil liability. *The FBI Law Enforcement Bulletin.* Retrieved June 2009 from http://libcat.post.ca.gov/dbtw-wpd/article/FBI/FBI70(07)16-21Jul2001.pdf.

Rosen, K. R. (2008). The history of medical simulation. *Journal of Critical Care, 23,* 157–166. doi:10.1016/j.jcrc.2007.12.004.

Sanderson, P., Mooij, M., & Neal, A. (2007). Investigating sources of mental workload using a high-fidelity ATC simulator. , In Proceedings of the 14th international symposium on aviation psychology, Dayton, OH (pp. 423–468), April 24, 2007, Human Factors and Ergonomics Society, Santa Monica.

Smith, R. (2010). The long history of gaming in military training. *Simulation & Gaming, 41,* 6–19. doi:10.1177/1046878109334330.

Webster's Ninth New Collegiate Dictionary. (1991). Markham, ON: Thomas Allen & Son.

Chapter 6
Redesigning Specialized Advanced Criminal Investigation Training in Germany

Norbert Unger

Introduction

This chapter provides an introduction to the process used in a joint Federation/ Federal state initiative tasked with the redesign of specialized/ advanced criminal investigation training in Germany.[1] Guided by a working group representing 13 federal states, the Federal Police, and the Federal Criminal Police Office (*Bundeskriminalamt*), the project objective was to devise an advanced training model that would take into account the professional needs of police services and the requirement for uniform standards covering various criminal investigation working areas and phenomenal domains.

The model was to reflect the objectives, target groups, content, and methodological approaches consistent with identified subject matter. The personal requirements (conditions of participation) and the underlying organizational conditions (duration, number of participants, and responsibilities) were also to be defined. The training model was to be given a modular didactic/methodological structure. It would also require a framework that was inclusive of introductory advanced training (basic principles/basic modules), refresher training (first specialization/extension modules), further professional development training (greater specialization/special modules), and, finally, the need to update acquired knowledge.

[1] The author would like to express his thanks to all those who took part in the working groups and thus made it possible to achieve the overall results.

N. Unger (✉)
Bundeskriminalamt (BKA), Wiesbaden, Hesse, Germany
e-mail: norbert.unger@bka.bund.de

M.R. Haberfeld et al. (eds.), *Police Organization and Training: Innovations in Research and Practice*, DOI 10.1007/978-1-4614-0745-4_6,
© Springer Science+Business Media, LLC 2012

German Police Context

In the Federal Republic of Germany, policing is a matter that falls within the remit of the federal states (*Länder*). This means that each of the 16 federal states has its own police force and settles the relevant issues internally. Pursuant to Article 87(1) and Article 73 of the Basic Law (the German constitution), the Federation has exclusive legislative power for, among other things, overseeing cooperation between the Federation and the German federal states concerning criminal police work (FRG, 1949a, c). In 2006, the legislature extended this competence and conferred on the Federation exclusive legislative power for protection against the dangers of international terrorism in prominent case configurations (FRG, 1949b). With regard to police training tasks, the constitutional rules mean that each federal state determines and conducts its own initial and advanced police training. The Federal Criminal Police Office (*BKAG*) sets forth the details on the Federation's legislative competence for cooperation between the Federation and the federal states in criminal investigation matters. With regard to the area of advanced criminal investigation training, the German Federal Criminal Police Office (*Bundeskriminalamt*) is responsible, as part of its duties as the central criminal investigation agency, for conducting initial and advanced police training events on special criminal investigation matters at the Federation and federal state levels (BKAG, 1997a, 1997b).

In practice, this means that the Federal Criminal Police Office organizes and runs centralized events in this area for its own criminal investigation officers and those in the German federal states. The federal states take advantage of this provision alongside or in addition to their own advanced training courses. There are distinct differences between the individual federal states regarding the extent of the training provision that they provide. On account of their size, some of the 16 federal states provide a very extensive range of initial and advanced training courses, including courses in the field of specialized advanced criminal investigation training, for their own officers. Other federal states limit themselves to providing courses on selected areas of criminal investigation in the specialized advanced training. The federal states consequently differ in the extent to which they take advantage of the training provided by the Federal Criminal Police Office in this field.

Background

The impetus for this initiative came from instructions issued by the head of the Offices of Criminal Investigation in the federal states and the head of the Federal Criminal Police Office. The initial objective was to set up a project group which represented both the Federation and federal state levels with the aim to devise a concept for specialized advanced criminal investigation training. This concept was to be geared to professional needs and to include the development of uniform national standards and courses for advanced training in various areas of criminal investigation work and phenomenal domains. These instructions specified a key element, the inclusion of the professional level members of the criminal police, who have to deal with actual criminal manifestations and fields of action in their daily work. At the same time, the advanced training courses were to be developed within a modular structure to ensure that criminal investigation staff were able to acquire skills that were specifically in line with requirements and their duties.

The development of standards implies the need to reach an agreement regarding content. It also requires communication between the various police forces within the stakeholder group. At the same time, it stresses the need for an agreement between the functional level and the scope of individual modules. In an effort to align these elements, the process of development required the following items:

- A survey of the current situation
- A review of previous modular teaching concepts
- Determination of the advanced training areas suited to a modular structure
- Establishment of the sequence, structure, and contents of and responsibilities for the modules
- Resource and cost-related aspects

Procedural Approach

In order to achieve the above noted objectives, the relevant areas of crime as well as the phenomena and areas of investigative support had to be identified; the current situation also had to be surveyed and previous (modular) concepts reviewed. The advanced training areas suited to a modular structure were then to be determined and the sequence, structure, and contents of the modules designed. Lastly, proposals were to be worked out regarding the organization and conduct of the modules and the resource and cost aspects were reviewed. Defining the tasks and implementing them in a federal structure such as that of Germany called for the extensive involvement of the police forces in all 16 federal states, the Federal Police, and the Federal Criminal Police Office. As a result, deliberations regarding a suitable method led almost inevitably to the need to develop a questionnaire.

The questionnaire was used to gather data on the current state of the specialized advanced criminal investigation training at the Federation level and in the federal states. It would also forecast what was required by way of specialized advanced criminal investigation training. Questions on cost and resource aspects were also included. The aim was to acquire as complete a nationwide list of training courses and their contents as possible. The Ministers/Senators of the Interior in the federal states, the Federal Police, and the Federal Criminal Police Office were given feedback in the form of a summary of the survey results. The response rate and attitude revealed that an approved, modular advanced criminal investigation training program was of considerable interest to all those concerned at the Federation/federal state levels.

In order to ensure that the procedural approach was effective, a coordination group comprising five members was set up. This group's task was to coordinate, summarize, and evaluate the tasks between the meetings of the entire project group (which consisted of 15 members) and to prepare the meetings of the project group. Specifically, this included summarizing the nationwide survey and evaluating it, acting as the contact partner for sub-working groups, and, lastly, preparing the meetings and draft reports of the project group as well as the advanced training concept. The project group also decided to make use of sub-working groups. This was necessary as the questions on the subject needs in the federal states and at the national authorities had shown that advanced training was needed in a number of criminal and phenomenal domains and investigative support areas.

A total of 23 sub-working groups were set up, 22 of which were to deal with phenomenal domains, while one was established to deal with the matter of "costs and resources." The sub-working groups included representatives of training facilities as well as subject-matter experts. This was a major criterion for the acceptance of the results and proved worthwhile as the conceptual work proceeded. For their specific areas, the sub-working groups were required to review whether the relevant crime and phenomenal domains were suited to a modular structure and to establish a modular advanced training concept. In this connection, it was important to take account of approved concepts or modular approaches that already existed.

A joint kick-off event was held for all heads of sub-working groups, the aim being to communicate the project group's objectives and clarify what was expected of the individual groups. This was to ensure that the results of the sub-working groups were consistent in terms of the structure and content of the modules – regardless of the specific topic covered. Furthermore, this would ensure that a standard depth of processing was adhered to for the targeted advanced training concept. It would further focus attention on the question of whether or not the proposed modules could feasibly be organized and put into operation. The work done by each sub-working group, its methods, and its results were to be documented. The following breakdown was prescribed in an advanced training summary sheet, the aim of which was to provide a brief overview of each module:

- Designation of the module
- Objective
- Target group
- Number of participants
- Personal requirements
- Content
- Method
- Conclusion
- Duration

In accordance with strict standards, the number of the modules to be devised by the sub-working groups was to be restricted to what was professionally necessary. The concept development work was not to be guided by what was professionally desirable but what was realistically feasible and professionally necessary. The report presented by the project group was to contain comments on the following points:

- Field of crime, phenomenon or area of investigative support
- The current state of specialized advanced criminal investigation training
- The envisaged training, based on the analysis of the current state of training provision
- Design of the sequence, structure, and contents of the future modules
- Classification of advanced training measures into the following categories:

  - Introductory advanced training
  - Advanced Refresher courses
  - Specialized professional development training

The coordination group's mandate was to compile and coordinate the results of the sub-working groups. The sub-working groups' reports were reviewed with regard to the prescribed structure and thus to suitability for the advanced training concept. The sub-working groups' reports were then discussed at the meetings of the entire Federation/federal state project group. In order to achieve as broad a consensus as possible before the sub-working groups' results were discussed, the members of the overall project group were advised to approve the forwarded reports with regard to the subject content in their own federal state or at the national authorities. Feedback to the coordination group was accordingly forwarded to the sub-working groups. If changes or additions were deemed necessary, the sub-working groups' results were modified.

In summary, the sub-working groups came to the conclusion that in all criminal and phenomenal domains and areas of investigative support considered, the advanced training measures should be modular. This also confirmed the views expressed in the Federation/federal state survey, in which a modular structure was essentially seen as positive.

Results

The main results of the survey showed that, compared with the list of courses provided by the Federal Criminal Police Office, there was a need for advanced training measures on all criminal investigation topics. Relevant advanced training measures were already provided at the Federation's advanced training facilities and in many of the federal states. In virtually all areas of specialized advanced criminal investigation training, a modular approach was seen as having an advantage. The federal states with their own advanced training facilities and extensive advanced training needs tended, first and foremost, to consider that the responsibility lay within their own state. The Federation was deemed to have central responsibility in special topic areas only. Existing cooperation agreements between individual federal states were based on regional initiatives and general declarations of intent. In a few cases, there were written cooperation agreements. The question about assuming a central coordination function as a means of satisfying a training need, together with the possible willingness to assume a specific professional or organizational "godfathering" responsibility, was answered with considerable hesitancy.

In devising the advanced training concept, the project group's intention was to determine knowledge standards, which were deemed, to be absolutely vital to processing in each crime or phenomenal domain. On the other hand, this was to ensure that almost identical previous knowledge would be available for subsequent advanced training measures (refresher and professional development training courses). In addition to what was desirable from a professional point of view, matters of feasibility and predictability were addressed.

The advanced training concept covered 22 crime or phenomenal domains and areas of investigative support. Each area was broken down into "basic modules," "extension modules," and "special modules." This concept formed the reference framework for specialized advanced criminal investigation training in the federal states and at the national authorities. The progressive implementation of the contents will lead in the medium and long term to an approved adjustment of the specialized advanced criminal investigation training. Due to the different police structures in the federal states and the Federation and the associated difference in the requirements for advanced police training, it is not possible or purposeful to achieve an overall harmonization of the corresponding advanced training measures. In its advanced training courses, the Federal Criminal Police Office already makes broad use of the modular advanced training concept.

The Advanced Training Concept

The findings of the sub-working group and ultimately of the project group are best presented by taking forensics (crime scene investigation) as a typical example of investigative support. The observations will clarify the structural sequence of the specialized advanced criminal investigation training concept as well as the contents of the individual modules.

For the purposes of specialized advanced criminal investigation training, the topic of crime scene investigation comprises the areas of tracing evidence, securing evidence, trace analysis, and evaluation at and of crime scenes. Owing to the significance of this topic area, it can be assumed that advanced training measures in this field are basically provided in all federal states and by the national authorities. The contents of these existing advanced training measures, some of which were modular, were taken as the basis for designing the modules in the national advanced training concept.

As increasing importance must be attributed to material evidence, and in connection with the ongoing further development of scientific and technical possibilities, crime scene investigation is of key significance in conducting investigations. The modular structure for the area of forensics (crime scene investigation) is comprised of:

- Basic modules

  - Crime scene investigation – securing evidence
  - Basic photography

- Extension modules

  - Police records department

- Practical module

  - Crime scene investigation – securing evidence
  - Photography

- Refresher course on crime scene investigation
- Special modules

  - Video technology in crime scene investigation
  - Fingerprints
  - Homicide
  - Sexual and criminal assault
  - Getter substances
  - Alternative light sources
  - Crime scene documentation, crime scene surveys, and reconstruction
  - Securing evidence of shots, arms offences
  - Car and truck screening
  - Safety at work and in the laboratory
  - Quality assurance/management in crime scene investigation
  - Corpse fingerprinting

Basic Module: Crime Scene Investigation – Securing Evidence

Aim

Participants should:

- Be able to understand and present the overall context of a crime scene investigation, the criteria for the appraisal and cooperation with the other organizational units
- Be familiar with how evidence occurs and its characteristics
- Master the relevant methods of securing evidence
- Be familiar with the appraisal options and be able to judge the results
- Find out about the latest developments in the field of fingerprinting and forensics

Target Group

Members of the police force who are in the future to be entrusted with the task of securing evidence and crime scene investigation.

Number of Places Available

15.

Personal Requirements

None.

Contents

Basic concepts

- Law (powers of intervention)

    - Evidence theory (types of evidence, difference between personal/material evidence, and value given to the different types of evidence)
    - Initial intervention systematics
    - Forensic tasks
    - Overview of the forensics structure
    - Reporting
    - Staff safety

- Track analysis

    - Types of tracks and their significance
    - Interaction when tracks are made
    - General principles of securing evidence

- Consolidation of the approach to securing evidence, also with regard to scenes specific to certain crimes
- Introduction to appraisal interventions
- Simple crime scene photography
- Evidence securing measures in the fields of fingerprinting, tracks left by tools, fiber traces, and biological traces
- Significance of and taking comparable fingerprints of appropriate persons

- Securing comparative material
- Preservation and packing
- Possible ways of identifying and evaluating said traces
- Preparation of trace maps, analysis reports, and mandates
- Hand-over of the crime scene
- Overview of current methods of securing evidence and applied aids
- Possible ways of evaluating DNA traces, fiber traces, fingerprints, form traces, and paint and glass traces
- Practical exercises/crime scene exercise

Method

Lectures, group work, and exercises.

Conclusion

Certificate of attendance.

Duration

15 days.

Extension Module: Crime Scene Investigation – Securing Evidence

Aim

Participants should:

- Understand the targeted procedure for recording objective evidence
- Be generally familiar with the methods/aids for tracing, rendering visible and securing evidence appropriate to various situations and be able to use them
- Find out about conditions, possibilities, and limits of trace evaluation

Target Group

Members of the police force who are to be entrusted full time in the future with the tasks of tracing and securing evidence.

Number of Places Available

No more than 15.

Personal Requirements

Basic course or similar knowledge, practical module.

Contents

- Crime scene analysis and methodology of crime scene investigation with the emphasis on evaluation intervention (objective appraisal of the (overall) evidence)
- Searching for and securing evidence in accordance with the nationwide, approved guidelines for crime scene investigation – evidence (ATOS)
- Forensic photography, traces/crime scene photography
- The preparation of records on the objective evidence
- Possibilities and limits of the value as evidence of traces and their usability
- Overcoming mechanical security facilities (door locks)
- Documentation and documentation systems
- Possibilities of crime scene assessment and reconstruction
- Practical exercises

Method

Lectures, group work, and exercises.

Conclusion

The course concludes with a certificate of qualification.

Duration

10 days.

Special Module: Fingerprints

Aim

Participants should be able to work independently in the field of seeking and securing evidence, broaden their knowledge, exchange experience, and analyze problems.

Target Group

Members of the police force who are entrusted full time with the tasks of securing evidence and crime scene investigation.

Number of Places Available

10–20.

Personal Requirements

Extension course on crime scene investigation/securing evidence, certificate of qualification.

Contents

- Latest methods of finding and securing evidence on absorptive and nonabsorptive surfaces (sticky tape, fingerprints with blood, metal, weapons, and munitions)
- Latest criminal investigation methods
- Presentations by participants on current procedures or problems for securing evidence; discussion of possible solutions
- Practical exercises

Method

Lectures, group work, and exercises.

Conclusion

Certificate of attendance.

Duration

5 days.

Quality Assurance and Continuation

Owing to ongoing technical and phenomenological developments, quality-assurance measures and continued work on the advanced training concept were needed. The standards developed were reviewed repeatedly and adapted accordingly. In practical terms, those responsible for advanced training at Federation level and in the federal states meet as necessary and discuss the need to update specific suggestions; they also organize the review of modules or supplementary material by the professionals (case processing) and the advanced training facilities. This process enables, as far as possible, work to be carried out on proposals regarding costs and resources and responsibilities. This means, for example, considering whether set numbers of places can be earmarked for participants from other federal states or from the national authorities and how the costs are to be shared or whether there is perhaps a willingness to assume responsibility for a phenomenal domain. In a complex process of this kind, only gradual developments can be expected in these particular matters. The federal states and the national authorities are also given an overview of the current nationwide advanced training areas covered by the specialized advanced criminal investigation training. Here, all advanced training measures provided in the federal states or at Federation level are fed into an existing platform that is accessible to all through a nationwide "police intranet."

The extensive work carried out by the police at Federation and federal state levels therefore enabled an important step to be made. Being aware of this extensive work, the project group realized at an early stage that the conceptual work did not end with the submission of the concept. The contents of the specialized advanced criminal investigation training are geared, as shown, to practical needs and are thus subject to an ongoing development and amendment process. In order to structure and design this process, working meetings of those responsible for advanced criminal investigation training at the Federation level and in the federal states are organized, as required, by the Federal Criminal Police Office. This ensures continuation of the work on the advanced training concept. A structured exchange of experience by those responsible is also encouraged and includes the state of implementation within the individual bodies involved. This leads to a well-founded discussion and continuation of the work. Further development of the concept thus includes the possibility of discussing how responsibilities should be further established for individual phenomena areas or modules.

Conclusion

The extensive work of the Federation/Federal state project group, its coordination group, and the sub-working groups had the common goal of devising an investigation training concept. It proved possible to present a framework of agreed contents that had an impact on advanced training measures and standards. At the same time, guidelines were set within the modular structure that enabled similar structures to be applied to tasks in other phenomenal domains covered by the police.

References

Bundeskriminalamtgesetz – BKAG, (1997). Law on the Federal Criminal Police Office and cooperation between the Federation and the federal states in criminal police matters. *Federal Law Gazette, I,* 1650.

Bundeskriminalamtgesetz – BKAG, (1997). Law on the Federal Criminal Police Office and cooperation between the Federation and the federal states in criminal police matters. *Article* 2(6), No. 4.

Federal Republic of Germany, (1949a). Basic Law, Article 73(1), No 10(a).

Federal Republic of Germany, (1949b). Basic Law, Article 87(1), (2006 amendment).

Federal Republic of Germany, (1949c). Basic Law, Article 73(1), No 9(a).

Chapter 7
The Evolution of Police Training: The Investigative Skill Education Program

Carol Glasgow and Cheryl Lepatski

Introduction

The education and professional development of police officers have undergone an evolution in the past century. The training of police officers must be reflective of the society in which they serve, and, as such, changes in police education have occurred in response to changing societal conditions and challenges. The traditional para-military behavioral training method that many police agencies in Canada have used "…may not be the best environment for the teaching-learning transaction to occur" (Birzer, 2003, p. 29). When trying to empower individual officers to respond to the changing demands of their profession, the flawed environment created by the para-military model limits the effectiveness of training initiatives. In response, police services are attempting to improve police training and education because there is a direct correlation between insufficient professional development and inadequate investigations. This chapter will examine recent challenges for police organizations in Alberta and the educational response of the Investigative Skills Education Program (ISEP). Also discussed, in relation to ISEP, are adult learning theory and methodologies for both classroom and online education as well as the structure, content, research, validation, and pilot phases of the program. Finally, we will examine the present and future outlook for the provincial competency-based educational program.

August Vollmer, a police chief in Berkeley, CA, between 1905 and 1935 advocated for the reform of police education (Dunham & Alpert, 2010, 2010a). Vollmer suggested that improving training for police officers would help legitimize the occupation as a profession. After Vollmer's plea for the amelioration of police training, police organizations in North America began to implement new methods

C. Glasgow (✉) • C. Lepatski
Edmonton Police Service, Edmonton, AB, Canada
e-mail: carol.glasgow@edmontonpolice.ca; cheryl.lepatski@edmontonpolice.ca

M.R. Haberfeld et al. (eds.), *Police Organization and Training: Innovations in Research and Practice*, DOI 10.1007/978-1-4614-0745-4_7,
© Springer Science+Business Media, LLC 2012

of training. The educational methodology of constructivism was adopted by police educators in response to the community-based policing philosophy that began in the 1980s. The introduction of constructivism, or problem-based learning, into the realm of police education was significantly influenced by Goldstein (1990) who recognized that effective policing consisted of the proper recognition and research of "problems" and the planning to try and solve those problems. This shift in how police officers were trained was a significant step forward for police education and helped to align the learning experience in the classroom with the work police officers would be doing in the field. However, constructivism as an educational methodology alone could not address all of the shifting demands placed on both individual officers and their respective police organizations. Interestingly, almost a century after Vollmer's plea for change, police training was still characterized as being rudimentary, fragmented, and reminiscent of a traditional, pedagogical, military model (Vodde, 2009). Critics point out that police organizations had not done enough to adequately change the way police officers were trained. Cleveland (2006) acknowledges that based on research about how knowledge is acquired and transferred the traditional Socratic and mimetic methods of police instruction were not effective.

Re-examination of the educational methodologies utilized for police training was warranted in response to increases in the complexity of criminal law, consequences of decision making relating to investigative procedures, the new demands on police services to help solve community problems, and the frequency of inter-jurisdictional investigations. All of these influences were exacerbated by the changes in police demographics, specifically the sharp increase in hiring in response to the retirements of experienced officers. To address these factors, police training began a holistic approach to police education that included a blended learning model (incorporating both online and classroom learning), the use of experienced officers to coach and mentor junior officers, and a spiral curriculum that centered on a constructivist design. This new approach also utilized proven, validated competencies and a program of professional development that spanned multiple years in a police officer's career. The ISEP addressed the challenges that faced policing through proven adult educational methodologies, competency-based curriculum, and a blended learning model in keeping with this newly formulated approach to training.

Challenges Facing Police Training

Investigative Complexity

The investigation of contemporary criminal offences required knowledge of criminal law, investigative procedures and techniques, and problem-solving capabilities. Furthermore, the complexity of investigative knowledge required by police officers continues to increase as they advance in their career and move into specialized areas. Failure to provide adequate education continuously throughout the span of an officer's career may result in prohibitive financial costs associated with inadequate investigations leading to case dismissals or wrongful convictions. New case law has set a precedent of increased liability for failed investigations. In *Hill v. Hamilton-Wentworth Regional Police Services Board* (2007), the Supreme Court of Canada stated that police officers can now be held liable for negligent investigations. By training members in anticipation of investigative responsibilities, police organizations can mitigate this risk and reduce potential loss of time and money.

Policing Conditions in the Province of Alberta

Large Geographical Area

Alberta is a large geographical area that encompasses 661,848 km² (National Geographic, n.d.). There are 12 municipal police agencies, the Royal Canadian Mounted Police (RCMP), and the Solicitor General and Public Security Sheriffs that all provide law enforcement services to large and small communities that encompass both urban and rural characteristics. Alberta's large land mass presented instructional design challenges in ensuring that all officers had access to standardized training, regardless of their location in the province or the size of their police agency. It was also noted that having multiple police organizations in one province meant that officers were working on inter-agency investigations when criminals crossed jurisdictional boundaries. To overcome the large geographical area and the need to service multiple police organizations, blended learning, which is a mix of online learning and classroom instruction, assisted with both issues. Advocates for distance learning, Moore and Kearsley (2005) describe how online learning provides students with access to quality education that they may otherwise not have had. With the advent of communication technologies, geographical barriers are no longer an insurmountable obstacle to participation in higher education or professional training.

Shift in Police Personnel Demographics

From 2002 to 2009 police organizations, like other industries in the province of Alberta, struggled with employment trends that saw an increase in the number of employees eligible for retirement. Statistics Canada (2004) indicated that an aging Canadian population means a shrinking workforce. This trend will continue as Statistics Canada estimated that the number of people eligible for retirement could reduce the workforce from 67 to 57% by the year 2025. For police organizations in Alberta, it meant increased hiring to match attrition rates. This resulted in organizational gaps in relation to mentorship, experience levels, and educational opportunities since there were fewer experienced officers in active service to pass along practical knowledge and provide mentorship and coaching. For example, from 2006 to 2009, the Edmonton Police Service hired 712 new police officers in order to keep up with attrition (Edmonton Police Service Recruiting Unit, 2010). In 2009, there were 1,447 police officers in the Edmonton Police Service, meaning that almost 50% of all sworn members had less than 3 years of policing experience (Edmonton Police Service and Edmonton Police Commission, 2009). The effects of this mass hiring will continue to be felt in police agencies for multiple years as the officers hired within this time frame advance in their careers through either promotion or transfer to specialized investigative areas where even more complex knowledge and skills will be required.

Andragogy: The Teaching of Adults

Characteristics of Adult Learners

Weinblatt (1999) supported the implementation of adult learning principles because he felt that it improved on the quasi-militaristic model of police training. Holden (n.d.) (as cited in Vodde, 2009) also indicates that officers "…should be taught utilizing adult education methodologies rather than behavioral techniques which are currently utilized in a fair number of police academies" (p. 286). In 1970, Knowles redefined adult learning by calling the adult learning methodology as "andragogy," as opposed to "pedagogy" (the teaching of children) (Mackeracher, 2004). Knowles's assumptions of adult learners define adult learners as being different because adult learners possess prior formal education and/or experience (Mackeracher). Another important distinction is that adults must apply their knowledge practically in order to learn effectively; they must also have a goal and reasonably expect that the new knowledge will help them reach that goal. "Teaching strategies that enhance adult learning involve real-life activities" (Cleveland, 2006, p. 52). Prior experience can assist with building on previous knowledge or assist with solving problems presented in class.

Constructivism in Policing

As previously mentioned, Goldstein (1990) recognized that problem-solving capabilities were crucial to conducting effective police work. This philosophy needed to be reflected in how police officers were trained if officers were to effectively solve problems in the community. As a result, constructivism, also known as problem-based learning to many police organizations, significantly and positively altered the way face-to-face learning occurred (Cleveland, 2006). According to Vygotsky's socio-cultural approach, there are several components required to develop an authentic learning environment in which problem-based learning can be applied (Honebein, Duffy, & Fishman, 1993). To begin, the cognitive demands placed on the student in the learning environment must be consistent with the cognitive demands the student will experience in the real-world environment for which they are being educated (Honebein et al.). For instructional designers, this means generating tasks for students to complete and problems for students to solve rather than supporting curriculum that relies on memorization and study from a textbook. Designing the tasks and problems for students to work through requires instructional designers to first consider the concepts or principles that students must learn and then generate real problems to be solved based on those concepts (Savery & Duffy, 2001). The problems generated should also fall within the zone of proximal development (ZPD). Vygotsky described the ZPD as the zone of interaction with a more experienced individual who assists the learner in solving a problem that he/she would not have the ability to solve on his/her own (Andrade, Jaques, Jung, Bordini, & Vicari, 2001). Working within the curriculum and using the authentic problem created by the instructional designer, the ZPD agent supports the learner by working at the edge of the learner's ability, providing appropriate resources, assistance, and challenges to assist the learner in finding their own solution to the problem (Andrade, Jaques, Jung, Bordini, & Vicari, 2001). The support of the ZPD should diminish as the learner moves closer to the solution eventually withdrawing completely. The final component in developing authentic learning is the creation of a collaborative learning environment where students can interact with each other. The importance of collaborative groups rests in the ability of learners to "…test [their] own understanding and examine the understanding of others as a mechanism for enriching, interweaving, and explaining [their] understanding of particular issues or phenomena" (Savery & Duffy, 2001, p. 2). Participants of learning groups benefit from varying perspectives, experience, and knowledge levels.

The use of a constructivist/problem-based learning curriculum helps officers utilize their diverse skill set and experience. Norman and Schmidt (n.d.) indicated that:

> The growing interest in problem-based learning comes from the integration of sound educational approach. This approach commonly consists of aspects of self-directed and life-long learning, with problem solving and critical thinking skills developed through facilitated group learning. A basic premise of problem based learning is that students take greater responsibility for their own learning, with the benefit that they develop a wider range of transferable skills such as communication skills, teamwork and problem solving (as cited in Savin-Baden & Wilkie, 2004, p. 11).

Blended Learning

What Is Blended Learning?

The term blended learning does not have a readily agreed-upon definition by either practitioners or scholars. "The definition of blended learning has been argued and debated at workshops and in print" (Albrecht, 2006, p. 2). Schooley (2005) also agrees that there is no one definition, but Schooley points to three key aspects of the blended learning models that are consistent: online self-paced learning (in an asynchronous online environment), offline instruction (classroom instruction), and, lastly, online synchronous learning. The use of online learning, whether it is asynchronous or synchronous, will overlap with classroom instruction. Schooley acknowledges that the characteristics of the blended learning method will vary between the participants, instruction, interaction, learning approach, and instructional leader. Similar to Schooley, Masie (2002) wrote that blended learning "is the use of two or more distinct methods of training" (p. 59) that may include combinations such as:

- Blending classroom instruction with online information
- Blending online instruction with access to a coach of faculty member
- Blending simulations with structured courses
- Blending on-the-job training with brown bag information sessions
- Blended managerial coaching with e-learning activities (as cited in Albrecht, 2006, p. 2)

Although there is no one definition of blended learning, typically it is acceptable to characterize blended learning as using Web-based or online activities, thus reducing the time required for classroom instruction. The ability of organizations to utilize two different approaches opens up more opportunities to utilize the strengths of each method to achieve the intended learning objectives.

Benefits of Blended Learning

Blended Learning Helps Organizations Respond to Change

Thorne (2003) suggests that blended learning is a natural evolution of a learning agenda. Schooley (2005), Albrecht (2006), and Thorne (2003) suggested that organizations utilize blended learning because it is a flexible solution that helps organizations meet their training objectives. Consequently, most blended learning programs are not driven by the learners themselves, but the institution or organization in which the blended learning program is created. For example, in 1996, the University of Central Florida (UCF) began to implement blended learning in large part to respond to enrollment that outpaced faculty capacity (Albrecht, 2006). Automakers are also utilizing blended learning to address corporate objectives. Schooley (2005) explains that the automakers and dealers determined that classroom training alone could not meet their demands in a timely way. The automakers acknowledged key reasons for implementing blended learning such as employees are constantly changing, products require up to date knowledge to provide an excellent product and customer service, and customers are demanding improved expertise and knowledge (Schooley). The blended learning programs comprised of classroom instruction, synchronous online instruction, and asynchronous online learning. The three approaches mentioned were utilized in different combinations depending on the employee that required training such as management, sales, and technicians.

Improving Student Learning

While organizations and institutions are utilizing blended learning to address corporate objectives, funding limitations, and space issues, the need to improve student learning is also a factor. According to Thorne (2003), blended learning "…suggests an elegant solution to the challenges of tailoring learning and development to the needs of individuals" (p. 16). Integrating the best technologies with the ability to have interaction and participation in a classroom setting allows blended learning to offer more experiential learning and encompass more learning styles than a nonblended approach (Thorne). C. Dede at Harvard University also agrees with the concept that blended learning accommodates more learning styles than a traditional classroom approach alone (Albrecht, 2006). According to Albrecht, few critics of the blended learning model have come forward. Albrecht explains "perhaps the concept of improving learning has discouraged potential criticism" (p. 4).

Benefits for Learners

Convenience

Combining online learning with classroom instruction reduces the amount of time that students need to spend in classrooms (Albrecht, 2006; Picciano, 2006). By having materials online, the learners can schedule their time and access the study material when it is most convenient for them. Distance education provides learners with "…flexibility in program structure to accommodate their other responsibilities, such as full-time jobs or family needs" (Howell, Williams, & Lindsay, 2003, p. XX). Adult learners require more flexibility because they have competing demands on their time. Many adult learners have increased responsibilities at work and at home. Partial delivery of ISEP through online learning gives police officers flexibility and options.

A direct benefit in the blended learning model that utilizes asynchronous learning (as opposed to synchronous learning which is real time) is that students can learn at their own pace (Schooley, 2009). A student can take more time to learn the material or they may challenge the assessment and complete the online course without reviewing all of the material in detail. Also, the learners benefit from the opportunity to review the material and have any new questions answered whenever they like, thus increasing their chances for success.

Success in Blended Learning

The success of a blended learning program is directly related to the quality of instruction. "Maximizing success in a blended learning initiative requires a planned and well-supported approach that includes a theory-based instructional model, high-quality faculty development, course development assistance, learner support, and ongoing formative and summative assessment" (Dziuban, Hartman, & Moskal, 2004, p. 3). Schooley (2009) agrees and suggests the effectiveness of blended learning is directly related to the course quality: "Whether content is classroom-based, online self-paced, or blended learning, it must be engaging and tied specifically to outcomes that are meaningful to the employees" (Schooley, 2008, p. 11).

Building the Investigative Skills Education Program

Identifying Competencies

The first step in ISEP's development was to identify the competencies required to conduct a superior investigation. "A competency is defined as, what a person is required to do (performance), under what circumstances (conditions), and to what level of competence this is to be done (standards)" (Edmonton Police Service, 2010a, 2010b, p. 8). Subject-matter experts from key investigative areas of the Edmonton Police Service were identified and asked to participate in the competency identification process. Through an ongoing series of interviews, meetings, and questionnaires, curriculum designers were able to identify performance gaps, processes, techniques, and methodologies of investigations.

Two types of analysis – task analysis and critical trait approach – were utilized to determine the technical processes associated with criminal investigations as well as the behavioral methodology. According to Dubois (1993), the task analysis is a compilation of tasks, processes, and responsibilities associated with the subject matter, which for the purposes of ISEP was criminal investigation. The critical trait approach method identifies the behaviors, skills, and methodologies that distinguish a superior performer from an average one. Based on the data collected, 14 main investigative competencies were identified as detailed below:

- Ethical Decision Making
- Note Taking
- Risk Effective Decision Making and Case Management
- Criminology
- Crime Scene Management
- Interviewing Victims and Witnesses
- Confidential Informant Handling, Search Warrant Drafting
- Photographic Lineup
- Report Writing, Court Testimony
- Judicial Administration
- Structured Interviewing: Suspects

Once the competencies were identified, the information was merged with the expertise of the curriculum designers to begin work on the program structure. It had already been noted that a multilevel program was required in order to provide

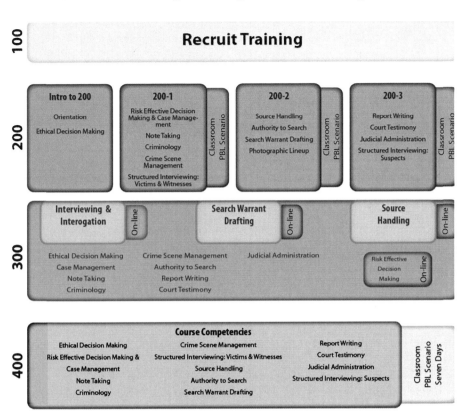

Fig. 7.1 Illustrates the four different levels that comprise the Investigative Skills Education Program (ISEP)

investigators with progressive education that spanned their investigative careers rather than singular training courses. Through ongoing discussion with the subject-matter experts, it was discovered that the competencies did not change from one level to another but the "level of competence…(standards)" increased in proportion to an increase of specialization or authority (Edmonton Police Service, 2010a, 2010b, p. 8). For example, officers participating in ISEP 200 began by learning to take comprehensive notes in their notebook. As they gain more skill and experience in investigations, they advance to ISEP 300 courses, where more complex dimensions are added to note taking such as how to properly record confidential informant information. Then, in ISEP 400, investigators learn to utilize a complex file management system with task logs and investigative summaries for investigating serious crimes such as homicides. While the competency performance remained the same (take adequate notes), the standard of the competency (what constitutes adequate) increased from level to level. As a result, officers work through each level of the program, first gaining fundamental competency, then going back to the field to apply this new knowledge before returning to the program at the next level for more complex skills and knowledge (Fig. 7.1).

Program Structure Overview

ISEP is comprised of four sequential levels, each consisting of curriculum based on core investigative competencies that increase in complexity at each level. This method allows investigators to obtain knowledge and skill from the program, apply that knowledge to practice in the field, and then build on what they have learned by proceeding to the next more complex level of education. Level 100 was the basic recruit training program that all Alberta police services utilize as required training for their newly hired police officers. ISEP Level 200 was for investigators who had completed recruit training, including the field training component, and had had some opportunity to begin to apply their investigative skills on the job. ISEP Level 300 was designed to hone specific investigative skills that concentrated on three key areas (confidential informant handling, interviewing and interrogation, and search-warrant drafting) while still including all other investigative competencies in the training. Level 300 prepares investigators for project teams, and secondments to specialized investigative units. ISEP Level 400 focuses on the processes, techniques, and strategies required by investigators for conducting complex and/or major crime investigations, known as Major Case Management. Participants in the Level 400 course were typically those who had achieved the rank of detective. This competency-based multilevel approach integrates formal education with field experience and assists officers in attaining the knowledge required to conduct criminal investigations appropriate to their current positions.

ISEP utilizes a blended learning model that maximizes the potential of both online and classroom learning. Providing a portion of the curriculum online ensured multiple benefits to the program and the participants. First, the online curriculum provided students with the theoretical component of each topic area. This meant that more time could be spent on practical application during the classroom segments. Also, having studied the online material, learners arrive for the classroom sessions with a similar level of knowledge and understanding of the required theory regardless of prior experience. The online modules are self-paced and students can work through them as time allows prior to the classroom segments. The online modules are readily available to everyone in the province regardless of their location, and the material is an information resource during and after participation in ISEP. Upon completion of the online modules, investigators from police agencies across Alberta attend the classroom sessions where they apply what they learned online in a problem-based learning investigative scenario.

As already mentioned, the principles of adult learning tell us that adults learn best when education is relevant to their work and they can practice applying the course content. The teaching methodologies of ISEP were based on the principles of adult education, for example; based on Vygotsky's ZPD theory,[1] one or two

---

[1] The concept of the zone of proximal development was originally developed by Vygotsky to argue against the use of academic, knowledge-based tests as a means to gauge students' intelligence. Vygotsky argued that, rather than examining what a student knows to determine intelligence, it is better to examine his or her ability to solve problems independently and his or her ability to solve problems with an adult's help (Berk & Winsler, 1995, p. 27)

experienced investigators were utilized in the classroom to serve as syndicate leaders to assist in guiding students through the learning and investigative process. Syndicate leaders coach, mentor, and, at times, challenge participants in order to impart the best understanding possible. This method helps transfer the knowledge of a few experienced and skilled investigators to a multitude of less experienced officers. Utilizing problem-based learning principles and constructivism theory, students are expected to work through practical investigative scenarios using real-world available resources. These resources include the theory and information from the online modules, supplementary material available in the classroom, the coaching and guidance of the syndicate leader, and the collective knowledge base of the other learners in the classroom. Under these conditions, training has real meaning for the adult learners and can be applied to similar situations that occur in the real world. The conditions and resources in the classroom sessions mirrored the conditions under which police officers functioned every day. For example, police officers work with other officers and members of the community to solve problems, a task most often accomplished in a collaborative fashion under the guidance and advice of those with more experience. For Alberta police officers, this learning theory provides police members with an opportunity to discuss, collaborate, and problem-solve with officers from other agencies across the province. As a result, the classroom is a safe, low-risk environment in which participants are able to learn how to investigate complex criminal occurrences utilizing new investigative methodologies.

Course Assignments

Each level in the investigative skills program requires the student to complete a number of assignments that assess their learning and ability to demonstrate competency. Each assignment was designed to mirror the investigative process and its inherent products. Students are required to meet the same standard set for each assignment as they would for a real investigation. The assignments include items such as: Information to Obtain a Search Warrant (ITO), Photographic Line-Up, Note Taking, Report Writing, Interviewing, Task Logs, and Executive Summaries for example.

Validation

It was identified that the feedback from multiple diverse stakeholders was required to validate the structure and methodology of ISEP. It was determined that focus group interviews were the most efficient and effective method of gathering the information. The focus groups were made up of the following stakeholders from the Edmonton and Calgary Police Services and Crown Prosecutors:

- Frontline patrol investigators (constables/sergeants/staff sergeants)
- Detectives from various investigative disciplines

- Staff Sergeants from various investigative disciplines
- Provincial Crown Prosecutors

The results of these focus group interviews confirmed the structure and methodology that had been developed and reaffirmed the dire need for this type of comprehensive curriculum.

ISEP Pilot

Each level of ISEP was piloted separately in order to assess the following:

- Appropriateness of the curriculum to the experience level of the student
- Alignment between course assignments and learning objectives
- Alignment between online learning and practical application in class
- Inconsistencies
- Effectiveness of the structure, scheduling, and logistics of each level for both the student and the facilitators

Students selected to participate in the pilot were a representative sample group from across the province and were deemed appropriate to the experience level being piloted. During the pilot, students were asked to complete both paper and online evaluations. This was completed as both a formative and summative evaluation process. Further evaluation was completed through facilitated discussions with the students, as well as debriefing sessions with the subject-matter experts, facilitators, and curriculum designers. All the evaluation data were compiled in order to begin a prioritization of edits and modifications to both the online and classroom material prior to implementing any revisions. Feedback from all stakeholders involved in the pilot was crucial to identifying the changes that were required in order to enhance the content and delivery of the program.

ISEP Level 200 Pilot

What Worked

ISEP Level 200 pilot was originally comprised of five classroom sessions and 15 online modules. The learners benefited from having a blended learning curriculum that allowed them to have access to online material prior to coming to class. The online content helped prepare students for classroom discussion and practical activities. The availability of syndicate leaders during the classroom instruction helped to provide necessary guidance when needed. Students felt that the use of syndicate leaders was unlike any other training they had received and valued the assistance and guidance of someone with investigative experience. The inter-agency groups allowed individuals an opportunity to gain a better understanding of the material through discussion and sharing of prior experience with one another. Students stated that they would not have thought of certain ideas had they been working alone. The classroom instruction allowed students more time for hands-on learning experiences and the learners could practice their skills prior to applying them in the field. Interestingly, students indicated that they did not have any exposure to some of the material before participating in ISEP. For example, some students had little to no prior experience in search warrants or managing confidential informants.

What Changed

After the ISEP Level 200 pilot, a number of changes were implemented based on evaluative feedback. Students indicated that there was too much time between the online and classroom components, and that this longer time span made it difficult to keep the online learning fresh in their minds. Thus, this timeline was reduced and, as a result, the overall length was compacted and the classroom sessions were reduced from five classroom sessions to three. In addition, some of the online material had not reinforced during the classroom instruction. Students became frustrated when the online assignments were not addressed in the classroom session or online content was not referred to in class. Details of the classroom problem-based learning scenario were brought into the online modules and assignments from online were discussed in the classroom. As a result, the online content became a continuation of the classroom scenario and vice versa.

Changes were also made to the method of delivery and content of the online modules. Because there was no provincial server available to host the online modules, each agency utilized its own internal learning management system or intranet to host the courses. This limited access for the learners made edits to the online material cumbersome to implement. An external Web-based provider was utilized to provide the learners with broader access and allowed for quick and easy course edits when necessary. Finally, course content was edited to reflect the provincial scope of the program. Agency-specific references to policies and procedures, language, and terminology were vetted and replaced with neutral language. Images and photographs were collected from agencies across the province and utilized in the online modules to ensure inclusivity.

ISEP Level 300 Pilot

What Worked

The ISEP level 300 pilot comprised of three topic-specific courses delivered independent of one another: Confidential Informant Handling, Interviewing and Interrogation, and Search-Warrant Drafting. Each course also included content that related to all of the other 11 ISEP competencies. ISEP level 300 development benefited from lessons learned in both the level 200 and 400 as both these levels preceded the level 300. Comprehensive online module completion and an exam were mandatory for students prior to participation in the classroom session. This ensured that students met the desired standard set for the training and were able to immediately engage in practical application through scenarios and simulations. As observed by Det. John Tedeschini of the Edmonton Police Service, one of the subject-matter experts for the program,

> Interview and interrogation courses in the past were dominated by lectures with the odd video clip included to highlight a point. Clearly, this was not an ideal learning environment. The [constructivist] learning approach taken in ISEP actively involved the learner. Not surprisingly, the feedback from participants…has been overwhelmingly positive in this respect.

Further, students were able to utilize investigative tools in order to determine strategies based on best practices taught online and in the classroom.

What Changed

The ISEP level 300 remained largely intact after the pilot. Small changes were required in the Search Warrant Drafting course relating to the concentration of some components in the online module. Through classroom observation, student feedback, and final assignment performance it was found that students required more guidance and they experienced some confusion with one segment of the course. As a result, this area was bolstered in the online module. Conversely, some material was eliminated from the course altogether because it was found that students would not have an opportunity to immediately apply this knowledge in the field.

ISEP Level 400 Pilot

What Worked

The target student for the ISEP level 400 were senior investigators, usually detective rank or equivalent, working or about to be working in a unit or area responsible for major case investigations. Therefore, principles of major case management, risk effective decision making, and case coordination were emphasized. The ISEP level 400 pilot was a 7-day classroom course with some self-study pre-reading information provided to students approximately 2 weeks prior to the start of the course. At the time of writing, there was no online component; however, the need for online pre-learning and pre-testing had been recognized and planned. Each day of the classroom session was comprised of a half day or less of presentations from subject-matter experts and the remainder of the day students worked within their major case management teams of five to seven and "investigated" a complex serious crime. The students were expected to utilize all resources that would be available to them during a real investigation, make critical decisions, and produce the required investigative material such as task logs, information to obtain, search warrants, investigative summaries, notes, etc. Students advised that they were completely engaged in the investigative process and benefited from the hands-on, practical application of investigative techniques that they had never utilized prior to the course. As with other levels of ISEP, an experienced syndicate leader worked closely with each group to guide the team, provide advice, and serve as the "devil's advocate" to ensure decision making was well thought out and followed appropriate process. The feedback received indicated that the students learned a great deal from the syndicate leaders regarding both content and the dynamics and challenges of working in a team environment.

What Changed

After receiving feedback from the ISEP level 400 pilot students and other stakeholders, little change was identified for this level of ISEP. Because of the complexity of the investigative scenario utilized during the course, there were some logistical details that were corrected but the structure and content remained the same. In order to reduce the requirement for lengthy subject-matter expert presentations and to ensure that students arrived in the classroom with the appropriate requisite knowledge, online learning modules are planned for this level.

ISEP Success

After the pilot courses and subsequent evaluation and editing processes, ISEP began full implementation on a provincial scale. As of March 2011, over 820 police investigators had successfully participated in one or more of the ISEP levels.

In 2010, ISEP had been identified by the Alberta Chiefs of Police as a priority and was being sustained financially by the Solicitor General and Public Security and each of the Municipal Police Services in Alberta and the Royal Canadian Mounted Police (RCMP). Support for the program is strong throughout the province and a provincial team will continue to manage the continuing facilitation and administration of the courses both online and classroom as well as the currency of the curriculum.

Conclusion

The history of police training illustrates the ongoing need to continually improve instructional practices in order to mitigate inadequate investigations, wrongful convictions, and to optimize organizational education. To address the ongoing challenges facing the police profession, the In-House Training Unit of the Edmonton Police Service identified a need for a more comprehensive curriculum that utilized blended learning, adult education methodologies, and a competency-based curriculum, through the development of the ISEP. ISEP's multilevel design provided Alberta police officers with the proper training at the appropriate time in their career. Because ISEP is a province-wide training initiative all police officers in the province are receiving the same investigative education and therefore able to provide a consistent standard of policing service to all citizens in the province. Further, the structure of ISEP provides a responsive curriculum framework that is able to adapt and evolve to meet any needed changes in the future.

References

Albrecht, B. (2006). *Enriching student experience through blended learning.* Boulder, CO: EDUCASE Centre for Applied Research.

Andrade, A. F., Jaques, P. A., Jung, J. L., Bordini, R. H., & Vicari, R. M. (2001). A computational model of distance learning based on Vygotsky's socio-cultural approach. In *Proceedings of AIED 2001 workshop papers: Multi-agent architectures for distributed learning environments, San Antonio, TX* (pp. 35–48).

Berk, L., & Winsler, A. (1995). "Vygotsky: His life and works" and "Vygotsky's approach to development". In *Scaffolding children's learning: Vygotsky and early childhood learning* (pp. 25–34). Washington, DC: National Association for Education of Young Children.

Birzer, M. L. (2003). The theory of andragogy applied to police training. *Policing: An International Journal of Police Strategies and Managment, 26*(1), 29–42.

Cleveland, G. (2006). Using problem-based learning in police training. *The Police Chief, 73*(11), 1.

Dubois, D. D. (1993). *Competency-based performance improvement: A strategy for organizational change* (1st ed.). Amherst, MA: HRD Press.

Dunham, R., & Alpert, G. (2010). *Critical issues in policing: Law enforcement training changes and challenges.*

Dunham, G. R., & Alpert, P. G. (2010a). *Critical issues in policing: Contemporary readings* (6th ed.). Long Grove, IL: Waveland Press.

Dziuban, C., Hartman, J., & Moskal, P. (2004). *Blended learning.* Boulder, CO: Educause Centre for Applied Research.

Edmonton Police Service. (2010a). *Adult education program: Characteristics of adult learners.* Edmonton, AB: Edmonton Police Service.

Edmonton Police Service. (2010b). *Edmonton Police Service: Course training standards manual.* Edmonton, AB: Edmonton Police Service.

Edmonton Police Service and Edmonton Police Commission. (2009). *Annual report to the community.* Edmonton, AB: Edmonton Police Service.

Edmonton Police Service Recruiting Unit. (2010). *Edmonton Police Service recruiting statistics.* Edmonton, AB: Edmonton Police Service.

Goldstein, H. (1990). *Problem-orientated policing.* New York, NY: McGraw-Hill.

Hill v. Hamilton-Wentworth Regional Police Services Board. (2007). 2007 SCC 41.

Honebein, P., Duffy, T. M., & Fishman, B. (1993). Constructivism and the design of learning environments: Context and authenticity activities for learning. In T. M. Duffy, J. Lowyck, & D. Jonasson (Eds.), *Designing environments for constructivist learning.* Heidelberg, Germany: Springer.

Howell, S. L., Williams, P. B., & Lindsay, N. K. (2003). Thirty-two trends affecting distance education: An informed foundation for strategic planning. *Online Journal of Distance Learning Administration, 6*(3), 1.

Mackeracher, D. (2004). *Making sense of adult learning* (2nd ed.). Toronto, ON: University of Toronto Press.

Masie, E. (2002). Blended Learning: the magic is in the mix, in A. Rossett (Ed.), *The ASTD e-learning handbook*. (P. 59) New York, McGraw-Hill.

Moore, M. G., & Kearsley, G. (2005). *Distance education: A systems view* (2nd ed.). New York, NY: Wadsworth.

National Geographic. (n.d.). *National geographic: Travel & cultures, Alberta map*. Retrieved April 15, 2010, from http://travel.nationalgeographic.com/places/map_province_alberta.html.

Picciano, A. G. (2006). *Blended learning: Implications for growth and access*. Newburyport, MA: The Sloan Consortium.

Savery, J. R., & Duffy, T. M. (2001). *Problem based learning: An instructional model and its constructivist framework*. Bloomington, IN: Center for Research on Learning and Technology.

Savin-Baden, M., & Wilkie, K. (2004). *Challenging research in problem based learning*. New York, NY: Open University Press.

Schooley, C. (2005). *Use blended learning to get dealer action: New techniques and technologies help dealers and OEMs make training stick*. Cambridge, MA: Forrester Research.

Schooley, C. (2008). *How to create a comprehensive, high impact learning strategy*. Cambridge, MA: Forrester Research.

Schooley, C. (2009). *The ROI of elearning*. Cambridge, MA: Forrester Research.

Statistics Canada. (2004). *Perspectives on labour and income: The near-retirement rate*. Ottawa, ON. Retrieved May 20, 2010, from Statistics Canada Website http://statcan.gc.ca/pub/75-001-x/10204/6790-eng.htm.

Thorne, K. (2003). *Blended learning: How to integrate online & traditional learning*. Philadelphia, PA: Kogan Page Limited.

Vodde, R. (2009). *The efficacy of an andragogical instructional methodology in basic police training and education*. Doctoral dissertation, University of Leicester, Leicester, UK.

Weinblatt, R. B. (1999). New police training philosophy: Adult learning model on verge of national wide rollout. *Law & Order, 47*(8), 84–90.

Chapter 8
The Professionalising Investigation Programme

Dan McGrory and Pat Treacy

Abbreviations

ACC	Assistant Chief Constable
ACPO	Association of Chief Police Officers
APA	Association of Police Authorities
CBA	Crime Business Area – ACPO
CCTV	Closed Circuit Television
CPD	Continuous professional development
CPIA	Criminal Procedure and Investigations Act 1996
CPS	Crown Prosecution Service
DC	Detective Constable
DAC	Deputy assistant
DCC	Deputy Chief Constable
DI	Detective Inspector
DIDP	Detective Inspectors Development Programme
DNA	Deoxyribonucleic acid
FLO	Family Liaison Officer
HRA	Human Rights Act 1998
HO	Home Office
HMIC	Her Majesties Inspectorate of Constabulary
HR	Human Resources
HWG	Homicide Working Group
ICIDP	Initial Crime Investigators Development Programme
IMSC	Initial Management of Serious Crime

D. McGrory (✉) • P. Treacy
National Police Improvement Agency (NPIA), London, SE1 9QY, UK
e-mail: danmcgrory@btinternet.com

M.R. Haberfeld et al. (eds.), *Police Organization and Training: Innovations in Research and Practice*, DOI 10.1007/978-1-4614-0745-4_8,
© Springer Science+Business Media, LLC 2012

IPCC   Independent Police Complaints Commission
IPLDP   Initial Police Learning and Development Programme
ISP   Implementation Support Plan
IT   Information Technology
MPS   Metropolitan Police Service
NCALT   National Centre for Applied Learning Technology
NCPE   National Centre for Policing Excellence
NIE   National Investigators Examination
NIM   National Intelligence Model
NOS   National Occupational Standards
NPP   National Policing Plan
NVQ   National Vocational Qualification
PACE   Police and Criminal Evidence Act 1984
PCSO   Police and Community Support Officers
PDR   Personal development review
PDP   Personal development plan
PIP   Professionalising Investigation Programme
POCA   Proceeds of Crime Act 2002
PSSO   Police Standards and Skills Organisation – (Now Skills for Justice)
PSU   Policing Standards Unit – Home Office
RIPA   Regulation of Investigatory Powers Act 2000
RDS   Research and Development Section – Home Office
SCAIDP   Serious Child Abuse Investigators Development Programme
SIO   Senior Investigating Officer
SOCPA   Serious and Organised Crime and Police Act 2005
SP   Significant point
STC   Standards training and competency (ACPO)
STO   Specially Trained Officer – Sexual Offences
STODP   Specially Trained Officers Development Programme
UAP   Unified Assessment Protocol

Introduction

The Association of Chief Police Officers (ACPO) and the Home Office commissioned the Professionalising Investigation Programme (PIP) in 2004. The aim of PIP was to improve the professional competence of all police officers and staff whose roles involved conducting supervising or managing investigations. The intention was to embed a national process, which integrated underpinning knowledge and published guidance on the best practice and principles governing investigation, which included investigative interviewing. The approach was to align existing learning and development programmes with National Occupational Standards (NOS) for conducting, supervising and managing investigations, thereby creating a robust and consistent process for developing and assessing investigators competence in the workplace. This would enable the police service to create local and national registers of competent practitioners, within defined levels, and consequently deliver improvements in investigative practice, generating improved confidence in the Criminal Justice System.

The Drivers for Change

The focus on improving effectiveness and efficiency in the public services was driven forward in the 1980s by the "new public management" approach to public service management defined by clear accountability for functions and performance. Moving forward to the 1990s concern for the way in which public services were managed and run was commonplace in all political parties with all asserting the view that improvement in the management of public services was as equally important as additional resources being committed to those services (Kerley, 1994). The police service of England and Wales was not immune to these concerns and, although the spotlight was focused on other public service organisations in the early part of the decade, events of the latter part of the decade were to seriously call the effectiveness and efficiency of police investigations into question. Rising levels of crime coupled with reducing numbers of crimes detected and offenders being brought to justice suggested deterioration in the effectiveness of the police in crime investigation an activity that many people saw as the primary role of the police (Audit Commission, 1993).

Added to this, at the end of the decade, police incompetence and failings in the conduct supervision and management of major investigations were exposed in the public enquiries into the death of 18-year-old Stephen Lawrence who was knifed to death at a bus stop in South London and the Shipman inquiry into the numerous killings carried out by Dr. Harold Shipman in the North of England, both of which were widely reported in the media.

The government had introduced a number of legislative changes designed to improve the conduct and practice of investigations and in particular to improve public confidence in the manner in which investigations, stop and searching interviewing and detention were conducted. Technology was developing new techniques in forensic science and advances in DNA techniques had created new opportunities for offenders and offences to be identified. Despite these positive changes, police performance in one of its core roles investigation was not improving.

The Government White paper published in 2001 "Policing a New Century; A Blueprint for Reform" (Home Office, 2004) advocated a number of radical reforms to policing which included:

- The police need a clear and common understanding of the theory and practice of investigation.
- There need to be clear strategies to tackle criminal gangs and persistent offenders.
- There needs to be a more effective means of spreading good practice in handling investigations.

Many of the recommendations included in the white paper were incorporated into in the Police Reform Act 2002. The focus was on bringing policing into the twenty-first century, improving effectiveness and efficiency as well as improving public confidence and satisfaction in the police. At the heart of the governments drive to reform policing was the concept that effective investigation was crucial to delivering the strategic objectives of reducing crime and the fear of crime by increasing crime detection and bringing more offenders to justice, thereby improving public confidence and reducing the fear of crime. The Police Reform Act 2002 introduced a number of policing reforms, which included the publication of a National Policing Plan (NPP) outlining the governments' strategic objectives for policing. This contained a set of performance measures and targets against which individual force performance would be judged. The act also required police authorities to create a 3-year local policing plan that outlined how forces would achieve the strategic objectives within the NPP.

The PIP was one of the key elements in the ACPO response to the reform agenda. The aim of the programme was to improve the professional skills and knowledge of all police officers and staff whose role entailed conducting, supervising or managing criminal investigations.

Stelfox (2009) identifies that the police service's capacity to carry out investigations across the spectrum of offending and its ability to respond to new challenges as they emerge consists entirely of the knowledge skills and understanding that individual investigators have developed of investigative practice. While the legislation, forensic and technical developments are important without competent practitioners capable of applying the correct techniques, making timely informed and appropriate investigative decisions in individual cases, all the developments would have little or no effect.

The Governance of Policing in England and Wales

There are currently 43 autonomous police forces in England and Wales (separate arrangements exist for Scotland and Northern Ireland), each of which is headed by a Chief Constable who is responsible for the leadership of the force in conjunction with members of their management team consisting of ACPO officers. The governance of policing in England and Wales is based upon what is commonly termed the tripartite structure which consists of the government Home Office (HO), the Association of Police Authorities (APA) and ACPO, whose roles are defined as follows: the Home Office is the government department with lead responsibility for law and order for the whole of the United Kingdom. It has national responsibility for the police service in England and Wales. The Home Secretary, a government minister, manages the relationship with the police service in a tripartite manner working with the ACPO and the APA. The Home Secretary has the overall responsibility for ensuring the delivery of an efficient and effective Police service in England and Wales. The Home Office sets the annual key priorities for policing in the National Community Safety Plan, which also details the means by which achievement of the priorities will be measured. The Home office also performs numerous other functions such as determining police pay and regulations, performance monitoring and funding.

The Police Reform Act 2002 gave the Home Secretary the power to directly intervene in underperforming police forces. Further subsequent reforms to the tripartite structure were introduced in the Police and Justice Act 2006, which gave the Home Secretary the power to intervene in underperforming police authorities. Home Office influence in policing has expanded in a variety of ways in recent decades, through issuing policy circulars in a number of areas, greater control over training and career paths of senior police officers, increases in central funding and from the late 1980s onwards the development of an increasingly vigorous national performance framework (Jones, 2003).

Police authorities are independent bodies consisting of locally elected and independent members. Their role is to set the force's strategic direction and to hold the Chief Constable to account on behalf of the local community. The strategic direction is set taking into account the national and local policing priorities determined after local community consultation. The police authorities also have the responsibility for setting the local policing budget and decide how much local (council) tax is raised to support local policing. Most police authorities have 17 members:

- Nine local councillors appointed by the local council.
- Eight independent members selected following local advertisements, at least one of whom must be a magistrate.

Chief Constables are the chief officers of police in England and Wales with the exception of the London Forces (Metropolitan and City of London) who are headed by Commissioners. They are the highest-ranking officers in their respective forces and are responsible to the police authority for the direction and control of policing in their force areas. All Chief Constables are members of ACPO, which consists of senior police officers or police staff who hold the rank or appointment above that of Chief Superintendent or equivalent police staff grade. The association focuses on the following:

- Providing strong and visible leadership.
- Developing policing doctrine in a professional and coordinated manner.
- Acting as the principal voice for the service.
- Supporting the continuous professional development of members and the achievement of the highest standards of performance.
- Coordinating the strategic policing response in times of national need.
- Developing its business activities to ensure that the ACPO brand is recognised globally as a mark of excellence in policing.

The Government via the Home Office and Home secretary-sets National Policing Plan with Objectives and targets

Police Authorities;

Locally elected councillors and magistrates-create three year local action plans to deliver against National Policing Plan

Chief Constables – responsible to the Police authority for the direction and control of individual police forces

Prior to the creation of the National Centre for Policing Excellence (NCPE) in the Police Reform Act 2002, one of the core activities of ACPO was in developing policing policy which was conducted through its network of regional and national business areas.

The bulk of this policy and practice was produced by working groups from within the various ACPO business areas, who would take responsibility for consulting within the service and elsewhere and producing draft policies. These policies were submitted for approval by ACPO cabinet which comprises the heads of each business area (or the Chief Constables council if appropriate) for discussion and approval before being disseminated to the 43 police forces of England and Wales and the Police Service of Northern Ireland. The ACPO cabinet meets monthly and is responsible for setting the business strategy for the organisation and managing the day-to-day business involved in developing policing policy and practice. ACPO was not solely responsible for producing guidance and practice for the police service. Her Majesties Inspectorate of Constabulary (HMIC), the Audit Commission and the Home Office Policing Standards Unit (PSU), together with the Home Office Research and Development Section (RDS), all produced reports influencing or recommending good practice for adoption by the service.

The government was responsible for producing new legislation, regulations and codes of practice which had a statutory effect. ACPO does not have a statutory function; it produces policy guidance and practice to coordinate policing activity (Stelfox, 2009). ACPO policy and guidance are endorsed by the service, and forms an authoritative guide to policing practice in a particular area, upon which inspections, reviews and audits of compliance can be undertaken by bodies such as HMIC.

Individual police forces will also be responsible for producing local force policy to ensure local compliance policing objectives. These policies will be linked to the achievement of local and strategic policing objectives outlined within the National and local policing plans.

Prior to the creation of the NCPE in 2004, while ACPO had responsibility for the dissemination of policing policy and practice, there was no national consistency in the implementation of this policy. The NCPE-assisted implementation had developed considerable experience emanating from delivering the National Intelligence Model (NIM) and ensuring compliance to national standards when the NIM was rolled out to all forces in 2000. The NCPE Assisted Implementation team was tasked with managing the national implementation of PIP as a project within the programme.

Professionalisation

While there are some obvious examples of recognised "professions" such as the medical, legal and nursing professions, they tend to be defined by certain common features which include:

- A body of professional knowledge and ethics.
- Defined standards of practice.
- Learning programme leading to qualification.
- Levels of expertise.
- Continuous professional development required to retain status.
- A professional body or institute that regulates and guides the membership.

While the police service is regularly described as a profession and members viewed themselves as being professionals, there was no established process that could be identified in light of the criteria described above. For example, outside of legislative training there was no definitive, published body of knowledge, which defined the process of investigation and the best practice and principles governing all criminal investigations. There was nonetheless a tradition of craft-based learning similar to an apprenticeship, learned through training and practice in the workplace; not all of this might be regarded as good practice.

Concerns were raised about the effectiveness of police investigations in the 1990s when a number of high-profile miscarriages of justice and failed investigations were publicised which highlighted widespread deficiencies in the knowledge, practice, supervision and management of investigators, creating a focus on the capabilities of the police service to investigate effectively.

It has been identified that as the processes of criminal investigation become more visible due to the changes in the speed and range of communication and the techniques of media presentation, the potential existed to demystify the police as effective crime fighters (Mawby, 2007).

This focus on effective performance had highlighted that there were obvious deficiencies in the practice, supervision and management of investigation at all levels of the service. There was an emerging opportunity with the creation of the NCPE in 2004 to professionalise all aspects of investigation and, in doing so, to improve investigative performance and achieve many of the national and local policing objectives.

The Professionalising Investigation Process

Origins of PIP

The ACPO Homicide Working Group (HWG) was a subgroup of the ACPO crime business area responsible for the development of investigative policy and practice. Prior to the creation of the NCPE, and influenced by recommendations from some of the aforementioned public enquiries (Macpherson, 1999; Smith, 2003), in 2002, ACPO (HWG) under the direction of Commander Bill Griffiths, of the Metropolitan Police, had begun work to scope how the skills, abilities and competence of investigators could be improved. Although the working group was predominantly concerned with major investigation, there was recognition that the investigative performance of all investigating officers and staff could be enhanced. "The investigation of murder should set clear standards of excellence that all other criminal investigation can follow" (HMIC, 2004, p. 115; Stelfox 2007, p. 632).

South Wales Police were undertaking a review of investigative performance at all levels and developing solutions to improve the skills and competence of investigators. They introduced a programme of supervisor-led assessments of competence against "seven significant points" in an investigation. The significant points covered all aspects of investigation from initial attendance at a scene through to case preparation and the disposal of a case at court.

SP1 – Initial contact and initial response
SP2 – Scene assessment
SP3 – Evidence gathering
SP4 – Victim and witness management
SP5 – Suspect handling
SP6 – Post charge
SP7 – File preparation trial

The significant points reflected common areas of poor investigative practice and supervision.

Their research had identified that investigation could be categorised by the nature of the offence and the perceived skills required. These fell naturally into distinct levels.

Level 1 accredited investigators include frontline officers who have completed their probation (including Sergeants and Inspectors), officers involved in road policing investigations, officers in more detailed community roles, civilian investigators and police staff involved in the investigation process.

Level 2 accredited investigators will, in addition to having *Level 1* accreditation, have received nationally recognised investigative training. They will be involved in the investigation of volume crime, serious crime or road death investigations.

Level 3 accredited investigators (traditionally referred to as Senior Investigating Officers) will be those officers investigating difficult or complex cases such as homicide, corporate killing and deaths in custody.

Level 4 accredited investigators will be those involved in cross-border-linked serious crime inquiries, as well as the investigation of those crimes whose severity is likely to significantly undermine public confidence.

The outcome from the assessment process was an "accreditation" of competence at each level. The ACPO HWG was later to adopt the principles of the South Wales initiative and named their project the PIP.

PIP Pathfinders

In order to test how the PIP accreditation model would work in practice, it was decided to pilot the first three levels of PIP (Level 4 was still under development at this stage) in a number of forces ("Pathfinder sites") prior to national roll-out. It was initially expected that there would be five Pathfinder forces in addition to South Wales but one of those initially selected decided not to participate and three other forces asked to be involved in the pilot. The eight Pathfinder forces were:

- Durham
- Hampshire
- Lancashire
- Merseyside
- Metropolitan Police
- Northamptonshire
- South Wales
- Staffordshire

The Pathfinder sites each planned to implement different levels (or combinations of levels) of PIP in different units or teams. An evaluation was undertaken by the Home Office, on behalf of the ACPO (Unpublished report, Home Office, 2004).

The evaluation highlighted that while there was widespread support for the concept of PIP, a range of issues appeared to affect the successful introduction of PIP in the Pathfinder forces. These included:

- The perceived benefit arising from the accreditation process from an individual and organisational perspective.
- Inadequacy of the assessment process including the bureaucracy involved.
- Skills of the assessors and supporting HR process, i.e., PDR.
- Lack of Integration with training programmes and other organisational processes.

The report made recommendations for implementing the project nationally. The establishment of the NCPE enabled ACPO and the Home Office to implement the programme nationally in 2004.

The Project Becomes a National Programme

The PIP was initiated by the ACPO crime business area as a key programme within the Police Reform Agenda. It was developed in consultation with a range of stakeholders including the Home Office, The NCPE and Skills for Justice (Formerly the Police Standards and Skills Organisation – PSSO, 2004). Deputy Assistant Commissioner (DAC) Bill Griffiths of the Metropolitan Police Service (MPS) was the original ACPO lead for the project and was instrumental in developing the original PIP concept as aforementioned.

The project was reviewed by ACPO cabinet on the 14th April 2004. Cabinet endorsed the concepts outlined within the project but noted that further work would be required before the processes could be implemented in the 43 police forces in England and Wales. It was proposed that further work would be taken forward by the newly created NCPE and ACPO requested that Chief Constable Ian Johnston crime business area lead on crime training should chair the PIP programme board which would be created to oversee the further development and implementation of the programme.

Programme Governance

A PIP steering group comprising of key stakeholders from ACPO, The Home Office, The Crown Prosecution Service (CPS) and Skills for Justice, HMIC, the Superintendents Association and Police Federation staff associations, together with the Metropolitan Police Service (MPS), and key project leads from the NCPE was created to provide strategic direction to the programme. It was agreed that the programme would be delivered through four interdependent projects of work and the timescales for this work to be completed together with the full implementation of the programme were agreed by ACPO cabinet as follows.

Project area	Start date	Finish date
Core investigative doctrine	May 2004	March 2005
Training and assessment	May 2004	July 2007
Communications products	May 2004	October 2006
Implementation products	October 2004	April 2007
PIP	May 2004	July 2007

The original completion date for the programme was set as being July 2007. This timescale was to be amended as the programme developed and challenges to the deliverables arose. In September 2006, the ACPO PIP lead CC Ian Johnston presented PIP implementation support plan (ISP) and timescales for delivery to ACPO cabinet. While wholly accepting the timescales for delivery of the PIP Level 3 investigator package, the cabinet members expressed concern over the capacity of forces to deliver to the timescales proposed within the ISP concern was also expressed in relation to the levels of bureaucracy associated with the assessment processes for existing staff at PIP Level 1 and 2. As a result of these concerns, cabinet requested that the NCPE examined whether the PIP and Personal Development Review (PDR) Processes could be more closely aligned to reduce the perceived bureaucracy.

As a result of this development the PIP programme team conducted widespread consultation with Skills for Justice, the Police Federation and practitioners. A proposal to assess existing staff against the NOS for the relevant investigative and interviewing standards applicable to their role was agreed. In March 2007, the amended ISP and timescales were again presented to ACPO cabinet for approval. Cabinet approved the changes to the assessment processes but extended the timescales for full implementation of the programme as follows:

PIP Level 3	All level three investigators to be assessed as competent against PIP standards by 31st March 2007
PIP Level 1 and 2	All "new to role" investigators at Pip Level 1 and 2 to have been assessed against PIP standards by 31st march 2008
All levels	All existing investigators "in role" to be assessed against PIP standards by 31st March 2009

The challenging programme of work would bring all elements of the newly formed organisation together to:

- Design and development of investigative doctrine.
- Design and development of investigative learning and development programmes based upon investigative doctrine specifically tailored to meet the needs of new to role and existing investigators and investigative specialists.
- Design and development of workplace assessments of investigative competence for all new to role and existing investigative staff based upon the integrated competency framework incorporating NOS.
- Development of a national register of competent investigators.
- Development of a communication strategy to provide regular and timely updates to the service and stakeholders – producing tailored marketing and communications products to promote awareness and ensure consistency and professionalism throughout the life cycle of the programme.
- Development of an ISP to ensure that the programme could be consistently implemented in all forces and supported by the required people, systems policies and practices.

Programme Deliverables

The Development of Investigative Doctrine

The ACPO (2005) Practice Advice on Core Investigative Doctrine provides definitive national guidance on the key principles of criminal investigation. It provides a high-level overview of the process of criminal investigation. It was written by the NCPE investigative doctrine team in 2005 as the first product for the PIP Programme. Essentially this document represented one of the foundation stones of the body of knowledge required by the police service to if it aspired to be professional. The dictionary definition of the term doctrine simply refers to teaching or that what is taught, a principle of belief. Investigative learning and development programmes that were developed prior to the publication of this document were based upon the acquisition of legal knowledge and practical skills based around investigative case studies. The publication of the doctrine provided definitive national guidance for all investigators irrespective of the nature or complexity of the investigation and articulated the principles which are the basis for all investigations. The document also highlighted the importance of decision making, recording and accountability in a single document aimed at investigative practitioners for the first time in the history of the British police.

- The Police service had previously published the ACPO Murder Investigation Manual in 1998 compiled by experienced senior investigating officers (SIOs) with support and advice from other professionals and experts from the criminal justice system. This document provides a reference point for the investigation of all types of major crime and underpins training and development of SIOs (Stelfox, 2009, p. 80). The ACPO Investigative Interviewing Strategy was published in 2000 following extensive consultation with practitioners and experts from the criminal justice system and research conducted by academics and practitioners. The strategy, which provided definitive guidance on the best practice relating to the preparation and planning of interviews with victims, witnesses and suspects, was also used to underpin the training of investigative interviewers. This combined body of researched best practice provided the foundations for all PIP learning and development programmes.
- The doctrine was produced following extensive consultation with expert practitioners and academics with a wealth of experience in the fields of criminology, sociology and psychology. It provides investigators with the knowledge, skills and understanding that they need to carry out investigations to the highest possible standards and to make choices about the objectives that are being pursued and the method of disposing of cases that are driven by consideration of the public good rather than expediency (Stelfox, 2009, p. 22).
- This document, the ACPO (2005) Practice Advice on Core Investigative Doctrine, represented the first publication by the police service for the police service on how to conduct and manage criminal investigations. The strength of doctrine lies

where high-value good practice impacts upon performance and where common standards and accountability of performance are needed. Doctrine also provides the blueprint for training programmes, information technologists, system designers, personnel and finance managers who can all do their jobs more effectively and efficiently if common standards are laid down for the service (Skills for Justice, 2004, p. 23).

The National Occupational Standards

The existing learning and development programmes for investigation were in need of review and revision in light of the publication of doctrine, which in turn this would lead to revision of the NOS for investigation and interviewing standards, which had recently been developed (2003) by the newly formed Police Skills and Standards Organisation (PSSO), now Skills for Justice.

It was agreed that the assessment of competence against the seven "significant points" from the original project was replaced with assessment against the newly defined NOS, produced by Skills for Justice. This organisation had been established and funded by the government in 2001 as the standards setting body for the police sector, with the remit of identifying learning needs in criminal justice organisations and linking developmental training programmes to the achievement of academic qualifications. The first NOS, published in June 2003, specified the standards of performance that staff were expected to achieve in their role, together with the knowledge and skills they required to perform effectively (NOS are subject to periodic review to ensure that they remain fit for purpose – the initial standards have been amended to reflect doctrine and professional practice.).

Learning and Development Programmes

There was a need to align national learning and development programmes to the new NOS to enable effective workplace development through an assessment process. The aim of PIP was to provide the police service with a process that imbued confidence in the competence of all police officers and staff whose role involved conducting, supervising or managing investigations, regardless of their nature and complexity. The programme would deliver a framework that enabled career progression based upon an objective assessment of practitioner's skills in the workplace and supported by relevant learning and development programmes that enabled all practitioners to continuously maintain their professional development. In simple terms, the inputs to the programme would be the publication of professional practice aligned to NOS and Learning and Development Programmes which incorporated consistent workplace assessment at all investigative levels. This would enable

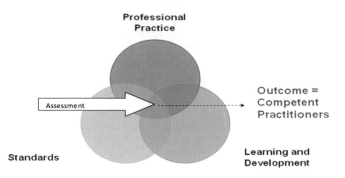

Fig 8.1 The tripartite structure

a practitioner's performance to be judged against objective criteria to assess their individual competence, such as their ability to apply their knowledge and skills to achieve and maintain consistent results at their level of investigation (see Fig. 8.1).

There were a series of learning and development programmes that provided access to the knowledge and skills for new to role investigators. All recruits to the police service undertake the Initial Police Learning and Development Programme (IPLDP) which is a 2-year modular development programme delivered within the trainees' home force. Some forces have entered into partnership with local education establishments and universities to deliver the programme and attain academic qualifications alongside the policing skills. Each trainee has to achieve competence against a range of NOS during this period, which encompasses classroom learning and community and workplace attachments in the company of a trained tutor constable, who is responsible for assessing and developing their practical policing skills. The trainee will undertake investigations and interviews with victims' witnesses and suspects during their tutor phase and they will be expected to achieve competence against the three PIP Level 1 NOS during the 2-year programme.

A stand-alone module was developed and designed for existing PIP Level 1 staff, which could be delivered in a 5-day classroom-based course, designed by NCPE and made available to all forces for delivery. This course was also available in an e-learning format on the NCALT database, which all forces have access to.

At PIP Level 2, the Initial Crime Investigators Development Programme was updated to concur with the Core Investigative Doctrine and NOS. NCPE updated the training curriculum and made this available to all forces; training for trainers was also undertaken to ensure that those tasked with training delivery were fully apprised of the new developments. A number of new learning and development programmes were designed for Level 2 investigative specialists and supervisors, together with a new programme, the Detective Inspectors Development Programme, designed specifically for investigative managers whose roles involved managing serious and complex investigations but did not require them to manage major investigations at

PIP Level 3 (Senior Investigating Officer). The design and development of this programme were undertaken in conjunction with Skills for Justice who created new NOS that covered the supervision and management of serious and complex investigations.

For PIP Level 3, the Senior Investigating Officers Development Programme was amended and following consultation with the ACPO HWG from within the ACPO crime business area agreement was reached on assessment, continuous professional development and registration process. This agreement led to the creation of a National Register of SIOs, which is managed and maintained by the NCPE in conjunction with the ACPO HWG.

The range of learning and development programmes that support the three levels of PIP is shown below.

PIP level	Learning and development programme	National Occupational Standards
Level 1	Initial Police Learning and Development Programme (IPLDP) designed for all new entrants into the police service A stand alone module was developed for existing investigators at PIP L1 Specially Trained Officers Development Programme (STODP)	Conduct volume crime investigation Conduct interviews with victims and witnesses in volume crime investigations Conduct interviews with suspects in volume crime
Level 2	Initial Crime Investigators Development programme (ICIDP) The foundation course for all those who are expected to carry out investigations at PIP Level 2	Conduct serious and complex investigations Conduct interviews with victims and witnesses in serious and complex investigations Conduct interviews with suspects in serious and complex investigations
Level 2 Specialists	For those experienced officers already at Level 2 but requiring additional specialist training, e.g. Serious Child Abuse Investigators Development Programme/Family Liaison Officers Training For supervisors the Initial Management of Serious Crime (IMSC), Detective Inspectors Development Programme (DIDP)	Assessed against above in context of their role
Level 3	Senior Investigating Officers Development Programme (SIODP), for those who will be leading major investigations, e.g. homicide, kidnap	Managing major investigations
Level 4	To be determined	To be determined

At the time of publication, work is still underway to determine the exact requirements of a PIP Level 4 investigator. The ACPO Standards, Training and Competency
group, who assumed responsibility for the programme post-implementation, are
taking this work forward.

The routes to registration for each level of PIP would be as follows.

New entrant to police service	New to role	Existing investigator
Learning programme	Selection	Initial assessment and development supervisor PDR
Workplace assessment – PDP	Learning programme	Registration
Tutor/supervisor assessment	Workplace assessment – PDP tutor supervisor	Assessment PDR
Registration	Registration	Maintenance – CPD

Communications

Throughout the lifetime of the programme, the communications strategy ensured
that developments on the programme were widely communicated and circulated to
the service. A dedicated website, www.deliveringchange.org, was established and
maintained throughout the lifetime of the programme. The website was designed to
reflect the projects within the programme and was used to consult with and update
practitioners and stakeholders on all developments within the individual project
work streams and overall programme.

All changes to the learning and developmental programmes, including the trainers guides, curriculum documents and case study materials, were published on the
website to ensure that force training staff were kept abreast of developments and
supporting material. The website contained a frequently asked questions section
which was regularly updated by the programme management team in order to promote consistency and inform practitioners, in relation to ongoing developments.

The implementation team and the programme manager conducted a number of
regional presentation days when they met with the relevant force PIP teams to discuss the programme and update them on progress and emerging good practice.

In addition, a quarterly newsletter was published by the programme team and
widely circulated to all stakeholders and police forces. The newsletter "Insight"
provided updates on all developments within the various project work streams; it
also contained articles relating to innovative good practice and benefits that had
been identified by individual forces in local implementation. The document also
allowed force implementation managers and individual staff to articulate their experiences of the programme and the personal and organisational improvements that
had been identified as a result of undertaking the programme.

A series of articles in national policing journals were compiled and released during the lifetime of the programme and numerous presentations were conducted at national conferences to stakeholders and practitioners to increase knowledge and communicate the aims and benefits of successful implementation.

The PIP assessment process and lack of knowledge and awareness of the NOS were identified as a potential challenge for practitioners and forces. The programme team developed a series of practical informative brochures for all PIP levels; the brochures outlined how effective assessment could be conducted in the workplace using realistic workplace examples to minimise the bureaucratic burden on practitioners and supervisors. A poster campaign was also conducted with a series of posters being produced aimed at promoting the benefits of being "fit to practice" which were published by the programme team and made freely available.

Communication is essential to promoting the benefits of implementing a major business change programme. PIP identified a number of challenges that would impact and potentially impede the successful implementation of the programme. The programme team also recognised that successful implementation would deliver a number of benefits that could be aligned to realise the strategic policing objectives outlined within the NPP. Throughout the lifetime of the programme, the board through its membership proactively attempted to identify and resolve risks, issues and challenges. Consultation and effective communication with stakeholders and practitioners were paramount in pragmatically resolving the majority of problems that arose during the implementation of the programme and creating synergy with the various interdependent projects that combined to deliver PIP.

Implementation

The implementation for PIP was established as a discrete project stream within the programme and followed a framework used within the newly formed NCPE. This format had been used to implement the NIM and so would be familiar to all forces.

The format included the development of an ISP, which had a dual function. First, it needed to describe the requirements of the programme in organisational terms taking into account the individual circumstances likely to be found in 43 HO forces in England and Wales. Second, it would serve as a self-assessment and action planning document against which progress could be measured.

The ISP allowed forces to consider a number of agreed criteria against their current position and where there were gaps to determine the action needed to achieve compliance. The criteria were a description of the organisational "Assets" under the following headings, Knowledge, People, Systems and Processes and Facilities, which would need to be aligned to support the professionalising model. The professionalising process was also described in the following categories: Selection, Learning and Development, Assessment, Registration and Maintenance of Registration. Again the criteria were defined within each area (see diagram below).

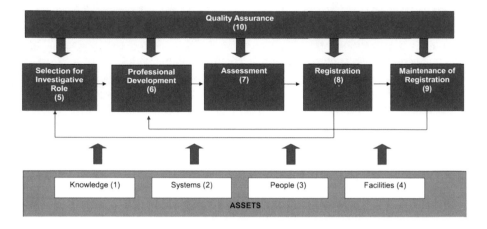

The ISP also outlined a series of milestones to be achieved over the 3-year implementation period, which had been agreed as achievable by ACPO (see table above).

From the above process it become clear that the programme originally conceived
in 2004 as a major "Learning and Development Programme" was much wider in
scope and reflected the need to integrate the process within business change, as
previously identified during the evaluation of the original Pathfinder Pilots.

The implementation began with a national capability assessment to gauge the
achievability of the plan. The response was that forces would be able to implement
the programme and the implementation process was commenced through establishing
local leads at the ACPO level for each force with a local designated manager for
implementation. The PIP programme board was the central reference point and
national implementation issues were managed on a daily basis though the project
lead from the Assisted Implementation Team in conjunction with the programme
manager.

A key feature of implementation was to undertake reviews of progress, known as
peer reviews. Two of which were conducted during the Implementation Project. The
reviews included a self-assessment document returned by each force followed by a
series of site visits to talk to implementation leads and practitioners on how PIP was
being progressed locally, to identify emerging good practice and to highlight issues
for escalation to and resolution by the programme board.

The outcome was a feedback letter to each ACPO lead within the force, detailing
progress and making suggestions for areas to develop in relation to compliance with
the ISP. The aggregated response from the peer reviews would be reported to the
programme board in order for strategic and local action planning to be undertaken
to manage or mitigate identified risks and issues.

The final peer review of forces was conducted during the period 2008–2009 set
against the timescales for implementation (see above) agreed by ACPO. While all
forces had not met the deadlines set for full implementation, the following results
emerged from the 41 forces which were reviewed.

Criteria	Forces satisfied this area
Investigation policy is aligned to guidance contained in Core Investigative Doctrine	87
Investigation processes aligned to Core Investigative Doctrine	84
Policy gives guidance on the standards of knowledge and skills required to undertake defined categories of investigation	81
Processes in place to quality assure policy is being applied effectively	84
Feedback from quality assurance processes to improve investigative performance	81
Investigators will be able to effectively maintain their skills through monitoring an review via PDR	74

	Total number of investigators	Number assessed	Assessed via initial development programmes
Level 1	22,403	8,890 (40%)	4,192 (47%)
Level 2	6,483	5,254 (81%)	2,460 (47%)
Level 3	208	108 (52%)	83 (77%)

Benefits and Challenges

A number of benefits were identified which would be realised on full implementation of the programme. These benefits were aligned to the strategic policing objectives articulated within the Government's NPP and would in turn help to achieve local policing priorities, thus satisfying the requirements of the tripartite governance structure for policing. The benefits which were identified included:

- Improved service to victims and witnesses in criminal investigations.
- Improvements in victim, witness and suspect interviewing.
- Improvements in victim and witness support.
- Improved conduct, supervision and management of criminal investigations.
- The prevention and early identification of poor practice and identification of individual or organisational developmental needs.
- Improvements in crime scene management, creating opportunities to maximise the forensic yield from crime scenes.
- Improved intelligence deriving from criminal investigations.
- Increases in the number of offenders being brought to justice.
- Improvements in public confidence in the Criminal Justice System.
- Improvements in staff confidence and competence.
- Improvements in local and national PDR processes.
- National and local registers of competence.
- More effective deployment and use of resources.

The programme also encountered a number of challenges to successful implementation at strategic and local levels.

The government had imposed a strict performance management regime with a focus on improving the number of sanction detections and increasing the numbers of offenders being brought to justice. In the early stages of the programme, there was an unrealistic expectation that PIP would begin to deliver instantaneous results in the sanction detection rate and the number of offenders being brought to justice. While successful implementation would inevitably lead to performance improvement, increasing the investigative competence of staff would create a gradual improvement in performance and was interdependent upon a number of other factors not least of which were changes in organisational and management culture that would enable the programme to flourish (Stelfox, 2007, p. 629).

The programme was perceived by many as an initiative to improve training rather than major business change. New to role investigators had to be given time to develop their skills towards competency and some existing investigators would require tailored developmental plans to refresh and improve their skills before significant improvements would be delivered. Delivering professional practice and amending learning, development and assessment processes would have little impact if senior management and staff did not demonstrate commitment to the programme by providing the appropriate organisational infrastructures to deliver and sustain improvements in investigative practice.

ACPO and senior managers were under pressure to achieve government targets aimed at improving volume crime investigations, increasing sanction detections and the numbers of offenders being brought to justice and rebuilding public confidence in the criminal justice system. There was cynicism within the service that fully adopting PIP would not deliver the anticipated benefits and was overly bureaucratic. Despite the ACPO mandate for the programme, some forces did not fully embrace it and only delivered the learning and development programmes for new-to-role staff. Delivery of training had always been of good standard; the key feature of PIP was workplace development and achievement of standards.

Coterminous with the delivery of PIP, the government and the police service had embarked upon programmes to dramatically reduce bureaucracy and return officers from form-filling duties to operational activity on the streets. The assessment processes were perceived by many to be adding to the bureaucratic burden on the service. The lack of a nationally consistent PDR created a major challenge. Many forces had recently developed their PDR processes and acquired IT frameworks to support their local systems. There was a reluctance to commit to further expenditure in a process which the management and staff had little confidence in. Despite numerous attempts by the Tripartite Structure and Human Resource specialists, the annual appraisal or PDR processes in many forces were failing due to a lack of buy-in from senior managers and staff (Baldwin, Strebler, & Reilly, 2007).

There was a perception that effective assessment required voluminous amounts of documentation and created bureaucracy. The programme team established that the bureaucracy was caused in the majority of instances by a lack of understanding of the requirements of the assessment process and the NOS. The production of the informative assessment leaflets was designed to address these issues and provide reassurance that assessment could be undertaken in the workplace by direct observation, questioning and/or reviewing documentation produced by practitioners in their everyday role.

Considerable effort was extended in consulting with stakeholders and practitioners to design the Unified Assessment Protocol (UAP), which defined a number of pragmatic approaches to assessment, which forces could choose to adopt. Unfortunately, this protocol was not ratified by ACPO during the lifetime of the programme; despite this what it advocated was welcomed by the service.

The production of the Core Investigative Doctrine in 2005 outlined the investigative process and articulated the best practice and principles governing all investigations. The best practice from the document needed to be reflected in the NOS for investigation and interviewing. This presented a challenge for the programme team and necessitated a reworking of the NOS for all PIP levels. This work also impacted upon the learning and development programmes which had to be amended to incorporate the knowledge requirements of the new investigative and interviewing standards and assessment processes. This entailed working with practitioners and key stakeholders from Skills for Justice to amend and publish the new investigative and interviewing NOS; this work was completed within the timescales of the programme but inevitably led to delay in the delivery of some of the learning and development products.

Information obtained from the peer reviews and via direct consultation with forces identified that there was an investigative skills gap in the knowledge and competence of frontline supervisors. The assessment of existing staff would rely heavily on effective assessments being conducted by these individuals.

Feedback from practitioners, supervisors and staff associations articulated a lack of competence in the investigative skills and ability of supervisors many of whom lacked ability in initial investigation, forensic awareness and interview techniques.

To address this skills gap, a stand-alone learning and development package was designed for Level 1 investigators and supervisors. This standalone module was made available on the National Centre for Applied Learning Technology (NCALT) IT platform, which enabled staff to undertake investigative development in the workplace. A 5-day, Level 1 development programme was also designed and delivered by the PIP learning and development project team.

In addition, the programme team together with Skills for Justice worked to design and develop a new NOS, tailored to reflect the knowledge and skills required to supervise or manage Level 2 investigators.

All these challenges created resource implications for the programme team but were completed within the timescales of the programme.

The timescale for implementation of the programme was challenging for the programme team in terms of product design and delivery.

As discussed earlier, on many occasions this required protracted consultation with stakeholders and practitioners in order to draft or amend the various products, which were produced to support the programme. Individual forces required time to build and finance the infrastructures to support full implementation. Some forces were not able to achieve full implementation within the timescales set by the ACPO cabinet when they ratified the ISP on 7th March 2007.

The fundamental reason for commencing a programme is to realise benefits through change. There was a wealth of evidence available that demonstrated the requirement for the police service to improve the manner in which it conducted one of its core business functions, the investigation of crime. The Policing White paper published in 2001 (Home Office, 2001) had outlined key requirements for the service, which included:

- The police need a clear and common understanding of the theory and practice of investigation.
- There need to be clear strategies to tackle criminal gangs and persistent offenders.
- There needs to be a more effective means of spreading good practice in handling investigations.

In project management terms, the early development of PIP lacked a clear business case and benefits realisation plan.

The initial planning for the programme took place in a period of dynamic change for the police service; the ACPO crime business area had initially instigated the scoping work, and commenced work with Centrex the National Police Training arm. The Police reform programme, instigated in 2002, created the NCPE who took on management of the programme shortly after their inception in 2003.

The programme was initially conceived as a learning and development or "training" programme. In reality, the programme entailed a great deal more than developing or tweaking investigative training programme. As the programme developed and the implementation plan was introduced to the service, it became more apparent that whilst the programme would deliver the capability to improve investigations fundamental business change processes would have to be put in place to embed the changes and deliver the anticipated benefits to the service.

Due to changes in programme structure and key personnel, a definitive benefits realisation plan was not unveiled to the service until 2007. The absence of clearly defined benefits and disbenefits was an inhibiting factor which prevented the early adoption of the programme in some forces. While it was plainly obvious there was a requirement to improve performance across the investigative spectrum, some used the lack of a benefits plan as a barrier to fully engage with the programme.

Conclusion

The programme was delivered to the service by the 31st March 2009. The final Peer Review report outlined that not all forces had achieved full implementation for the reasons outlined above, but most had made significant progress in achieving the criteria outlined in the ISP.

It has established a body of knowledge for investigative practice; adopted the NOS for investigation and interviewing as the benchmarks of competence; aligned learning and development programmes to the knowledge and standards; established the basis for career pathways for investigators; and introduced a national register for SIOs and created the framework for forces to establish local registers of competent investigators.

The programme has established a recognisable framework to professionalise investigation, which had been absent previously. It has provided the opportunity to deliver the right people, with the right skills in the right place at the right time (Flanagan, 2008).

The programme board acknowledged that there was further development needed to ensure that PIP became fully embedded within the fabric of the police service as business as usual.

To that end, it was agreed that the ongoing support and guidance for professionalisation would transfer to the ACPO crime business area, Standards, Training and Competence (STC) group supported by the National Policing Improvement Agency, which had subsumed the NCPE by 2007.

The work to build upon and further develop professional investigation in the service carries on under the guardianship of the STC.

References

ACPO. (2005). *Practice advice on core investigative doctrine*. Wyboston: National Centre for Policing Excellence.

Audit Commission. (1993). *Helping with enquiries: Tackling crime effectively*. London: HMSO.

Baldwin, S., Strebler, M., & Reilly, P. (2007). *Police federation: PDR research; Final report*. Brighton: Institute for Employment Studies.

Flanagan, R. (2008). *The review of policing: Final report*. London: HMIC.

HMIC. (2004). *Modernising the Police service: A thematic inspection of workforce modernisation – The role management and deployment of Police Staff in the Police Service in England and Wales*. London: HMIC.

Home Office. (2001). *Policing a new century: A blueprint for reform*. London: Home Office.

Home Office. (2004). *National policing plan*. London: Home Office.

Jones, T. (2003). The governance and accountability of policing. In T. Newburn (Ed.), *Handbook of policing*. Willan: Cullompton.

Kerley, R. (1994). *Managing in local government*. London: Macmillan.

Macpherson, W. (1999). *MacPherson report. The Stephen Lawrence inquiry: Report of an enquiry by Sir William MacPherson of Cluny*. London: Her Majesties Stationery Office.

Mawby, R. (2007). Criminal investigation and the media. In T. Newburn, T. Williamson, & A. Wright (Eds.), *The handbook of criminal investigation* (pp. 146–170). Cullompton: Willan.

Newburn, T., Williamson, T., & Wright, A. (2007). *Handbook of criminal investigation*. Cullompton: Willan.

Police Standards and Skills Organisation. (2004). *Skills foresight report*. London: HMSO.

Skills For Justice (2004), Police Sector Skills Foresight 2004. Identifying the current and future skills needs of the police sector: A report on the Skills Foresight Program, London, UK.

Smith, D. (2003).*The Shipman Inquiry second report: The Police investigation of March 1998*. London: HMSO.

Stelfox, P. (2007). Professionalising criminal investigation. In T. Newburn, T. Williamson, & A. Wright (Eds.), *Handbook of criminal investigation* (pp. 628–651). Cullompton: Willan.

Stelfox, P. (2009). *Criminal investigation: An introduction to principles and practice*. Cullompton: Willan.

Further Reading

Stelfox, *Criminal investigation an introduction to principles and practice* (Cullompton: Willan, 2009) provides useful background to the development of professional practice in criminal investigation, written by a former senior investigator and academic who is the NPIA lead on Investigative Practice. Another useful publication that provides a broad overview of a wide range of perspectives that influence criminal investigation in England and Wales is Newburn, T., Williamson, T., and Wright, A. (2007) *Handbook of criminal investigation*. Cullompton: Willan.

Chapter 9
The Generational Gap: Values and Culture-Building in the Hong Kong Police Force

K.C. Cheung

Introduction

Hong Kong, like many countries and large metropolitan areas, has undergone significant changes in recent decades. Demographics, political and social expectations and the growth of information technology have reshaped the perceptions of public and police officers alike. For Hong Kong, the kind of generational changes witnessed across the globe have resulted in the staff of the Hong Kong Police Force being made up of three distinct generations, each having its own recognisable set of values and assumptions.

The more senior in age and service are the "Baby Boomers" born to the immediate postwar generation, roughly between the years 1943 and 1960. This generation tends to define themselves through their work, and they are competitive and team-oriented. They place faith in the structures of an organisation without necessarily trusting those who populate those structures. Generation X is next, born between 1961 and 1981. This generation are usually characterised by their independence and self-reliance. They are somewhat less regarding of hierarchical status than their forebears, enjoy independence and prefer the freedom to work with minimal regulation. Finally, and increasingly, are the representatives of the so-called Generation Y, sometimes also referred to as the Millennium Generation, born after 1982. They are the most supervised generation, subject as they are to very much more parental focus, and benefiting from greater family resources (Deloitte & Millard, n.d., as cited in Hong Kong Police Force, 2008). They are characterised by their ease with technology, their idealism and their desire to be listened to.

Currently, members of Generation Y account for 13.7% of the Hong Kong Police Force Force's personnel, and clearly this is going to rise (Tam, 2009). The older generation still predominates in positions of both formal and informal authority and there

K.C. Cheung (✉)
Hong Kong Police College, Hong Kong, People's Republic of China
e-mail: kccheung@police.gov.hk

M.R. Haberfeld et al. (eds.), *Police Organization and Training: Innovations in Research and Practice*, DOI 10.1007/978-1-4614-0745-4_9,
© Springer Science+Business Media, LLC 2012

is potential for friction between the generations due to their different conceptions of authority and the way it should be exercised by management. Conflicts, misunderstanding and inappropriate behaviour, all symptoms of a potential generation gap, may sour relations between cohorts. This in turn has implications for Generation Y in two areas: the acquisition of policing knowledge and skills, without which new entrants cannot engage their future as police officers, and perceptions of individual and organisational values. The current composition of the Force and the increasing proportion of Generation Y, while not yet leading to significant internal problems, do present important questions: how to address the gap in attitudes and understanding between the generations, and defining the role to be played by training in this strategy.

Role of Force Values

A logical appreciation of this development dictates that closing the generational gap must be approached from both ends, i.e. the younger and older generations should be addressed simultaneously in order to align them in a common culture, one that is committed to striving for excellence. The unifying element in both approaches must be the essential values inherent in the organisation. In the 1990s, like many organisations, the Force set out to encapsulate its organisational culture and aspirations. The result was the Force Vision and Statement of Common Purpose and Values, which is commonly referred to throughout the Force as the "Values" or "Force Values". Through the Values, the Commissioner of Police stated the philosophy underpinning the organisation and its goals, and set the standards of behaviour for individual officers in order to ensure the quality of the services delivered by the Force (see the Hong Kong Police Force Values, Appendix 1)

Effective organisational identity requires the sharing of common assumptions and values. Having three generations represented within the same organisation increases the diversity of assumptions and values, reducing the commonality of approach to the Force's core mission. Therefore, moulding an inclusive identity that allows the different generations to function together with common values and purpose has now become an important objective. In the following two sections, we will consider how training at both entry level and throughout an officer's career, informed by organisational values, plays its role in closing the generational gap.

Foundation Training

Mission of the Hong Kong Police Force College

Police officers work in a very challenging environment. They are expected to be impartial servants of the law but at the same time exercise discretion and maintain the highest possible standards of professional and personal conduct. They are expected to be largely autonomous in the exercise of their powers, but at the same time subject to the law and strict discipline. Increasingly in the modern police force, officers are under scrutiny from within and outside, and, despite an excellent record in the area, questions of police integrity continue to arise in the mind of the public. The Force Values provide the framework for addressing these challenges in modern policing.

The mission of the Hong Kong Police Force College is "To develop police officers with the professional ability and integrity to better serve the community". Traditionally, police training focussed on the knowledge and skills necessary for police officers to discharge their duties, but, increasingly, the attitudes and values of the individual officer are being given at least equal weight. It is important to establish the right attitudes at the beginning of an officer's career, as early experiences will have a profound impact on attitudes and behaviour exhibited later (Tam, 2009). Foundation (basic) training is the means by which the force prepares its new entrants to take on the responsibilities of a police officer and socialises them to the norms and values of the organisation. Candidates may enter foundation training at two levels: as a recruit police constable (RPC) or as a probationary inspector (PI).

There is little doubt that if the candidates for entry into the force already display many, if not all, of the qualities sought, then most of the work will already have been done. Therefore, it is essential not only that the force has a high degree of certainty that the candidate it is recruiting is the right one, but also that the candidate understands (as far as is possible without actually being a member of the Force) what a police career entails and the level of expectations the organisation places on its members. The Personnel Wing of the Hong Kong Police Force and the Police College have collaborated in order to enhance understanding amongst pre-appointment candidates prior to the commencement of foundation training. This better prepares the new entrant for the culture shock of a disciplined training environment. Once the recruitment process is completed, the objective becomes one of education and practical application.

Role of Force Values

At foundation level, Force Values are key to recruit training. Curricula of both PI and RPC courses are subject to continuous review to ensure that Force Values are at the core of each subject covered. Study notes have been updated to ensure they not only are in keeping with the Values, but also place emphasis on them at appropriate junctures. Leadership and command training for PIs incorporate the application of Force Values in decision-making scenarios, as do practical beat incident exercises for RPCs. Trainees also take part in Living-the-Values Workshops, a compressed form of an ongoing Force-wide programme to reinforce the Values amongst all officers, from Constable to Commissioner.

Attitudinal Training Programmes

In recent years, many programmes have been designed for commercial, educational, police and military organisations to provide staff with training in values, ethics, morals, leadership, integrity, character, etc. The focus is often on one particular feature, such as integrity management or ethics, with other aspects, for example, leadership, being referred to tangentially. However, a careful examination of these programmes reveals two consistent facts. Firstly, values, character, ethics, leadership, etc., are inextricably linked and cannot be effectively separated, either organisationally or for the purposes of training; secondly, it is the character of the individual staff member regardless of position in the organisation which is the pivotal element, since values, ethics, leadership, integrity and so on can only be made real by individuals.

Mindset Development

To address attitudes, the Police College has instituted a programme known as Mindset Development (MD). This is a programme specifically aimed at the holistic development of trainees' attitudinal characteristics. MD develops mental attitudes and qualities in officers to strengthen them in their commitment to their duty, to the community and to the Force; to aid them in resisting the pressures encountered in their professional life and to align their personal values with Force values and promote the professionalism of the individual. It represents a structured mechanism for developing the mindset of police trainees (Hannaford, 2009).

Mindset Objectives

MD, which was initially introduced into the PI training programme early in 2009, has three principle objectives. In the past, the PI syllabus provided the trainee with professional and practical training, teaching a set of skills; the internalisation of which can be tested and verified. In general, the attitude of PIs had been taken into account in the preparation of training reports. However, in terms of mental or attitudinal qualities, there had been no formal instruction and no means to test and verify mental attitudes. The first objective of MD is therefore to make what was previously implicit explicit, so that it can be formally assessed.

The second objective is intended to build a system that works on the mind to enhance desirable qualities and minimise or remove undesirable ones. It should be stated here that it is *not* intended to dictate to trainees what they should think, or to produce "clone" police officers who cannot think critically. Rather "mindset" is considered to mean a set of mental attitudes and qualities held by an individual that are likely to produce particular behaviours in that individual. They are the mental tools that allow a person to interpret and respond to the environment and to particular incidents within that environment. The bedrock of the desired mindset is the Force Values. In addition, MD seeks to develop the attitudes and qualities, particularly of leadership, determination and problem solving, which enhance the professionalism of the officer. Taken as a whole, these attitudes and qualities can be said to add up to an ideal "police mindset". The ideal mindset promotes enactment of the Force Values while at the same time preparing the individual for the requirements and expectations under which police officers conduct their professional life. It therefore provides guidance for development not only throughout training but also throughout the rest of the officer's career.

The third objective is to strengthen officers' resilience in preparation for the real pressures of police work, with the purpose of making him or her less susceptible to stress and poor motivation, and the possible consequences of these. A police officer's professional life tends to be a series of so-called "wicked problems"; that is, messy, circular problems that are usually inter-related with other problems where solutions are often difficult to recognise (Conklin, 2008). Such problems often have an ethical dimension and can produce a highly ambiguous environment that can induce situations of stress, low motivation, and challenges to an officer's integrity. MD is designed to counter this by developing physical, mental and moral resiliency.

There is little that is radical or new in MD. MD provides a context for existing subjects and activities, allowing reorganisation of course content for the purpose of further reinforcing the appropriate mindset. With such a framework, all aspects of training, including more informal elements such as social and ceremonial occasions, can be described in definitive terms and meshed together in a holistic training programme.

The MD Template

A number of characteristics and qualities have been identified and associated with the ideal police mindset. These characteristics tend to be intangible – values, mental qualities and character traits – that makes them difficult to assess and quantify. However, having established which traits and behaviours exemplify the ideal mindset it is possible to formulate a "template". The template allows training staff to recognise and encourage positive traits and behaviours when they are exhibited by trainees and similarly to discourage the opposite (i.e. undesirable) traits and behaviours; in doing so, the various positive qualities and traits expected in a police officer are integrated into foundation training in a coherent and structured manner (see Mindset template, Appendix 2).

Execution

The MD element of the Probationary Inspectors' course is executed in three phases, generally corresponding to the three stages of training – Junior, Intermediate and Senior – which comprise the PI course.

In the initial phase, the PIs are introduced to the concept of MD and the standards expected from them during training. This is done through an introductory talk and discussions with the instructing staff. Also in this phase, the PIs are given an initial assessment against the MD template, the primary purpose of which is to begin the reflective process. In addition, and early in the training, the trainees take part in the Outdoor Personal Development Adventure Training (OPDAT) programme, which includes leadership and command tasks set in an environment that is challenging for many new recruits. This is the first close observation of the trainees' mindset under adverse conditions.

Phase 2 involves all the usual activities of the PI course, such as lectures on law and procedures, command exercises, weapon and physical training, foot drill, and social and sporting activities, etc., and also includes a structured programme of specific MD activities such as research projects, debates, role play, team building and so on. The whole is integrated and built up incrementally from Phase 2 through the final phase. The core of Phase 3 is "Exercise 48", which brings together all aspects of the PI course in a physically and mentally challenging 48-h period.

"Exercise 48" is aimed at assessing the mindset development of the PIs to ensure that when faced with adversity they still show the appropriate mindset characteristics and qualities. It is also intended to enhance the officers' self-esteem by giving them a realisation of their own capabilities and resilience, thereby increasing their confidence. A blend of individual leadership and group tasks requires the trainee to demonstrate and apply police knowledge and procedures, command and managerial skills and the personal qualities encapsulated in the MD template. This demanding programme runs over 2 days and two nights during which trainees are restricted to a maximum of 5-h sleep per night. The programme commences with a prolonged physical endurance session (i.e. night hikes, long-distance rescue tasks, long-distance runs, swim–run–swim, circuit training, etc.) after which the PIs have to perform assessed leadership exercises that test leadership and management abilities. In between leadership assessments, the trainees are tasked to perform physical and group tasks, offering opportunities for staff to observe individual attitudes while the PIs are working in situations which attempt to replicate stressful, unpredictable situations.

Although the mindset of the PIs is assessed, it is not a stand-alone pass/fail test. A PI's mindset is under constant observation in all activities throughout the 9 months of the training course. However, if observation of a PI's mindset has led to questions regarding his or her attitudes or motivation, then this phase of training is considered a key element in deciding whether or not they have a suitable mindset to progress further in training.

Assessment

Assessment of mindset presents a particular problem. Values, traits and qualities are difficult to assess due to their intangible nature. To test a person's knowledge of the subject is merely to test their ability to memorise a list of words and their ability to reproduce them when questioned. Since the development of a particular mindset is designed to influence the individual's behaviour, the assessment system concentrates on the behaviour *exhibited* by the trainee rather than his/her knowledge of the subject. It is accepted that any assessment system is highly subjective and that the assessment is used only as a tool to guide the development of the trainee without becoming directly a means of deciding if the PI should graduate or not.

The assessment is based on the template of MD traits and qualities. Reports contain standardised assessments of the trainees' performance in the areas identified in the template. In addition, at the commencement of the course, in each phase and at the end of training, the trainee assesses his/her own subjective views on the development of various dimensions of the mindset, and how they have attempted to apply them during the course. This is done via a questionnaire and self-reflection exercises.

Extension of MD to Recruit Constable and Continuation Training

Measures are already in place to extend the MD concept in RPC and continuation training run by the Police College with the objective of creating a binding experience structured around the Force Values and the Mindset template. The various units responsible for different areas of Force training have already identified the modes of delivery of the MD concept and are implementing the template in methods tailor-made to their own training needs and content.

Dangers

There are dangers inherent in inculcating a standardised set of mental attitudes in individuals within a single organisation, the principal one being "groupthink". In MD, there is a counterweight to ensure that both the excessive conformity and poor decision making associated with groupthink do not become the norm, and that officers have the critical faculties to reason from evidence rather than prejudice or the pronouncements of authority. Therefore, a key element inbuilt into MD is critical analysis and critical thinking.

Other areas of foundation training have been re-aligned with a view to support the objective of reducing the generational gap by preparing new entrants for life in the Force. One key area, and one which dovetails closely with the MD strategy, is in the area of psychological competency training.

Psychological Competency Training

In formulating the Force's Strategic Action Plan for 2005–2008, the need was identified to improve human interaction skills in police officers (Hong Kong Police Force, 2005). A set of well-defined competencies was established covering the broad range of knowledge and skills, behavioural patterns and lifestyle management strategies required for effective performance in the human aspects of policing. The objectives of such training are to enhance professional standards, reduce complaints and improve customer satisfaction levels and address the psychological aspects of the generation gap.

Eight specific psychological competencies were identified:

- Stress management
- Emotional regulation
- Conflict management
- Counselling skills as a supervisor or colleague
- Interpersonal communication skills
- Healthy lifestyles
- Victim psychology
- Psychological skills in interviewing suspects

Training in these competencies is delivered during foundation training in partnership with the Hong Kong Open University over a period of 15 weeks.

Integration of PI and RPC

In a system that has two entry points, at constable and inspector, it is important that the two groups of trainees do not diverge from each other, creating a distance that continues into working life. To ensure this does not happen measures are taken to bring all officers undergoing foundation training together. The RPCs and PIs are involved in a number of exercises while under training, are jointly responsible for the security of the campus outside training hours, have organised experience-sharing sessions and also meet on social occasions. The objective is to forge links across ranks and also to reinforce a sense of esprit de corps that will continue into future working relationships.

Use of Practical Exercises

Preparation for, and assimilation to, the wider organisational environment of the Force has recently encouraged a move towards problem- and scenario-based learning. Practical exercises are increasingly being used in all aspects of foundation training, for both PIs and RPCs. Generation Y is less inclined to traditional forms of learning and benefits greatly from multiple modes of training. They prize practical forms of learning above all, and they want to be able to apply what they have learned in a realistic training environment. In the Police College, trainees are frequently put through practical exercises to enhance their ability to both assimilate and apply knowledge learned through a variety of methods. Many of the scenarios used come from recent police cases. As policing emphasises practical fieldwork in an environment that is in a constant state of flux, police training is placed in close proximity to the real world to prepare officers psychologically for their new roles and to address the complex needs of the community. Context-based authentic learning that makes use of real cases gives trainees a taste of work in the real world in a training environment where mistakes are never costly but are instrumental to future performance. Real scenarios generate focussed discussions, empathy and understanding of the roles of police officers and highlight practical considerations in reaching decisions. By evaluating and living through the experience, the officers not only gain confidence in discharging their duties but also become more attuned to the police ethos.

Community Service to Reinforce Values

Community service is also seen as a key aspect of a new officer's assimilation into the Force and as a means to give expression to the Force Values. In the later stage of training, PIs and RPCs form teams to visit the elderly and nonethnic Chinese communities. The experience broadens perspectives on social issues, reinforces the key role of the police in society and emphasises the importance of the mutual support between the police and the community that is at the heart of community policing. It also creates common bonds through shared experience in a context where the Force Values are being "lived".

Instructor Experience

An equally important facet in the process of preparing new generations of officers is the capturing of the experience of their instructors. The instructional staff of the Police College is composed of general service officers who, after an attachment of approximately two-and-a-half years, will return to operational duties. It is essential therefore that the experience they have gained is passed on, not only to new instructors but also to Force management in order that it can be used to inform policy decisions that impact on training and the generation gap.

Course Accreditation: Lifelong Learning

In order to promote convergence of the generations within the Force through the medium of shared education, the Force has set out to foster a culture that encourages, facilitates and supports continuous professional and personal development through lifelong learning. While under training at the Police College, Recruit Constables and Probationary Inspectors receive modules on Psychology in Policing and Sociology in Policing delivered by the Open University. Credits are awarded for these elements of the foundation training course, which officers may then use in pursuit of a B.Sc. in Law Enforcement and Security Management in their later career. The Force provides administrative, financial and logistical support for those officers pursuing courses provided externally. Academic accreditation of foundation training courses is a further step to encourage officers to pursue higher university qualifications in policing and police-related areas. In addition, the Police College is actively negotiating for credit exemption from local universities for its training programmes.

Integrated Integrity Management

The Force has long recognised the importance of promoting a culture of integrity and honesty and has a long-term commitment to reducing corruption and misconduct in all its forms. There is also recognition that the promotion of integrity as a key value is, in itself, an important support to officers in dealing with the stresses of their future career and an important element around which to build organisational identity. The Force's strategy is constructed of four pillars, and each of these has been translated into the training environment:

1. Education and culture building. In foundation training courses, briefing sessions are held regularly on integrity issues and easily accessible resources are provided to trainees.
2. Governance and control. Cases involving integrity issues are reviewed and lessons learned. These then form the basis of case studies for trainees.
3. Enforcement and deterrence. In Probationary Inspector courses (as well as in continuation courses for in-service supervisory level officers), emphasis is placed on developing the skills necessary for managing integrity amongst subordinate staff, including the effective use of the Force's disciplinary system.
4. Rehabilitation and support. For trainees at supervisory level, there is emphasis on taking responsibility for managing rehabilitation plans for staff with integrity issues, and for effectively employing support services.

Beyond Foundation Training

The means of approaching the younger generation through the medium of foundation training has already been discussed. We will now turn to how the Force influences the views and values of in-service officers.

The aim of promoting convergence of the generations outside the Police College is built, as with foundation training, around the Force Values. While foundation training lays the basis for socialisation into the Force, beyond foundation training the Force has sought to address the need to promote the changes in policing styles and techniques that all officers require to stay abreast of, while at the same time shaping the perceptions of the generations towards each other, and in particular of the older generations regarding the new entrants.

The Force has recognised that training takes place not only in the classroom but also in the workplace and through individual self-learning. As a result, the Force has adopted the "Learning Trio". This developmental strategy is made up of workplace learning, self-learning and formal training. Workplace learning in particular provides an ideal platform for sharing between the generations, since a mixing of life experiences brings with it benefits that can strengthen the organisation and its members. The strategy focuses on upgrading the knowledge and skills of officers by strengthening internal communications to keep in-service members of the Force abreast of developments and raise awareness. Most importantly, the strategy emphasises empowerment and motivation manifested through tutorship and mentorship schemes designed to bring the generations into closer contact. The aim is to promote a convergence of attitudes under the "roof" of the Force Values.

How the Old View the Young: Implications for Training

Older hands tend to regard the new generation as more "academic" and less in touch with the qualities needed for the "real world" of "frontline" policing (Tam, 2009). The older generation finds it difficult to communicate with the younger members of the Force due to differences in education, socialisation and life experiences, and this has implications for the transmission of the distilled experience necessary for organisational effectiveness. The younger generation, on the other hand, has high expectations and often finds it difficult to adapt to the pre-existing culture.

Coaching as a Core Competency

Coaching is seen as an important method of achieving communication across the generation gap. It is also an extremely effective developmental tool, consolidating performance effectiveness and raising professional competency standards and skills. Mentorship helps raise the younger generations to learn, grow and mature in a workplace environment that understands and nurtures their particular characteristics. It is no surprise therefore that coaching has become a core competency for officers at the supervisory level. In particular, sergeants, who are the immediate supervisors of newly graduated police constables, receive training to enhance their personal effectiveness, psychological competencies and supervisory skills, reinforcing their role as mentors, coaches and role models.

At the same time, the responsibilities of all officers in influencing their new colleagues have been recognised. Continuation training programmes are the key element in this approach, and, in recent years syllabi, have been revised to strengthen this concept. By creating an enhanced role for everyone in the shaping of new officers, the younger generations can more quickly learn the norms of behaviour in the "real world", thereby increasing their confidence about how others will behave and how organisational processes will be carried out. Good practices can be shared and at the same time such a strategy makes it important to all the representative generations to understand and engage with the newcomers.

Tutor Police Constables and Familiarisation

On graduation from the Police College, recruit constables undertake a four-week on-the-job familiarisation and tutelage programme. During this time, they are coached and developed by a Tutor Police Constable (TPC) who has received special training in order to fulfil the tutor role. Traditionally, the focus has been on transmitting practical policing skills. However, recently the TPC scheme has been strengthened with the intention of providing a well-structured tutelage content that works to mitigate the gaps between the younger generation and the "real" world of policing. TPCs now are key players in the task of building meaningful relationships with the new officers by reinforcing organisational goals and Force Values, and encouraging strong interpersonal skills.

E-Learning

If communication and education are important in the forming of a common culture and building bridges across the generational gap, then it is vital to disseminate knowledge and skills to all Force members. The potential of learning technologies to augment training cannot be ignored. The interactive nature of e-learning has the advantage of generating learner interest and adding an authentic flavour to the training scenarios. To enable easy access, e-learning packages are uploaded to the Force intranet system's Learning Portal that allows access even from the learner's home. By making e-learning materials and training information readily available and maintaining a well-managed training record system for Force members, individual officers can monitor and build their competencies according to their preferences and at their own convenience, a mode which suits all generations equally.

Other supplementary ways are employed to strengthen awareness and knowledge and to spread the fundamental concepts of Force Values and the Police Mindset beyond new trainees. Training packages have been developed for use in scheduled training sessions so that the awareness of all frontline officers can be raised to the existence of generational gaps, their causes and likely impact on the Force. Ideas as to how they can be bridged can then be elicited and shared across the organisation.

Lifelong Learning

Building on the foundations laid at the very beginning of an officer's career, the Force promotes continuous learning through organising formal seminars and providing financial subsidies. Programmes such as the "Learning and Development Opportunities for Junior Police Officers and Junior Inspectors Project" and the "Management Development Programme" for middle and senior management are delivered through a variety of media and are frequently organised outside office hours so that interested officers attending the programmes may do so in their own time. Financial subsidies in the form of reimbursement of course fees for short local courses provide an impetus to officers of junior service to engage in learning in their own time and at their own pace, whilst having the opportunity to collaborate with colleagues and mentors.

Structured Career Path

Management of the early years of an officer's career are especially important in the process of inculcating a shared value system. A new early career management mechanism, known as the Structured Career Path, aims to ensure that junior officers acquire the necessary fundamental knowledge and skills for uniform patrol operations and crime investigation in the years immediately following foundation training. A standardised and consistent approach has been adopted towards career development through a common platform of opportunities that also helps prevent possible mismatch of jobs, people and training resources. The mechanism covers the first 7 years of an officer's service and is divided into two phases. Phase I is a 3- to 4-year compulsory path for all junior officers comprising a number of mandatory course attendances and postings with a specified minimum length of attachment. Phase II is a flexible path allowing for the preparation of selected officers for specialised posts.

Mental and Physical Health and Wellness Support

Physical and mental fitness are important facets of building an organisational culture that is healthy, pro-social and united. The Force has therefore adopted an integrated approach to Physical Fitness and Health Management (PHM) by treating physical fitness and general health in a holistic manner. It strengthens and emphasises a culture of support and well-being by providing resources, facilities, training and information on PHM supplemented and supported by the voluntary sports and arts clubs. By promoting sports, fitness and healthy lifestyle activities among officers and their families, members of the Force find common activities and interests across generations.

A volunteer cadre of police officers, supported by clinical psychologists from the Force Clinical Psychological Services Group, was formed in 2004 to promote mutual care amongst officers, enhance mental health awareness and increase sensitivity to counselling and the need for help when problems arise. Both trainees and in-service officers form the target group. The emphasis is on personal and positive growth and self-actualisation as a means of preventing stress-related issues, and in order to promote a strong and resilient workforce. In addition, the cadre gives support to training at the Police College and to tutoring and mentoring programmes in frontline units.

An Integrated Approach to Integrity Management

New members of the Force are introduced to the concept and importance of integrity while still in foundation training. It is here that the formation of a culture of integrity begins. The emphasis is continued outside the foundation training environment, where honesty and integrity become a key unifying theme for all the members of the Force. The challenges faced by the Force are the same for all of its members. Isolated incidents of misconduct reflect equally badly on all officers, as do issues that may compromise integrity. Public expectations make no distinctions between officers of different generations. In order to maintain an organisation of the highest integrity in the face of organisational and societal change, the Force has developed an integrated integrity management system to address these issues. The system not only lays emphasis on education, enforcement and deterrence, but also incorporates the key areas of culture building, governance, rehabilitation and support. Leadership, responsibility and effective training underpin all the components of this strategy. Through this, and with the determination and commitment of all members of the Force, unity behind the key Force Value of integrity is ensured.

Conclusion

Generational change, and the acknowledged gaps this produces between generations, has wide-ranging implications for any organisation where maintaining pace with societal change is essential. This is particularly true of police organisations where responsiveness to change is essential for their efficacy in rapidly changing environments. Such implications, though, do not necessarily signify problems; they also represent challenges to an organisation that can cause it to reflect upon itself and its role in society and subsequently take action that will strengthen and invigorate it in its mission to provide key services to the public.

In Hong Kong, the police have been through this process and found that it has added new impetus to the inculcation of Force Values, while at the same time firmly fixing the Values as central to the creation of a common culture that binds the generations together in a unified commitment to serving the public in evermore effective and efficient ways. The Values, through the medium of integrated training and career development strategies, are the reference point for all police officers, regardless of the generation into which they were born.

Appendix 1   Hong Kong Police Force: Vision and Statement of Common Purpose and Values

Vision

That Hong Kong remains one of the safest and most stable societies in the world.

Statement of Common Purpose

The Hong Kong Police will ensure a safe and stable society by:

- Upholding the rule of law
- Maintaining law and order
- Preventing and detecting crime
- Safeguarding and protecting life and property
- Working in partnership with the community and other agencies
- Striving for excellence in all that we do
- Maintaining public confidence in the Force

Our Values

- Integrity and honesty
- Respect for the rights of members of the public and of the Force
- Fairness, impartiality and compassion in all our dealings
- Acceptance of responsibility and accountability
- Professionalism
- Dedication to quality service and continuous improvement
- Responsiveness to change
- Effective communication both within and out with the Force

Appendix 2   Mindset Dimensions

Mindset Dimensions

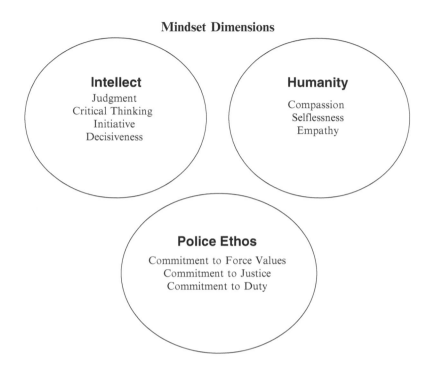

Intellect
Judgment
Critical Thinking
Initiative
Decisiveness

Humanity
Compassion
Selflessness
Empathy

Police Ethos
Commitment to Force Values
Commitment to Justice
Commitment to Duty

References

Conklin, J. (2008). Wicked problems and social complexity (Chapter 1). *Dialogue mapping: Building shared understanding of wicked problems*. CogNexus Institute. Retrieved on September 13, 2010, from http://www.cognexus.org/wpf/wickedproblems.pdf.

Hannaford, S. (2009). *Mindset development*. Unpublished thematic paper. Hong Kong Police Force College, Hong Kong.

Hong Kong Police Force. (2005). *Strategic action plan 2005–2008*. Author: Hong Kong.

Hong Kong Police Force. (2008). *Environmental scan 2008*. Combined data from Deloitte Development LLP and Robert Millard, Edge International. Hong Kong: Author.

Tam, C. H. (2009). *A study on the generation and knowledge gaps in the Hong Kong Police Force*. Unpublished Research Paper. Hong Kong Police Force College, Hong Kong.

Chapter 10
Learning to Deal with Potentially Dangerous Situations: A Situation-Oriented Approach

Otto Adang

Be careful. Do not approach too quickly. Give yourself more time to assess the situation.
If you respond to a call without thinking, you will be confronted with unexpected things.
By allowing yourself that time, you can reduce the risk.

Advice of Amsterdam police officer Jan Redegeld (Amsterdam) after a shooting incident
where his fellow officer almost lost his life and he himself could barely save himself
(ANPV-Magazine, 1997).

Introduction

In 1986, Fyfe drew attention to what he called the split-second syndrome: the feeling that since no two street situations are alike, it is impossible to train officers in other than very broad tactical skills. The split-second syndrome is based on the mistaken idea that decisions officers make in dealing with dangerous situations are typically made in a fraction of a second; that there are no principles that may be applied to the diagnosis of specific situations; that police operate under such stresses and time constraints as to create a high percentage of inappropriate decisions and that assessments of the justifiability of police conduct are most appropriately made on the exclusive basis of the perceptions of the immediate situation in which a decision has to be made (Fyfe, 1986). Analyses of incidents where police use force or are confronted with violence, tend to focus on a small, final, portion of a situation that actually begins when police become aware of the likelihood of confronting a violent person or dangerous situation. The work of Fyfe builds on the notion that in a potentially dangerous situation the final decision to shoot or to use force always follows earlier decisions taken in the situation.

O. Adang (✉)
Politieacademie, Appeldoorn, Netherlands
e-mail: Otto.adang@politieacadie.nl

M.R. Haberfeld et al. (eds.), *Police Organization and Training: Innovations in Research and Practice*, DOI 10.1007/978-1-4614-0745-4_10,
© Springer Science+Business Media, LLC 2012

Research shows that in practice, "many officers manoeuvre themselves into situations where the only option left to them is to shoot" (Fyfe, interviewed in de Jong & Mensink, 1994). Fyfe (interviewed in de Jong & Mensink) points to the fact that "shooting is the result of ...", and usually the result of a situation where an officer had better acted differently. On the basis of data from the then Belgian Gendarmerie, Pauwels, Helsen, and Wuyts (1994) state that many situations where officers used their firearm could have been resolved with less use of force. They mention several examples of "sins" against rules that should apply in potentially dangerous situations, such as:

- Jumping (or remaining standing unnecessarily) in front of vehicles
- Giving chase at any price
- Disregarding opportunities to take cover
- Underestimating the risks attached to use of the fire-arm
- Neglecting the division of tasks with fellow officers

For the Netherlands, these findings were confirmed by Timmer (1999).

It is therefore important to realise that there are different phases in potentially dangerous police–citizen encounters. Scharf and Binder (1983) distinguish the following phases:

1. Anticipation – the interval between becoming aware of the situation and arriving on the scène.
2. Entry and initial contact – the interval between arriving on the scène and approaching the civilian.
3. Information exchange – the phase during which, through verbal or nonverbal communication, officers and civilians assess each other and the situation by orders, threats or negotiations.
4. Physical tactics of regulation – that may or may not include the use of (less-lethal) weapons.
5. Final frame decision, where officers decide whether or not to use their fire-arm.
6. Aftermath – this phase includes both the period directly after the shoot–no shoot decision as well as the period thereafter, such as judicial inquiry, prosecution, future contacts between the officer and civilian concerned, contacts with colleagues, medical and psychological help, tactical analysis and reflection. This phase is not to be neglected due to the potential for post-traumatic stress reactions.

Pauwels et al. (1994) distinguish between just two phases, the initial and the situational phase. They show that when initial judgement – meaning decisions taken before first (eye) contact with the suspect has taken place – has been correct (i.e. effective), situational judgement is greatly simplified (Pauwels et al.). They concluded that education should therefore explicitly address the initial judgement phase (Pauwels et al.). Pauwels et al. (1994) recommend a learning setting that starts when officers become aware that they may encounter a potentially dangerous suspect. Compared with the Sharf and Binder model, these moments and circumstances are to be found in the first two phases of that model (anticipation and arrival, *before* initial contact). Fyfe, interviewed in de Jong and Mensink (1994), made a similar proposal. He concluded that it is beneficial to include the approach phase of use-of-force situations (the phase between becoming aware of a situation that requires attention and arrival at the scene) in training situations "the moment officers are confronted with a life-threatening situation/suspect, they no longer act on the basis of cognition but mechanically and instinctively" (de Jong & Mensink, p. 42). Education and training should therefore address those moments and circumstances where they still have a choice what the best possible next step can be.

This chapter deals with the implications of this vision for police education and training. First, the results of a field study are presented that looked specifically at the way in which officers approached potentially dangerous situations. Next, an educational vision on a situation-oriented use-of-force training will be presented and attention will be paid to training tools that contribute to an effective transfer to professional practice. Finally, implementation of the situation-oriented approach and some initiatives that have been taken in the Netherlands as a result of this approach are presented.

Field Study in the Netherlands

Adang et al. (2006) report on a field study where they went along with 57 beats at 12 police stations in ten different police forces in the Netherlands. In 467 observation hours, they observed and interviewed 119 different patrol officers and witnessed 67 situations that were assessed as potentially dangerous beforehand (afterwards it turned out that in 35% of these cases officers were confronted with verbal aggression, in 3% of the cases threats were uttered against officers and in 3% of the cases violence was directed at officers). The times and locations for the observations were chosen in such a way that the likelihood of specific types of potentially dangerous situations occurring was expected to be relatively high. Based on Timmer (1999), the study specifically focused on three specific types of situations that were associated with an increased level of danger or conflict: policing of night-time districts, dealing with disturbed individuals and dealing with (groups of) problematic youths. The study specifically looked at the way in which officers approached these situations as they presented themselves and did not preselect situations that had escalated in some way. The results of the study showed that even though (obviously) no two situations were exactly alike, it was possible to identify a limited number of typical situations that recurred again and again (with some variation) and constitute the larger part of potentially dangerous situations officers face (Adang et al., 2006). In the situations that formed part of the study, the following typical situations were identified

Regarding disturbed individuals:

- Responding to a nuisance in public space
- Responding to a nuisance inside a building
- Helping a disturbed or suicidal individual
- Searching for, arresting or transferring a psychiatric patient to an institution

Dealing with (groups of) youths

- Responding to a nuisance in public space
- Giving a ticket or a warning as part of a zero-tolerance policy

Policing night-time districts

- Responding to a fight in the street
- Responding to problems at the door of an establishment
- Giving a ticket or a warning as part of a zero-tolerance policy

The observations indicated that, on average, there was a 5-min interval between police officers receiving a call from the control room and their arrival on the scene (range 0–15 min). The study showed that, in general, during this interval, officers did not formulate what the goal of their intervention should be (only in 18% of the cases did they formulate a goal), nor did they proceed methodically (only in 10% of the cases did they make some kind of plan) or use the opportunity to gather additional information prior to their arrival on the scene (only in 13% of the cases was additional information requested). Generally, the officers in our study did not communicate with each other about how to act in the specific situation they were going to face (only in 13% of the pairs did). As a consequence, cooperation between the officers seemed to occur "spontaneously". This might seem logical where officers are used to working with one another, but of the 51 observed pairs of officers, only 25% worked together regularly (i.e. on a weekly basis), 36% had never worked together before, 25% worked together once or twice a month and 14% less often than that. Contrary to what could maybe be expected, officers that were more (rather than less) used to working together had a more explicit common methodical approach than officers not used to working together: they more often checked what was possible (Chi-square test, $p < 0.05$) or asked for additional information (Chi-square test, $p < 0.05$). Officers treated the situations in which they intervened as stand-alone incidents, rarely made connections with previous situations involving the same individuals or locations and made limited use of information that was or could have been available to them. After the situations were dealt with, officers hardly ever reflected with each other about what had happened or about the best approach to specific types of incidents. The interviews with officers made clear that they did have opinions about what constitutes "good practice", but that they rarely, if ever, communicated with each other about this.

The study concluded that officers often do not use (or make) the time available to them to anticipate on potentially dangerous situations, even though similar types of situations occur regularly. The study also concluded that it is possible and feasible to formulate practically useful rules-of-thumb/good practices for regularly occurring typical situations that would help officers being confronted with problematic situations or facing tough choices.

More specifically, the study made the following recommendations:

- For each police station/district/department to analyse what the most typical potentially dangerous situations are in its working area.
- On the basis of this analysis, to structurally reflect on and discuss good practices for dealing with potentially dangerous situations in briefings and debriefings and to ensure that these good practices are being applied.
- On the basis of this analysis and a network analysis, to come to agreements with relevant third parties (local council, health services, etc.) about responsibilities, division of tasks, exchange of information and cooperation in relation to identified potentially dangerous situations.
- To avoid treating incidents on a stand-alone basis and make sure relevant information is recorded and used.
- To do research into what constitutes "good practice" in dealing with specific types of potentially dangerous situations.
- To match advanced training to local needs and locally occurring potentially dangerous situations. To this purpose, police trainers should become involved in analysing police interventions in potentially dangerous situations and in reflections at police station level.

The conclusion is justified that police officers can do a better job anticipating potentially dangerous situations. This raises the question how best to prepare them to intervene in these types of situations.

Learning to Deal with Potentially Dangerous Situations: An Educational Vision

How best to prepare officers to deal with potentially dangerous situations requires an educational vision. The vision formulated below is based on Adang, ter Huurne, Liempt, and Spaans (1996), de Jong and Mensink (1997), Pauwels et al. (1994), and Timmer, Naeyé, and van der Steeg (1996). A potentially dangerous situation represents a problem to a police officer every time it occurs. To teach police officers to manage dangerous situations, their education and training should be aimed at increasing their problem-solving skills. Skills in shooting/handling weapons are only part of what is needed. Important is that actual transfer to practice takes place. This vision recognises the difference between the initial and situational judgement phases of police–citizen encounters and emphasises:

- The importance of gaining experience
- The importance of linking to practice
- The role of emotions
- That to manage dangerous situations, officers do not only need motor skills but also judgemental and decision-making skills and perceptual skills

Gaining Experience

It is important for police officers to experience success, so that they learn what they *can* do in dangerous situations. Overwhelming officers with complicated life-threatening situations contributes more to creating feelings of fear and failure than to developing the practical intelligence needed for safe and responsible action. Using simulated problematic situations, allowing for positive, nonfatal outcomes, self-confidence may be enhanced. From this perspective, shooting practice at the shooting range in itself contributes little to shooting skills in practice, where more complex and wide-ranging situations will be encountered. The emphasis in increasing experience should be on the build-up from simple to more complex.

Linking to Practice

For optimal transfer, the specific characteristics of real-life situations has to be taken into account. In training, these specifics have to be respected as much as possible. Characteristics of the most common dangerous situations encountered in practice should be dealt with. Especially in-force follow-up training should include local or regional characteristics and situations (de Jong & Mensink, 1994; Fyfe, 1989; Pauwels et al., 1994).

Role of Emotions

Stress and emotions play a big role in dangerous situations. It is a well-known fact that decision making and judgemental processes are influenced strongly by stress and emotions. It is also known that, in stressful or fearful conditions, shooting accuracy of police officers declines. The education and training of officers should pay attention to these effects and skills should be taught to deal with stress and emotions. Solomon (n.d.) (as cited in de Jong & Mensink, 1997) distinguishes six stadia that officers need to understand to help regulate themselves and others in threatening circumstances:

1. Awareness of danger and problems
2. Awareness of vulnerability
3. Recognition of threat and a shift of attention from personal risk to conditions causing the threat
4. Choosing between a violence-reduction strategy and a self-defence strategy
5. Mental commitment to the chosen strategy and gathering courage to implement it
6. The response: the physical attempt to carry out the strategy

The six stadia can be compressed in a short time span and will most often not be gone through in a conscious manner.

Skills Needed

Police officers need certain skills to be able to solve problems in dangerous situations.

de Jong and Mensink (1997) point to Doerner (year), who indicates that manipulating the fire-arm and shooting accuracy may be compromised progressively in function of the way in which the learning situation approaches reality more closely. This is an indication of the fact that in shooting situations not only shooting accuracy, physical condition and contextual factors exert an influence, but also the judgemental skills of officers. Pauwels et al. (1994) characterise the firing of a shot as a failed attempt to gain control of a situation and they propose that training should therefore be aimed at gaining control of dangerous situations by way of preventive and positive actions. They distinguish between three types of skills (see also de Jong & Mensink, 1997).

1. Perceptual skills
   Pauwels et al. (1994) show that differences exist in the way in which officers perceive potentially dangerous situations. The perceptions of highly experienced officers form a useful starting point for learning the assessment of situations. Their viewing patterns and judgement schemes on the relevance of information may serve as an example. Officers should be trained in observing potentially dangerous situations: what is relevant, where to look at, how to recognise danger?
2. Judgemental and decision skills
   Learning problem-solving skills for dangerous situations is an ongoing process. Both attitudinal aspects as well as a methodical mindset are important. Attitudinal aspects include the basic principles for use of force, such as force as a last resort, legitimacy, reasonableness and proportionality. Decision making and judging situations are founded on these principles.
3. Motor skills
   Officers need to know and understand each other's actions unequivocally. Whether or not they include the use of force, all actions to be used in dangerous situations need to be practiced. In addition to motor skills in the social context, motor skills related to manipulating use-of-force means/weapons should be practiced. From the point of view of safety and shooting accuracy, technical and shooting-related motor skills need to be practiced (see also de Jong & Mensink, 1997).

Traditionally, use-of-force training is focused on motor skills and much less on judgemental and decision-making skills, whereas minimal attention is given to training perception skills. Fyfe, interviewed in de Jong and Mensink (1994), makes the case for a shooting training that starts at the moment:

> Officers become aware of the fact that they may be going to confront a potentially dangerous suspect. Starting from this awareness, the goal of the training is to teach officers to approach the situation in such a way that their protective task is maximised while their exposure to danger is minimised. This has to be done especially by restructuring the situation in such a way that shooting becomes less likely.

To make this happen, it is imperative to pay more attention to the preliminary stages of potentially dangerous situations: from information gathering to making a goal/means assessment, to assessing the risks involved in the situation, the recognition of emotions involved and the consideration of alternative options. On the basis of what we know about didactics and about shooting incidents, officer training in use of force should therefore not focus one-sidedly on "final frame decisions" (e.g. shoot/don't shoot) but start with perception and preparation and include decision making.

In this vision, education and training for the management of potentially dangerous police–citizen encounters have to be *situation-oriented* training in the sense that they are based on situations as they are encountered in practice, with the most typical situations included. Furthermore, the learning trajectory has to have a careful build-up: it should not be too complicated at the start (as this is too overwhelming). It is important that officers experience what they can achieve/do and to avoid a wrong conditioning. Learning has to be integrated in the sense that it does involve not only controlled use of force but the management of potentially dangerous situations. Shooting is only a part of that. Specialist weapons and tactics teams (SWAT teams) are used to this kind of approach and seldom have to fire their weapon (Timmer, 1999). It is also important that learning is treated as a continuous process. The development of police officers towards problem-solving managers of dangerous situations should never stop and periodically, officers should be tested if they meet the demands for a safe practitioner. The learning process that starts at the initial education should be continued within forces, both through advanced training as through learning in the work environment.

Learning Tools

There are several learning tools that need to be used with care with an eye to a correct transfer to professional practice. The main ones are:

- Traditional shooting range (training cognitive and motor skills in relation to shooting accuracy)
- Shoot simulators (training cognitive and motor skills in relation to shoot/no-shoot decision making)
- Hypermedia and network applications (independent learning and knowledge construction)
- Role play (training all necessary competences with a high level of realism)

Shooting Range: Limitations

Traditionally, fire-arms training takes place at the shooting range. In a general sense, it can be said that fire-arms training where students use their own weapon with live ammunition is preferable. However, this goes along with severe limitations: training can only be done at shooting ranges and it is not possible to train interactively (it is only possible to shoot at inanimate objects). To a certain extent and with some creativity, it is possible to progressively increase the difficulty and complexity of the training. This can be done by introducing time pressures and by varying the amount and complexity of information.

Shoot Simulation

To avoid the limitations of shooting ranges, interactive shooting-simulation systems have been developed. In a study on the use of a shoot-simulation system (Fire-Arms Training System, FATS), de Jong and Mensink (1994) concluded that within a given time frame, at least 20% more shots can be fired in a training session compared to a shooting range training session. Given the goal of training for shooting accuracy – to hit the intended target – especially learning gains in relation to shooting with live ammunition are relevant. In that respect, de Jong and Mensink (1994) found no differences between the different types of training: only using live ammunition, only simulated shots or a combination of the two. Based on these outcomes it is difficult to say how much use should be made of traditional shooting ranges for training in shooting accuracy. However, where shoot/don't shoot decisions are concerned, de Jong and Mensink (1994) found clear differences between the different training conditions. The combination group (25% live, 75% simulation) showed the best results and the live-only group the worst.

The use of shooting simulation in the curriculum means increased reality in education and as such fulfils the function of experience-based training. Certain conditions have to be met for a successful inclusion of a simulation system (de Jong & Mensink, 1994). The situations included in the simulations should be constructed for optimal learning effects, the system should be taken seriously and not treated as a game and the level of artificiality should be kept low. Fyfe, interviewed in de Jong and Mensink (1994), critically commented the use of shooting simulators. According to him, shooting simulators maximise artificiality. There is no interaction with real individuals (although this can be countermanded in part by human contact in front of the screen) and even with branching, the system does not react the way real-life situations develop. Digital shooting simulators are more flexible than the first-generation shooting simulators. They allow a much more rapid and flexible production of scenarios that can more easily be adapted.

Of course, the need depends on the goals of the fire-arms training and the teaching aids deployed. As of yet, there is no comparative research into available digital shooting simulators. Shooting simulators can be used to teach both shooting accuracy as well as shoot/no-shoot decision making. It is important to distinguish between these two types of use in relation to the difficulty of the information offered. In learning to shoot accurately (hitting the target one aims at), the difficulty of the information provided may range from simple circles to complex life-like situations where a suspect who is located within a larger group of people has to be hit.

With regard to the last type of situation, it can be questioned in how far this is a realistic option, given criteria for legitimate use of lethal force. The training of shooting decision making does not benefit from these types of "duck-shooting". The danger is that a shooting simulator becomes or is seen more as a game than as a learning tool and that practicing shooting accuracy has a negative impact on training shooting decision making.

As far as the difficulty of the information presented for the training in shooting decision making, shooting simulators have less to offer. The amount of information, time pressure in the strength of stimuli can be varied through different scenarios. However, the artificiality of the information or stimuli may restrict transfer to practice. The information is presented interactively. However, interaction only takes place as a result of the decision to shoot or not to shoot, i.e. through the firing of the gun (be it a laser-gun or live fire). A more indirect form of interaction can be achieved when the trainer responds to the behaviour/decisions of the officer (verbal commands, movement, etc.). This type of interaction is difficult to achieve in a more direct manner, especially because it is virtually impossible to embed all possible verbal and nonverbal actions through branching. For this type of interaction, role play is much more adequate, because interactions develop much more naturally. The real power or benefit of shooting simulation can be found in the professional conversation, the evaluation of the actions of police officers in the simulated situation.

de Jong and Mensink (1997) tried to answer the question with what intensity simulation-aided instruction could be incorporated responsibly in the initial training of police students. An experimental group received 34% traditional shooting range training and 66% simulation training, a control group received 50% traditional shooting range training and 50% simulation training. There were no clear differences in results. The main conclusion of the researchers was that the breaking up of initial education into separate sequential modules (with shooting training concentrated in one module) could lead to diminished learning outcomes (especially in relation to safety procedures) compared to a situation where shooting training occurs over a longer time period through the course of initial education over. The authors therefore recommended to regularly repeat training of safe handling of the weapon.

As a result of the training, students became more aware of the criteria and reasons they use in justifying their decisions in life-threatening situations. There were no indications that use of simulation was more effective in this respect compared to other forms of instruction.

Because of the difference between students that followed the module and experienced officers, de Jong and Mensink (1997) recommend advanced training that includes more than shooting accuracy training. The training for experienced officers should focus especially on decision making in different phases of dealing with potentially dangerous situations and include inter-vision and exchange between colleagues.

In an interesting paper on use-of-force simulation training, Bennell, Jones, and Corey (2007) note that cognitive load theory suggests that in order for this training to be effective, instructional methods must facilitate the acquisition and automation of task-relevant schemas without overwhelming the limited processing capacity of the learner. They pointed to the urgent need to assess how the knowledge gained from cognitive load theory might serve to enhance the effectiveness of use-of-force simulation training as, currently, there is little evidence that use-of-force simulation training is effective in minimising unnecessary cognitive demands, enhancing schema acquisition, or carefully managing the inherent complexity of the to-be-learned material (Bennell et al.).

Role Play

According to Fyfe, interviewed in de Jong and Mensink (1994), in role play, officers have more options to choose their own approach and to respond to real (unpredictable) (re)actions of an opponent than in a "videogame". In other words, role play gives the best opportunities to simulate reality, without sacrificing credibility. Of course, effectiveness depends on the way in which role play is organised and implemented. Fyfe (1998) did research on the effects of a training in Florida where dealing with potentially dangerous situations was practiced using role play. First, an explanation was given, after which several role plays were executed. These were recorded on video and discussed afterwards. The result of this training was a reduction of violence used against these officers with 30–50%. Fyfe (1998) concluded that, in addition to a good introduction, the discussion after role play was a critical success factor. Pauwels et al. (1994) add to this "combined exercises with use of tactical procedures are best done on suitable terrain using role play" (p. 73).

Role play can be used very flexibly when one pays attention to the different aspects related to the difficulty of the information presented. In role play, it is easy to vary on all relevant aspects (amount and nature of information, stimulus strength, time pressure). Only the way in which the information is presented is fixed: interactively. Role play can be used at any time to teach police officers to deal with potentially dangerous situations.

Multimedia–Hypermedia Applications

Computer-assisted learning provides many opportunities. Multimedia applications make use of animations, moving images, video and sound. Hypermedia refers to texts connected via links in combination with multimedia elements. In addition to tailor-made educational programs, digital works of references can be used either online or offline to assist learning. Given the place of computers and the internet within present-day society, these types of independent learning, where the responsibility for the learning process lies with police officers themselves, offer many possibilities for the future. The power and flexibility of multi- and hypermedia applications makes it easy to vary the difficulty of the information presented. The power and flexibility of these applications are also their main pitfall. Often, too much is expected from these applications by teachers, end-users and decision makers. This is especially true when they are implemented as stand-alone learning tools, where the programmes serve to replace part of the curriculum. Given the learning goals, it is only to be expected that a multi- or hypermedia application can never fully replace an existing learning means, but rather has to serve to support and strengthen other elements of the curriculum.

Networks

National and international networks can provide access to a variety of knowledge centres. These knowledge centres can relate to laws and regulations, jurisprudence, information on relevant topics, etc. Just as is the case for multi- and hypermedia applications, no general criteria exist for these types of applications. Information may be bought or developed dependent on officers' information needs. The flexibility of the information offered depends on two factors: on the way the database is built and on the program providing access to the network.

Teachers

Use of new teaching tools within a curriculum will involve a larger amount of integration within use-of-force training than is currently the case. As far as network and computer-assisted applications are concerned, the role of teachers will shift from source of knowledge and being responsible for the transfer of knowledge to coaching officers in knowledge construction. This is the logical consequence of the increasing independence in the learning process typical for these learning tools. In addition to this shift in tasks, the task of teachers who are involved with simulation-aided training in marksmanship and judgemental will remain essentially the same.

According to Pauwels et al. (1994), the core of the task of teachers in this respect is to reduce the amount of information into meaningful chunks and to focus on the core aspects. Fyfe, interviewed in de Jong and Mensink (1994), emphasise that simulation, in whatever form, is an artificial representation of reality and that it is the task of the trainer to minimise that artificiality.

It is not reasonable to expect from teachers to possess all professional skills in addition to their didactic/pedagogical competences. Their task in the learning process of officers is to explicitly link the different areas to optimally integrate different skills and to achieve maximum transfer to practice. Before using any learning tool, the goal of the tool, its place in the curriculum and the way it is used should be made clear to officers, teachers and supervisors.

Implementing the Situation-Oriented Approach

As a result of this vision, over the past few years several initiatives have been taken in the Netherlands. In 1998, the Dutch Police Inspectorate noted that the use of fire-arms is the ultimate means of coercion available to a police officer and recommended that fire-arm proficiency should no longer be viewed in isolation, but should be seen as one aspect of a broader form of in-service training including practice in other professional police skills, such as situation management techniques, use of other means of coercion, theoretical knowledge, etc. (Lucardie, 1998, p. 79). The entitlement to carry and use a fire-arm should be subject to the possession of a fixed term certificate following the assessment of professional skills (not just fire-arms proficiency). Accordingly, a nationally mandated compulsory test was introduced (RTGP), which officers had to pass twice yearly. The test included fire-arms proficiency, theoretical knowledge related to use of force and a test of self-defence and arrest skills. Granting that this test was an advance, unfortunately, it did not require police officers to show they were able to manage potentially dangerous situations adequately. The test was seen as addressing minimum requirements and fear was that a more practice-oriented test would require more training hours (Stel, de Groot, Bervoets, van der Torre, & Visser, 2009). However, in recent years the need for a more practice and situation-oriented approach to testing was felt and competencies were formulated for officers dealing with (potentially) violent situations.[1]

These competences involve: problem-analytical skills (e.g. the ability to recognise problems or critical situations at an early stage and the ability to process information), communication skills, operational-effectiveness skills (e g., the ability to deal with stress, the ability to act decisively), motivational skills (e.g. the ability to focus on getting results, self-reflection abilities) and cooperative skills. As from 2011, as a first step, the 2-yearly proficiency test includes a situation in which officers have to intervene. They can only pass the test if they show the competencies mentioned above. In the meantime, several forces have taken initiatives to do more than the minimum requirements and provide additional situation-oriented learning opportunities for their officers, e.g.

- By requiring patrol officers to train together with other officers from their police station (including their commanding officer) rather than having officers attend training on an individual basis.
- By focusing more on role play than on simulations.
- By organising team-based reflections on the professional approach to the management of specific incidents or potentially dangerous situations in general, and include police trainers in these reflections (de Blauw, Holvast, & Algra, 2008).
- By preparing officers specifically for situations they will encounter on a regular basis, e.g. in night-time districts (van der Torre, van Duin, & van der Torre-Eilbert, 2004).

---

[1] In 2002, all education at the Police of the Netherlands became competency based. Strangely enough, it took until 2010 before specific competencies were formulated in relation to dealing with (potentially) dangerous situations.

To be easily applicable at the level of patrol officers, the principles of the situation-oriented approach were formulated in the form of an easy to internalise "goal-approach analysis" (Adang & Timmer, 1998). This "goal-approach analysis" now forms the basis of all use-of-force education and training (both basic and advanced) in the Netherlands and every officer is taught that before approaching a potentially dangerous situation, he should answer five basic questions to himself (which can be done in a minute, if needed, but usually there is more time): (1) what is my goal? (2) what are the risks involved in this situation? (3) do I have the authority to act? (4) do I have the skills/equipment/possibility to act? (5) how do I approach the situation/what is my plan? Partners should then communicate with each other about their goal-approach analysis. To assist this development, several CDs have been produced for officers to practice with the methodology in a safe way. Also, a learning text was produced for teachers with cases derived from practice to be used in police officer training. The learning tools and a database of good practices are made available through a nationally available *Police Knowledge Net* maintained at the Police Academy.

The learning text provides representative situations where police officers felt that at some point they had to resort to use of their fire-arm are presented in different phases:

• Initial phase: a description of the initial situation or report made to police.
• Situational phase: entry, arrival on the scene and first contact, gathering of information. The situational phase starts as soon as the danger becomes manifest, the first contact is made with the suspect and there is an exchange of information
• Situational phase part two, where police actions take place
• Aftermath

The description of each situation is followed by questions that specifically relate to the situation and can be used by teachers to start discussion and address knowledge-related aspects. Every situation finishes with relevant points of attention that can be used in discussing the specific case. The points of attention always include judicial, technical/tactical specs, organisational aspects and behavioural perspectives. Teachers are suggested to use the cases in such a way that students first make a goal-approach analysis, phase by phase, in a classroom setting and that after discussing their answers, they are then presented with other learning situations achieving a careful build-up from simple to complex by varying the amount of information offered to students, the nature of the information, the strength of stimuli, time pressure and the way in which information is presented: static (slide, video still), dynamic (video) or interactively (simulator, role play). Eventually, students will be given the opportunity to implement their own action plan with teachers providing feedback. Dependent on the goal perception, motor skills, judgement and decision-making skills or a combination of these will be emphasised.

In addition, the research program "Managing dangerous situations" has been set up with the specific purpose to study the interaction between police and civilians in a variety of potentially dangerous conflict situations. It includes research on use-of-force issues (e.g. the use of fire-arms and less-lethal weapons), crisis communication and hostage negotiation, riots, public order management and crowd management. The research program analyses how police and citizens regulate their position in cooperation and in competition with each other by means of their communicative and interactive behaviours. The aim of the research program is to gain insight into the regulation of conflicts and social tension and to contribute to a better management of potentially dangerous situations. It has already led to a large number of publications and examples where good practices have been identified and implemented in practice, e.g. in relation to the introduction of pepper spray in the Dutch police, dealing with interethnic tensions and dealing with small and large-scale public order problems around New Year's eve (Adang, Quint, & van der Wal, 2010; Adang & Mensink, 2004; Adang & van der Torre, 2007; Kop & Euwema, 2007).

References

Adang, O., Quint, H., & van der Wal, R. (2010). Zijn wij anders? Waarom Nederland geen grootschalige etnische rellen heeft. Apeldoorn: Stapel & de Koning.

Adang, O. M. J., ter Huurne, J., Liempt, F. H. A. J. v., & Spaans, D. (1996). Kwaliteit in Veiligheid. Leren met betrekking tot geweldstoepassing door de politie: een nieuwe visie. Hoogerheide: PIOV.

Adang, O. M. J., Kop, N., Ferwerda, H., Heijnemans, J., Olde Nordkamp, W., de Paauw, P., & van Woerkom, K. (2006). Omgaan met conflictsituaties: op zoek naar goede werkwijzen bij de politie. Politie en Wetenschap nr 30. Zeist: Uitgeverij Kerkebosch.

Adang, O. M. J., & Mensink, J. (2004). Pepper spray: An unreasonable response to suspect verbal resistance. *Policing: An International Journal of Police Strategies & Management, 27*(2), 206–219.

Adang, O. M. J., & Timmer, J. S. (1998, revised version 2005). Beheersing van gevaar. Praktijkboek voor de opleiding van vuurwapendragenden en de toetsing van geweldstoepassing. 's-Gravenhage: Elsevier bedrijfsinformatie.

Adang, O. M. J., & van der Torre, E. J. (Eds.). (2007). *Hoezo rustig?! Een onderzoek naar het verloop van jaarwisselingen in Nederland.* Apeldoorn: Politieacademie.

Bennell, C., Jones, N. J., & Corey, S. (2007). Does use-of-force simulation training in Canadian police agencies incorporate principles of effective training? *Psychology, Public Policy, and Law, 13*(1), 35–58.

de Blauw, H., Holvast, R., & Algra, S. (2008). Professioneel handelen. Evaluatie workshops, juni 2007 – januari 2008 Regiopolitie Haaglanden, bureau Zoetermeer. Apeldoorn: Politieacademie.

de Jong, F. P. C. M., & Mensink, J. (1994). Scherp of niet scherp...: Een onderzoek naar het gebruik van een schietsimulator. Amersfoort: Landelijk Selectie en Opleidingsinstituut Politie.

de Jong, F. P. C. M., & Mensink, J. (1997). De complexiteit van geweldsbenadering, -instructie en de noodzaak van (onderwijskundig) onderzoek. Amersfoort: LSOP.

Fyfe, J. J. (1986). The split-second syndrome and other determinants of police violence. In R. G. Dunham & G. P. Alpert (Eds.), *Critical issues in policing: Contemporary readings* (3rd ed., pp. 531–546). Prospect Heights: Waveland Press.

Fyfe, J. J. (1989). Police/citizen violence reduction project. *FBI-Law Enforcement Bulletin, 5*(58), pp. 18–23.

Fyfe, J. J. (1998). De "split second beslissing is een mythe". Politieel geweldgebruik in kritieke situaties is vaak te voorkomen. Algemeen Politieblad, nr. 9, 14–16.

Kop, N., & Euwema, M. (2007). Conflict op straat: strijden of mijden? Marokkaanse en Antilliaanse jongeren in interactie met de politie. Apeldoorn: Stapel & de Koning, Politie & wetenschap.

Lucardie, R. J. J. (1998). Schietvaardigheid. Een onderzoek naar de mate van geoefendheid van de Nederlandse politie in het gebruik van het vuurwapen. Den Haag: Ministerie van Binnenlandse Zaken.

Pauwels, J. M., Helsen, W., & Wuyts, P. (1994). *Perceptie en actie in gevaarsituaties. Een onderzoeksproject van de Generale staf van de Rijkswacht in samenwerking met de*. Rijkswacht/KU Leuven: Katholieke Universiteit Leuven, Brussel/Leuven.

Scharf, P., & Binder, A. (1983). *The badge and the bullet*. New York: Praeger Publishers.

Stel, E. L. A. C., de Groot, R. M., Bervoets, E., van der Torre, E. J., & Visser, J. M. I. (2009). *De Regeling Toetsing Geweldsbeheersing Politie Een evaluatie en behoefte- onderzoek*. Den Haag: COT Instituut voor Veiligheids- en Crisismanagement.

Timmer, J. (1999). *Politiewerk in gevaarsituaties. Omgaan met agressie en geweld van burgers in het basispolitiewerk*. Alphen aan den Rijn: Samsom.

Timmer, J. S., Naeyé, J., & van der Steeg, M. (1996). *Onder Schot Vuurwapengebruik van de politie in Nederland*. Deventer: Gouda Quint.

Van der Torre, E. J., van Duin, M. J., & van der Torre-Eilbert, T. B. W. M. (2004). Beproefde patronen: de politiële aanpak van geweld op de Korenmarkt. LokaleZaken.

Chapter 11
INTERPOL: An International Perspective on Police Training and Development

Dale L. Sheehan

Introduction

As the world's largest international police organization with 188 member countries, INTERPOL is committed to international police cooperation. Its mission is "connecting police for a safer world" (INTERPOL, 2011). Given the rapid expansion of technology, communications, and transportation, INTERPOL's mandate of facilitating cross-border police cooperation is not a simple task. One can readily recognize the unique challenge INTERPOL faces in achieving its mandate. In response to this challenge and the need to set a broad strategic direction, Secretary General Ronald K. Noble noted:

> The more we examine the challenges confronting us in the 21st century, the more that we see the need for a systemic and coherent global police training strategy. INTERPOL has to step out and be heard, so we have added police training as our fourth core function. (2007a).

In the following chapter, we examine the evolution of INTERPOL and its strategic implementation of an international police training and development model.

A Brief History of INTERPOL

In 1914, the first International Criminal Police Congress met in Monaco. Police officers, lawyers, and magistrates from 14 countries reviewed international arrest procedures, criminal identification practices, and the potential to create centralized, international criminal records systems, combined with a coordinated and standardized extradition process (INTERPOL, 2011). Under the guidance of

D.L. Sheehan (✉)
INTERPOL, Police Training and Development, Lyon, France
e-mail: D.Sheehan@interpol.int

M.R. Haberfeld et al. (eds.), *Police Organization and Training: Innovations in Research and Practice*, DOI 10.1007/978-1-4614-0745-4_11,
© Springer Science+Business Media, LLC 2012

Dr. Johannes Schober, president of the Vienna Police, the International Criminal Police Commission (ICPC) was created.

At the 1925 ICPC General Assembly, a recommendation was forwarded that each member country establish a central point of contact within its police structure. This set the direction for the establishment of INTERPOL's current structure of National Central Bureaus (NCBs). The NCBs are the main conduit between INTERPOL and its member countries. INTERPOL expanded its horizons in the 1930s by creating specialized crime departments, for example, currency counterfeiting and passport forgery. INTERPOL was granted consultative status as a nongovernmental organization by the United Nations, after which it modernized its constitution and took on its current constitution (International Criminal Police Organization – INTERPOL). In 1971, the United Nations recognized INTERPOL as an intergovernmental organization. This was followed by a headquarters agreement with France recognizing INTERPOL as an international organization in 1972. In 1989, the General Secretariat was relocated from Paris to Lyon (France), where it currently remains today (INTERPOL, 2011).

INTERPOL is currently governed by an annual General Assembly, comprised of delegates appointed by each member country, a 13-member Executive Committee elected by the General Assembly, a Secretary General elected every four years, and a General Secretariat which operates 365 days a year, 24 h a day, in four official INTERPOL languages, English, French, Spanish, and Arabic. The General Secretariat is also comprised of nine regional offices in Africa, Asia, America, and Europe, as well as Special Representatives at the United Nations in New York and at the European Union in Brussels. Each of INTERPOL's 188 member countries maintains a National Central Bureau (NCB) staffed by national law enforcement officers. The NCB is the designated contact point for the General Secretariat, regional offices, and other member countries requiring assistance with international investigations, the location and apprehension of fugitives, intelligence sharing and communication, all with the common goal of enhancing international police cooperation (INTERPOL, 2011).

A New Dimension in International Police Training

In November 2000, Ronald K. Noble was elected Secretary General. Mr. Noble's tenure as Secretary General was made even more complex with the changing social and law enforcement reality brought on by the events of September 11, 2001. These events gave INTERPOL a purpose to pursue a major path of rejuvenation, relevance, and expansion of service to its member countries. One of the areas of service redevelopment INTERPOL would align itself with was the provision of training and development. As an advocate of higher learning and professional development, Secretary General Noble recognized the importance of training. In an address to the 2005 Heads of Police Training Symposium he stated:

Policing is a difficult and dangerous job. There is no doubt in my mind of the dedication to public service of each individual who puts his or her life on the line each and every day. The strength and effectiveness of policing depends on each individual officer and staff member being willing to sacrifice everything to protect his or her fellow citizens and to serve his or her country or law enforcement organization. By concentrating on how to design, deliver and improve police training, we will help them, you and all of us to become more effective, to exercise better judgment, to make sound decisions, and to improve the safety of us all. Simply stated, well trained and well educated Police officers are the key to ensuring safe societies.

Following on this direction and an increasing need to meet the demands and requirements of its member countries, INTERPOL's Secretary General announced at the INTERPOL General Assembly in 2007 that INTERPOL had created a fourth core function, Police Training and Development. Placing this function in context, INTERPOL Chief of Staff, R. Andriani noted:

While the organization has significantly enhanced its operational support to law enforcement in recent years, police training and development activities are currently the fastest-growing components of INTERPOL's services. Taking advantage of the wealth of expertise and skills found across its member countries – and acknowledging that the chain of international police cooperation is only as strong as its weakest link – the organization has placed capacity building at the top of its agenda. The current emphasis is not on merely supporting the police of today, but developing the police of tomorrow (2011, p. 5).

The objective of the core Police Training and Development function was to assist member countries in bridging the gap between national and international police training. Moreover, it would provide member countries an opportunity to share knowledge, skills, and best practices in an effort to address the policing challenges of the twenty-first century. It would also ensure law enforcement agencies are fully aware of and take advantage of the tools, services, and databases provided by INTERPOL (2011). In context to this function, the Police Training and Development Directorate was to act as a conduit to both facilitate and expand the international best practices in police training programs and to establish global standards in partnership. In order to accomplish this, INTERPOL required an organizational transformation in the development and delivery of its training programs. By creating a standalone Directorate and standardizing the development and delivery of police training programs, INTERPOL expanded and solidified a role in international police training.

Further organizational change unfolded with the creation and implementation of an INTERPOL Training Quality Assurance (TQA) process, with the aim of ensuring the General Secretariat training programs applied a standardized process as outlined in the "INTERPOL Guide to Effective Training" (INTERPOL, 2011). By formalizing a needs analysis, design, delivery, and evaluation approach, the training cycle would ensure quality and the effective use of resources. Building upon this initiative the PTD Directorate aligned the structure of training in each Directorate and regional bureau by implementing a network of Training Resource Persons (TRPs). These individuals would act as a "liaison officer" to PTD Directorate. In 2010, the Directorate further developed the TRPs' skills and knowledge in the area of collecting training data, new developmental training initiatives and the registration process, police training initiatives, I-24/7 training, language training, and familiarity sessions on the INTERPOL Global Learning Centre. The TRPs also provide input on future training activities and events. The linking of staff from each Directorate to the Police Training and Development Directorate has brought about a transformation both in terms of improved communication and harmonized standards.

In a further effort to encourage member countries to form partnerships, the Secretary General stated:

> I mentioned the need for us to think and act beyond national and regional boundaries if we are to more effectively combat international terrorists and transnational organized criminals, who do not respect such jurisdictions. But what has changed since then? How have we moved forward? Have we broken down the barriers? Are we prepared to share our knowledge, skills and competencies with one another? (2007a).

Drawing upon that philosophy, the INTERPOL General Secretariat, with the strategic intent of supporting international police collaboration in combating international crime, developed the INTERPOL International Police Training Program (IIPTP). This advanced program was to provide training and development to qualified officers who have, or will have, responsibility in dealing with international police cooperation. Here, participants gain knowledge and skills in the field of international cooperation, as well as in specialized crime techniques including the utilization of the network of INTERPOL's National Central Bureaus (NCBs) and INTERPOL's numerous systems and services. The program combines familiarization, theoretical training, and practical working experience in a fully international environment.

Initially, the IIPTP sessions were conducted in English and French. To meet an increasing demand from member countries, a subsequent session of the IIPTP was implemented in Spanish in 2010. In describing the program, John Casey suggests:

> Education and training are important for the direct knowledge acquisition and skill building that result from program delivery, but participation in these programs also provides the opportunity for police from different countries to exchange impressions and create the personal networks that can be key to developing more effective collaborations. (2010, p. 86).

In order to streamline an effective delivery mechanism, INTERPOL modified the IIPTP into the INTERPOL Mobile Police Training Programme (IMPTP), a 3-week mobile activity designed to better meet the needs of its member countries.

This program is a condensed and modified version of the IIPTP, oriented to the regional needs and priorities where training is delivered. Like the IIPTP, it is aimed at training qualified officers who are responsible for dealing with international police co-operation, utilizing the National Central Bureaus (NCB) network as well as INTERPOL's numerous systems, such as I-24/7. By delivering the programs to the field offices, INTERPOL was able to provide the courses in a cost-efficient manner in the four official languages, Arabic, English, French, and Spanish. The following are the Learning Objectives of the IIPTP and IMPTP.

1. Improve international cooperation and communication skills
2. Raise awareness of national users as to the services and best practices provided by NCBs and the General Secretariat, in particular INTERPOL's Global Police Communications System I-24/7
3. Understand the respective roles of, and cooperation between, the General Secretariat and member countries through the NCB network
4. Provide up-to-date information with regard to the Organization's priority crime areas and gain expertise in specific crime areas that affect the region where the training takes place
5. Describe and understand international crime trends. (INTERPOL, 2010)

INTERPOL delivers these programs in various regions, utilizing regional and national subject matter experts as well as examined priority crime areas in the region. Utilizing some instructors and subject matter experts from the General Secretariat not only enhances the link to the latter, but also allows for tailoring of services to meet the needs of the member countries (INTERPOL, 2010).

The INTERPOL Global Learning Centre – A New Era of Technology-Based Learning

In 2008, INTERPOL launched the INTERPOL Global Learning Centre (IGLC), a web-based learning platform, which facilitates the delivery of timely and efficient capacity-building programs internationally. The IGLC is a centralized portal providing access to INTERPOL police training information, a library of e-learning modules, a calendar of training events, and a list of online links to law-enforcement-related websites. In launching this program, the Secretary General stated:

> I point in particular to one initiative from INTERPOL's side that we hope will be paradigmatic for developing global partnerships. This initiative, the INTERPOL Global Learning Centre (IGLC), will provide an electronic platform that allows the sharing of knowledge, expertise, best practices and training, including e-learning between member countries, well beyond the NCBs (INTERPOL, 2009).

Although the IGLC content is primarily aimed at INTERPOL's National Central Bureaus, the wider international police community and staff at the General Secretariat in Lyon also benefit. A knowledge bank allowing member countries to input and share their training resources and feed the repository of research papers and best practices has been built into the IGLC, permitting the exchange and access of best practices in training material, research and development in policing. At the demand of member countries, a site was added on to host Police Research to enhance the ability of national law enforcement areas to exchange best practices in this area.

In a short time, the organizational change in the delivery of training at INTERPOL developed into a blended format utilizing the IGLC. 2010 saw a significant shift in training delivery at INTERPOL, with over 6,000 e-learning modules completed by staff, comprising 3,000 h, using the IGLC (INTERPOL, 2010). The IGLC further expanded its reach with the translation of all content and interface into Spanish and French. A wide range of INTERPOL e-learning modules were developed and made available to member countries, on a variety of topics including Bioterrorism Awareness, the I-link Red Notice, as well as development courses for General Secretariat and Regional Bureau staff on topics such as the IRMA Portal, Budget Management, and Performance Assessment.

In further support of this e-learning vision, the Secretary General stated "establishment of a global learning community will allow for the growth of long-lasting meaningful partnerships, ones that will not be restricted to biannual conferences, to our geographic locations, or to our respective law enforcement or academic institutions" (INTERPOL, 2009). INTERPOL continued to partner with member countries in a variety of crime areas, hosting shared e-learning courses in areas such as Human Trafficking and Dispute Resolution. By facilitating access to subject matter expertise and materials, INTERPOL has acted as a platform for international exchanges and best practices in training curricula.

Knowledge Transfer: Putting Partnerships in Action

The foresight of the General Secretariat, during a period of global fiscal restraint and a weakened economy, provided INTERPOL with an opportunity to think beyond how it was currently delivering training services. The role of partnerships and the need to share resources is echoed in Secretary General Noble's statement that:

> Through committed partnerships, we can harness each other's strengths and learn from each other as we take up our shared fight against crime. Co-operation permits us to draw on each other's expertise and experience on a more regular basis, resulting in increased resources and well-rounded approaches in police training. It creates a synergy that propels us to achieve a much higher standard of training and cooperation for our police officers. (Noble, 2009).

The need for partnerships resulted in the creation of, in 2009, the INTERPOL Group of Experts on Police Training (IGEPT). The purpose of establishing the IGEPT was twofold; to partner with police, academic and private training experts, and to assist the INTERPOL Police Training and Development Directorate in the execution of its mandate. This would be achieved by facilitating the deliberations of the INTERPOL Senior Management, as well as encouraging and updating INTERPOL stakeholders in regard to police training content and delivery. The structure of the IGEPT would consist of individual members drawn from the public sector Law Enforcement and Police Training agencies, academia, and other international or regional organizations, all of whom have experience in Police Training (INTERPOL, 2009). The objectives of the IGEPT are as follows:

1. To foster and encourage cooperation, sharing of knowledge, and practical experiences in relation to Police Training and related matters, to develop

solutions to the problems that have been identified, and to propose recommendations to the PTD

2. To advise and assist generally in relation to the International Police Training interventions, its financing, organisation, and operation
3. To gather, compile, inform, and update training practices and guidelines for relevant training managers and make them available to INTERPOL and its stakeholders (e.g., through IGEPT's Library of Best Practices)
4. To consider and promote other ways of assisting INTERPOL and its stakeholders in Police Training matters
5. To consider, deal with, develop educated opinions, and report on any matters that may be referred to it by the PTD
6. To advocate and otherwise support the implementation of appropriate international instruments whether conventions, protocols or otherwise, that deal with Police Training (INTERPOL, 2009)

By developing and utilizing a network of training institutions and universities, INTERPOL created a network of informed and professional individuals. A clear indication of this direction can be noted in the fact that INTERPOL has entered several cooperation agreements with external agencies and organizations. An example of this process can be drawn from IGEPT's expanded mandate. Here, IGEPT organized a Working Group meeting on Police Research, drawing on both academic and operational institutions. The goal was to foster a dialogue with respect to international police science and law enforcement technology. Recommendations resulting from this meeting pertained to the international scope of police research, knowledge transfer, research projects of common interest, the feasibility and practical relevance of international police science, and creating future partnerships to enhance police training research.

In a 2010 annual report, John Newton stated:

> We have further developed a worldwide Intellectual Property crime training capability by extending a series of completed and ongoing activities to every INTERPOL region. ......This year we have worked closely with local law enforcement colleagues to translate strategy into action and deliver integrated training and proactive interventions in transnational organized IP crime (INTERPOL, 2010).

By providing training which immediately followed investigational and operational support, the cycle of Capacity building and training became complete. INTERPOL also partnered with the International Intellectual Property Crime Investigators College (IIPCIC), to develop and deliver training programs worldwide. Other training initiatives such as Wildlife Crime and Pharmaceutical Crime came about as a result of partnering with nongovernment Organizations, public, private, and international institutions. An excellent example of a joint training venture, INTERPOL's Medical Product Counterfeiting and Pharmaceutical Crime (MPCPC) brings together police, customs, health regulatory authorities, scientists, and the private sector to carry out effective training and operations.

INTERPOL Staff Development: A Unique Challenge

With approximately 700 employees from 80 different countries across the - General Secretariat and nine regional hubs, staff development training has also undergone significant organizational change since the inception of the Police Training and Development Directorate in 2007. One of the specific objectives of the INTERPOL Training Strategy is to enhance staff effectiveness through structured training programs addressing management development, information technology (IT), and job-related functions (INTERPOL, 2010). INTERPOL not only assumes the responsibilities of seconding officers and staff with a variety of skills and competencies, but also the responsibility of developing, mentoring, and training them. The end goal is that they will be better officers when they return to their respective countries, having gained new dimensions and views of international policing and cooperation.

In a paper entitled "Emotional Intelligence in International Police Cooperation," INTERPOL's Chief of Staff writes:

> Police officers who work at Interpol's General Secretariat offer a wealth of experience and expertise, but normally these will have been developed almost exclusively in a national setting. This means that there may be some critical issues to resolve if the officers are to integrate into a completely different work environment that is hugely varied on both a human and a professional level. In practical terms, it is necessary to strive to adapt to a multinational police culture that requires flexibility, adjustment to change and the ability to communicate. These skills are different from the technical capabilities traditionally associated with police work (Andriani, 2011 p. 6).

Building on this reality, INTERPOL took the step of developing a Staff Continuum of learning, which commenced with an Introductory "Getting Started" session at INTERPOL, basic and advanced budget courses, supervisory and management programs, and other courses that are delivered as a result of a needs analysis with staff, supervisors, and managers. With the continuum, staff and supervisors have the ability to plan out career development and progression. In another step toward improving the management of staff development, senior management designated that a Security Awareness e-learning course be made mandatory for all staff and management, thus commencing a process that tracked and reported on staff development (INTERPOL, 2010). The PTD also recognized that it needed to develop internal training capacity. Utilizing its vast network of resources, PTD designed the INTERPOL Instructor Development Course in partnership with the Federal Bureau of Investigation. A select number of staff from the General Secretariat qualified as "INTERPOL-certified instructors" and a train-the-trainer format was implemented.

2010 A Renewed Mandate: An Ambitious Future

In 2010, Secretary General Noble was elected with an overwhelming majority to serve a third term. With a new mandate, INTERPOL has entered an era of ambitious growth (INTERPOL, 2010). The General Assembly also unanimously voted to support the development of an INTERPOL Global Complex (IGC) to be constructed in Singapore and opened in 2014–2015 (INTERPOL, 2010). The center's mandate will focus upon capacity building, training, cyber crime, and advanced innovative methods for identification of crimes and criminals. In taking on this initiative, INTERPOL placed itself in a strategic and tactical position to enhance the delivery of its services. With an even stronger and enhanced organizational direction in the field of training and capacity building, INTERPOL extended its ability to form private and public sector partners. One example of these new partnerships can be noted in the joint INTERPOL/FIFA announcement of a 10-year, 20 million Euro investment, in a global effort to prevent corruption in football (FIFA, 2011). INTERPOL and FIFA agreed to dedicate a FIFA Anti-Corruption Training wing within the INTERPOL Global Complex (IGC) in Singapore. The importance of this initiative is summarized in the following FIFA media release:

> As INTERPOL and FIFA look to the future, basing this anti-corruption initiative at INTERPOL's upcoming Global Complex in Singapore while delivering training programs from INTERPOL Regional Bureaus and offices all over the world will help both INTERPOL and FIFA achieve their common goal of keeping the world's most popular sport free of the corrupt influences of transnational organized crime syndicates (FIFA, Media Release, May 2011).

Conclusion

Under the stewardship of Secretary General Ronald K. Noble, INTERPOL has undergone a major transformation, which is particularly evident in the area of Police Training and Development. INTERPOL has made significant advances in the delivery of police training to member countries, partners, and its staff at the General Secretariat and regional offices. As Martha (2010) stated, "the aim is to help officials in INTERPOL's membership to improve their operational effectiveness, enhance their skills, and build their capacity to address the increasing globalized and sophisticated nature of contemporary criminality" (p. 68).

In a world with stretched horizons and borderless capabilities, INTERPOL's role on the international stage of training and development is limitless. The realm of international police training has entered uncharted areas, and as the world's largest police organization, INTERPOL's mandate to meet its clients' needs remains paramount. INTERPOL is perfectly situated as a global hub for international police cooperation in police training.

References

Andriani, R. (2011). Emotional Intelligence in International Police Cooperation. http://www. policeprofessional.com. Accessed 21.04. 2011.

Casey, J. (2010). *Policing the world; the practice of International and Transnational Policing.* Durham, NC: Carolina Academic Press.

FIFA's historic contribution to INTERPOL in fight against match-fixing, http://www.fifa.com, FIFA Media Release, Accessed 09. 05. 2011.

Martha, Rutsel Silvestre, J (2010). The legal foundations of INTERPOL. Oxford: Hart Publishing and Portland, OR.

Noble, R. K. (2007a). Speech 76th INTERPOL General Assembly Address, Morocco, November 5.

Noble, R. K. (2009). Speech 17th INTERPOL Training Symposium, Edmonton.

INTERPOL Group of Experts on Police Training Terms of Reference 2009.

INTERPOL Guide to Effective Training, 2011.

INTERPOL Annual Training Report, 2010.

INTERPOL Police Training and Development Directorate, Staff Training Manual, 2011.

Chapter 12
Developments in United Nations Police Peacekeeping Training

Andrew Carpenter and Chris Sharwood-Smith

Introduction

International police peacekeeping has expanded dramatically in both function and responsibility. It is a rapidly growing aspect of the United Nations (UN) peacekeeping operations; its role has become complex and essential to the UN mandate. To respond effectively to these changes and associated expectations, the Department of Peacekeeping Operations (DPO) continues to grapple with the importance of articulating and implementing a strategic training model. In the following chapter, we highlight a number of the issues, objectives, and outcomes overseen by the UN DPO in its effort to address the need for standardized training, equitable program delivery, and specialized skill development.

Historical Context

While the origins of international police peacekeeping can be, at the very least, traced back to multinational interventions in the nineteenth century, the very first UN Police officers were a contingent from Ghana deployed to the UN Operation to Congo (ONUC) in 1960 to assist their host-state counterparts in maintaining public order in the conflict-torn country (Ennals, 1959). This beginning of UN Police Peacekeeping is all the more miraculous when it is considered that only a decade

A. Carpenter (✉)
Department of Peacekeeping Operations, Office of Rule of Law
and Security Institutions, New York, NY, USA
e-mail: carpentera@un.org

C. Sharwood-Smith
UNAMID Police Training, New York, NY, USA

M.R. Haberfeld et al. (eds.), *Police Organization and Training: Innovations in Research and Practice*, DOI 10.1007/978-1-4614-0745-4_12,
© Springer Science+Business Media, LLC 2012

earlier, the then UN Secretary-General Trygve Lie had concluded "the time was not ripe" when his proposal to establish a "small internationally recruited [police] force which could be placed by the Secretary-General at the disposal of the [UN] Security Council" had been firmly rejected by the UN Member States (Ennals, p. 1).

However, half a century later, attitudes had changed decisively with a radical shift of emphasis in favor of an expanded and enhanced role for UN Police in peacekeeping. On 15 May 2000, the Civilian Police Unit was established as a headquarters element in the UN DPO; this would later develop into today's UN Police Division within the Office for Rule of Law and Security Institutions and at the World Summit in September 2005, UN Member States endorsed the creation of a permanent Standing Police Capacity in response to unprecedented demands for police peacekeepers (United Nations, 2005). The number of deployed UN Police officers has grown dramatically from 1,169 in January 1995 to 14,037 by October 2010 (United Nations, 2010a, 2010b).

Traditionally, during the Cold War Era, police peacekeepers were deployed in a passive, unobtrusive manner to observe, monitor, and report on their local host-state police counterparts in order to verify police performance and its impartiality of service to the local population, to observe and ascertain police strengths and weaknesses, and to report and document police infractions (Ennals, 1959). This classical type of police peacekeeping deployment would be well after the shooting had stopped and benefited from little standardized training or commonly agreed guidance (Ennals). At the time, it was considered that the UN Police officers who carried out these missions did not require any specialized skills, only a good grounding in general police duties and, as such, officers were appointed to a generic role where their rank and specialist training were not considered as being particularly relevant (Ennals).

However, in the post-Cold War world of the 1990s all this began to change; UN Police peacekeepers were required to undertake more dynamic roles of mentoring, training, and advising their host-state counterparts in order to build up the domestic operational capability in less peaceful contexts. While this began initially with the UN Police assuming a lead role in the training of the host-state police, it was steadily recognized that there was also a need for the UN Police to become involved in assisting the reforming, restructuring, and/or (re)building of the institutional capacity of their local counterparts. However, the building of institutional police capacity in postconflict environments requires experts in a range of specialisms and not just larger numbers of general-duties police officers being deployed (United Nations, 2006).

Therefore, as both the number and complexity of the tasks mandated to the UN Police have grown dramatically in recent years, so has the understanding that structure of the UN Police components must change to reflect these realities.

While in the early days there was little need for UN Police to have anything more than a knowledge of general police duties, the new missions require trained and experienced first-line supervisors, middle managers, investigators, planners, logisticians, specialist trainers, gender experts, crime analysts, human resource, and IT experts among others. Moreover, in a majority of cases, these expert personnel need not only to be able to practice their specialism in the unfamiliar surroundings of a field-based mission in a foreign country, but pass on relevant aspects of their experience and knowledge to their host-state police colleagues too.

Moreover, in 1999, UN Police were authorized to undertake executive policing missions in Kosovo and Timor-Leste, where they would be responsible for carrying out interim policing and other law enforcement functions until such time that new police services could be trained and equipped to take over. This marked the first time in UN Police history that its personnel would be doing actual hands-on policing tasks in two postconflict societies, and while this could be considered as the UN Police simply undertaking regular policing duties, there is nothing "regular" about postconflict policing in a foreign country half a world away in an entirely different jurisdiction with colleagues drawn from similar but equally different policing traditions. Thus, police peacekeeping in a UN or other peace support operation differs significantly from the tasks, priorities, and challenges of regular domestic policing (United Nations, 2009).

As of October 2010, UN Police officers from 86 countries were serving in 12 UN Peacekeeping Operations and five UN Special Political Missions around the world, with 12 missions in Africa – including the largest ever authorized deployment of 6,432 UN Police for Darfur – as well as in Afghanistan, Cyprus, Haiti, Kosovo, and Timor-Leste (United Nations, 2010a, 2010b).

However, a UN Police peacekeeping academy where such specialized and appropriately tailored training could be offered to enable future police peacekeepers to transform their domestic skills and convert their professional experience to the requirements of international postconflict policing is yet to exist.

Previous Police Peacekeeping Training

Traditionally, UN Police were deployed with passive, nonintrusive mandates and acted as "police observers" merely monitoring and reporting on the behavior of the host-state police and other law enforcement agencies, lacking both the mandated authority and appropriate means to proactively protect or serve the host-state populace (Ennals, 1959). Thus, in a majority of cases, very little thought had been given to any additional preparation or further training of these police officers beyond what they had received in the course of their domestic police training and careers.

An internal UN report[1] in 2006 highlighted that only 32% of deployed UN Police peacekeepers had received any form of police-specific predeployment training (PDT). Therefore, the Police Division conducted its own survey of Member States and international peacekeeping training centers during the first half of 2007, which identified that while many of them did not have the capacity to conduct general PDT and/or specifically for police peacekeepers, a small number of countries had been actively undertaking police peacekeeping training for many years, but according to their nationally specified parameters rather than those clearly defined by the UN Police.

---

[1] Report of the UN Office of Internal Oversight Services, *Effectiveness of Peacekeeping Training in Peacekeeping Operations*, 19 Sept 2006, UN, New York (OUSG-06-751).

Thus, while there was a significant amount of police peacekeeping training being conducted, it was not resulting in any discernable positive outcome for UN Policing (United Nations, 2006).

Therefore, it was a matter of priority for the UN Police Division to clearly articulate what were the minimal professional requirements for a UN Police peacekeeping PDT curriculum, given that the Police Contributing Countries were not unwilling to adjust their training regimes to meet the UN's requirements; particularly so since UN Policing had begun to develop dynamically away from the traditional role of "observe, monitor, and report" into new complex areas of mandated activity, including responsibilities for interim policing and other law enforcement (executive policing) and the reform, restructuring, and (re)building of police institutions within postconflict societies (United Nations, 2008).

Moreover, often small groups of police officers were invited to attend these peacekeeping courses in these foreign countries, but eventually very few of these police officers were ever nominated by their country or selected by the UN Police to serve in a peace operation. However, this dire situation presented a potential "win-win-win" situation for the UN Police, the training centers, and police contributing countries, where the development of a common curriculum could be operationalized via regional training hubs to serve the needs of those police officers who would otherwise be deployed without the benefit of having received the appropriate police peacekeeping PDT.

Recent Police Peacekeeping Initiatives

The UN, recognizing the inherent differences from the "day job," has sought to develop standardized UN Police PDT packages for use by each of its 192 Member States and regional police training centers in order for them to train their own as well as other countries' police officers – both individuals and formed units – before they deploy as UN Police peacekeepers.

Predeployment Training for Individual UN Police Officers

The PDT of UN Police personnel is a crucial step before their deployment to a peacekeeping mission. While the training is a responsibility of the Member States, a number of General Assembly resolutions have recommended to Police Contributing Countries the need for them to conduct such training.[2] The Police Division, Office of Rule of Law and Security Institutions of the UN DPO has recognized and reflected this by incorporating it into its mission guidance and directives.

---

[2] General Assembly resolutions 46/48 of 1991, 48/42 of 1993 and 49/37 of 1995.

The UN DPOs' Police Division, in cooperation with its Integrated Training Services, developed Interim Police PDT curriculum for UNAMID. This curriculum was begun at a UN Police Training Workshop in Beijing, China in September 2006 and was circulated to all 192 UN Members States in November 2007 (UNAMID, 2011). The Police Division chose to select the African Union/United Nations Hybrid Operation in Darfur (UNAMID) as a pilot for addressing the issue of police PDT in all UN peace operations since less than 10% of the first UN Police officers deployed there had received any form of police PDT and its UN Police component was the largest in UN Policing history, comprising of 3,772 individual police officers and 19 Formed Police Units (FPUs) consisting of 140 officers each (UNAMID).

UNAMID had taken over from an African Union Mission which had been heavily criticized both by the people of Darfur and the international community for failing to provide the necessary protection to the local communities. It was therefore vital that new police officers selected for deployment to UNAMID received appropriate training to prepare them for what was undoubtedly to be a difficult and testing mission (UNAMID, 2011).

The pilot UNAMID Police PDT initiative had three objectives:

1. To provide Member States with an interim standardized police PDT curriculum for UN Police officers. This has been created by Police Division and Integrated Training Services personnel and reflects the latest developments in UN policies and international standards with regard to international policing, police peacekeeping, and other critical rule of law issues.
2. To link the already existing bilateral police training partnerships and extend them to other police contributing countries interested in accessing such support.
3. The strategic initiative is to ensure that up to 70% of individual police officers to be deployed in UNAMID will receive the standardized 2-week long police-specific PDT package.

The first step was to establish a dedicated working group consisting of a small number of interested Member States to assist in coordinating the training of police officers through existing bilateral agreements and by the use of international peacekeeping training centers. This would allow the reorientation of these preexisting national schemes to ensure that the right people were trained on the right things at the right time and at virtually no additional cost. It would also link incoming requests for assistance from police contributing countries with training offers from others.

During the initiative, the Police Donor Working Group developed a database which collated all donor activity conducted through bilateral agreements as well as through funding of international peacekeeping training centers and national police and military training centers.

The database also included all of the deployments to UNAMID and indicated those police contributing countries that had requested assistance with training and the training provided. This allowed the group to be updated on the numbers of police officers that had received training and analyze the results. The database also held data on courses currently being run, to enable the 3PDTID Coordinator to match the supply and demand and ensure that the process was kept transparent among the Member States of the UN. The database enabled the Police Donor Working Group to monitor who was trained using donor funds and ensure that they were in fact deployed to UNAMID. It also allowed the UN Mission Managers within Police Division to track those police officers who had been cleared for deployment but who had not yet arrived in Darfur and ascertain the reasons for their delay (most often due to difficulties with travel, i.e., passport, visa, etc.) (UNAMID, 2011). Part of the process built in at the start was a requirement for training centers to submit a monitoring form for every course run. This has enabled the UN Integrated Training Services to monitor and evaluate the process. The success of the UNAMID pilot has led to its adoption as the standard generic police PDT curriculum for all UN police peacekeeping missions (UNAMID).

In November 2007, the Chief of the Strategic Policy and Development Section, UN Police Division, co-chaired a meeting with his Integrated Training Services' counterpart with Member States who had displayed an interest in assisting with the initiative; it comprised representatives from Australia, Canada, France, Germany, Norway, Sweden, UK, and the USA; subsequently Denmark, Finland, and Italy also joined this grouping. Concurrently, a seminar was arranged for all interested parties from Member States and peacekeeping training centers to convene at the Kofi Annan International Peacekeeping Training Centre in Accra, Ghana, to discuss and ratify the draft curriculum for 3PDTID.

At the ensuing seminar, 20 participants attended from Bangladesh, Canada, Finland, Germany, Ghana, Mali, Nigeria, Norway, South Africa, Sweden, United Kingdom, and the United States. There was also the acting head of the police training in UNAMID and the European Union training adviser represented the African Union.

The seminar resulted in:

1. Determination of one standard training curriculum with course specifications, learning objectives, and assessment criteria;
2. Enhancement of the draft standardized generic training modules for UN Police;
3. Facilitation of the exchange of training methodologies in accordance with adult learning principles.

In March 2008, the donor countries met and ratified the outcomes of the Seminar at the Kofi Annan Centre. The UK agreed to provide an officer to act as 3PDTID Co-ordinator to the Group and administer its daily working in conjunction with UN Police Division. At this meeting, the Group also looked at its constitution and became designated the UNAMID Police Donor Working Group. The UN Police Division would nominate individual police officers from each of the police contributing countries at least 3 months prior to their actual deployment to UNAMID. This allowed for the Police Donor Working Group to discuss and allocate the appropriate training resources where necessary. Included in the process was a requirement for every training center to complete a debrief report of the course which would allow for analysis and evaluation of the system.

The UN Police Division had circulated a Note Verbal to all UN Member States alerting them to the work of the Police Donors Working Group and the potential to obtain assistance in the provision of standardized police peacekeeping PDT for their officers if they were unable to provide such a facility. Deployment to UNAMID steadily grew throughout 2008 until by December 2008; it had reached just over 1,000 individual police officers. Of these officers, 418 had been trained at international peacekeeping training centers and 346 within their own countries, both using the Interim Police PDT curriculum for UNAMID. This indicates that the initiative was evaluated and was assessed as having reached its strategic target, since over 76% of the deployed police officers in UNAMID had received the new standardized police peacekeeping PDT (UNAMID, 2011). By October 2010, the UN Police component in UNAMID had grown to 4,747, with 83% of UN Police officers now having benefited from this standardized training. Additional officers have also received training, but, at this time, are still waiting to be deployed. Once this occurs, this will further increase the percentage of those trained police officers who have been deployed.

Throughout its implementation, the UN Integrated Training Service in liaison with the peacekeeping training centers has been monitoring and evaluating the process through the reports submitted. Within the first year of the initiative's implementation, the emphasis was in ensuring that the police officers deploying to UNAMID have been adequately prepared, and this has been achieved through the willingness of the countries with international police training establishments to adopt and deliver the pilot Interim Police PDT curriculum. Moreover, the pilot Interim Police PDT curriculum for UNAMID had been so successful that it has been further developed in order that it could be adopted as the standard generic police PDT curriculum for all UN police peacekeeping missions and won a Webber Seavey Award for Excellence in Law Enforcement from the International Association of Chiefs of Police in October 2010. Therefore, the number of countries with training establishments capable of delivering the new standardized police peacekeeping PDT for all UN peacekeeping missions will steadily increase.

That process is now being progressed through the use of mobile training teams (MTTs) being deployed from donor countries or the regional peacekeeping training centers to conduct "Train the Trainer" courses. These are specifically designed to provide support for long-term sustainable institutionalized national capacity in individual police contributing countries through direct training assistance and ongoing mentoring.

This capacity building will allow those countries with high numbers of individual police officers deployed to become self-sufficient in their training, and, in time will mean that they themselves will have a sustainable means of providing new standardized police peacekeeping PDT for all their own police officers deployed to peace operations. Furthermore, in due course and over time, the 3PDTID steadily increase the number of police officers trained for peacekeeping overall and, in some cases, allow for ready reserves and/or standby forces to be maintained. There will always remain the need for the international peacekeeping training centers to run courses for those countries that do not have the facilities to run training or supply such small numbers of individual police officers that it would not be economically viable for them to run their own courses.

The UNAMID deployment has now been running for over 2 years and will not reach full deployment until late into 2010. UNAMID alone is likely to be mandated for several more years during which time the 3,772 individual police officers will rotate out every 12 months, add to that an additional 7,877 in 16 other missions, all creating a continuing demand for police officers well-prepared for the challenges of police peacekeeping by having successfully completed the new standardized police peacekeeping PDT for all UN peacekeeping missions which began with the UN Pilot Police PDT initiative for UNAMID (UNAMID, 2011; United Nations, 2010a, 2010b).

Predeployment Training for UN Formed Police Units

The FPU Review and Standards Team held its first meeting in New York, New York, on October 24–26, 2007 and second in Vicenza, Italy, on February 4–6, 2008. The team was co-chaired by the then Police Commissioner of the United Nations Interim Administration in Kosovo, Richard Monk, and Andrew Carpenter, the Chief of Strategic Policy and Development Section, Police Division, Office of Rule of Law and Security Institutions, UN DPO, and was comprised of policing experts from UN headquarters and field missions.

The team members examined the official reports on deaths of the two demonstrators in Kosovo, the operational orders, plans, and reports of all recent operations and shared concerns experienced first-hand related the deployment of FPUs – at that time – in seven UN peacekeeping missions (MINUSTAH-Haiti, MONUC-Democratic Republic of Congo, ONUCI-Côte d'Ivoire, UNAMID-Darfur, UNMIK-Kosovo, UNMIL-Liberia, and UNMIT-Timor Leste). The team found that there are wide variations and omissions in the procedures and practices pertaining to the deployment and use of FPUs.

The team concluded that there was no doubt that FPUs play an important role in international peacekeeping, since they are an important, robust policing capacity and provide some much-needed security support to both UN missions and the host-state police and other law enforcement agencies. In many instances, FPUs had been effective despite serious operational deficits, such as during the early 2008 evacuation of UN staff in Kinshasa, Democratic Republic of Congo.

However, it was clear that UN police components often struggled with unclear mandates and widely diverging views on what tasks the FPUs should or could take on. Within the FPUs themselves, this was coupled with a limited knowledge of the mission mandate, policing skills, and experience, as well as of UN guidelines and regulations.

The team determined the questions were: How to address immediately these shortfalls in order to secure the security framework of each of the seven missions with FPU? How to do this in such a manner that each FPU had every opportunity of living up to their potential? How to avoid triggering widespread panic and further insecurity while openly and transparently addressing a very real, but extremely sensitive security risk to UN peacekeeping operations worldwide?

Considering the absence of any standardized UN PDT and the ever-increasing demand for FPUs, the next step in the FPU Review would move away from the table-top review of collected materials and first-hand experiences and look to provide a comprehensive assessment of the then deployed FPUs in order to determine their actual operational proficiency, any gaps, and needs. The concept of Proficiency Testing and Training Teams (PT3s) was developed in response to these needs, and the UN Police Division began work with the UN Member States to identify appropriately qualified, skilled, and experienced personnel to administer the in-depth verification of operational capacity in all field missions with FPUs.

In mid-September 2008, after a selection process and 2 weeks of specially designed 2-week training course, delivered by the UN Police Division at the Centre of Excellence for Stability Police Units (CoESPU) in Vicenza, Italy, seven teams comprised of three experts each (21 experts total) were deployed in DPKO's field missions for 3 months for the purpose of conducting assessments. The assessment process involved testing and evaluating FPUs on a broad spectrum of categories: crowd control and public order management, firearms proficiency, command and control, logistics and equipment; as well as an overall operational capacity assessment.

The PT3s upon completion of their assignment returned to Italy for debriefing. Their findings and recommendations were delivered to Police Division representatives from 13 to 17 December 2008 and subsequently shared with experts in the Doctrine Development Group (DDG) charged with creating the new FPU doctrine. On average, the PT3s found that only 37% of the then deployed FPUs were operationally competent in the conduct of basic policing tasks and the other 63% posed an unacceptable security risk. The PT3s also confirmed that there was a critical need for standardizing capacities and skills as well as creating doctrine for all FPUs.

During February 2009, this frank and thorough analysis of the PT3 findings was presented "without fear or favor" to representatives of all 192 UN Member States, Heads of UN Police Components, and the UN Under-Secretary-General for Peacekeeping and his Senior Management Team identifying the most significant risks and immediate needs with regard to FPUs. This analysis of the cross-cutting thematic issues provided a comprehensive account of all the challenges facing the UN DPO and its FPUs.

Naturally, while not all of the issues identified by the PT3s were a concern for all units, the overall picture was extremely grim and called for short-, medium-, and long-term responses. After considering what alternative solutions were both available and practicable, an immediate action was presented to and approved by the UN Under-Secretary-General for Peacekeeping: the UN Police Division would create MTTs to provide remedial in-mission skills enhancement training to already deployed FPUs in the short- and medium-term and a standardized UN FPU PDT Curriculum would be developed as a sustainable long-term solution.

Thus, a pilot MTT was formed from former PT3 personnel who underwent a specially designed 3-week training course delivered by the UN Police Division in Fort Indiantown Gap, USA, and in a record-breaking time on 14 March 2009 deployed to UNMIL-Liberia, since this was judged to be the mission most at risk.

Another five MTTs were created from a pool of firearms trainers and public management instructors provided by the UN Member States and, after a specially designed 6-week training course, informed by the ongoing lessons of the pilot MTT and delivered by the UN Police Division at the All-Russia Advanced Police Peacekeeping Training Centre in Domodedovo, Russian Federation, the 32 MTT personnel (representing 29 countries) were deployed in July 2009 for 5 months to the remaining missions with FPUs (MINUSTAH-Haiti, MONUC-Democratic Republic of Congo, ONUCI-Côte d'Ivoire, UNAMID-Darfur and UNMIT-Timor Leste). All six MTT leaders were fully debriefed in person after they had completed their assignments and, while the MTTs were deployed as a temporary remedial measure to address immediate areas of underperformance, each of the teams was requested by their respective UN Head of Police Component to extend their deployment in order to continue delivering needed skills enhancement training.

The long-term approach of a standardized UN FPU PDT curriculum was intimately tied to the newly developed UN Policy on FPUs, since this would provide a solid and officially recognized basis for refining training modules and the criteria for unit readiness standards to determine whether the required learning outcomes of the curriculum had been realized. Both the policy and the FPU PDT curriculum (with its integral unit readiness standards) were critical for the UN to be able to fulfill its duty of care and ensure that every FPU deployed in the context of UN peacekeeping operations is as safe and effective as possible. The 3-month deployment of the very "hands on" PT3 verifiers and their extensive catalogue of digital photos produced an incontrovertible, if not unassailable, account of the operational status of FPUs deployed in the UN peacekeeping operations. The deployment of the MTTs resulted in the operational capacity of all currently deployed FPUs being raised from an average of 30% to over 74.5% in the six UN peacekeeping missions with FPUs.

The new UN FPU Policy was declared on 1 March 2010 and provides clear, unambiguous guidance on what a FPU is and the nature of tasks it is designed specifically to address. FPUs are now defined as follows:

1. FPUs are defined as cohesive mobile police units, providing support to UN operations and ensuring the safety and security of UN personnel and missions, primarily in public order management;
2. As a coherent part of the UN police component, FPUs work in support of the establishment and maintenance of safe, democratic, and human rights abiding communities by delivering professional, responsive, and more robust policing in accordance with the mandate; and
3. FPUs consist of a minimum operational capacity and command and logistics elements to make up an approximate total strength of 140 police officers.

The standardized UN FPU PDT Curriculum provides an "industry-standard" for UN Member States to contributing not only fully functional and operationally capable FPUs, but ones which will have a common operational basis and tactical philosophy which are fully in compliance with UN norms and standards of human rights and criminal justice.

The methodology designed and implemented by the UN Police Division for the FPU Review has not only been widely recognized by the UN Member States and their police and other law enforcement agencies, as well as by regional and professional organizations as highly innovative, dynamic, medium cost–high yield, and ultimately successful in achieving its objectives within the time and resources available to it, but has also been adopted by the UN Under-Secretary-General for Peacekeeping as part of his "New Horizons" vision for peacekeeping in the twenty first century and is the basis for the UN DPO' newly unveiled "Capability-Driven Approach" – a framework that links baseline operational standards for each core element of a UN peacekeeping operation with the training, equipment, support, and incentive structures it requires to be fully operationally capable (Le Roy, 2009).

Moreover, the standardized UN FPU PDT curriculum created by the UN Police Division will be shared with all 192 UN Member States, the African Union, the European Union, as well as other regional or professional organizations. In addition to being strongly endorsed at the Third DDG Meeting in Bangladesh, a number of countries and organizations have already incorporated this curriculum in their own training regimes based on the consultative draft that was shared with them, and a jointly conducted Train-the-Trainer course is being planned by the UN with the African Union to work hand-in-hand with FPU contributing countries to ensure they have the much needed and appropriately trained FPU instructors capable of building sustainable national and regional capacity in order to produce fully operational FPUs for use in international police peacekeeping operations.

Conclusion

These police predeployment courses seek to operationalize the good practice identified during the first half-century of UN Police peacekeeping operations and as such ensure that these hard-won lessons are not only learned but actually applied. Naturally, there is more work to be done in the field of international police peacekeeping training, particularly with regard to specialized courses, given that a UN Police Commissioner has a very different mix of concerns and responsibilities from his/her domestic counterparts, a UN Police Planner is likely dealing with a much wider field of activities in much less permissive settings than a police officer planning for a local event such as a major football match or pop concert or even a cross-border operation involving police and other law enforcement agencies from more than one country.

In order to address these and other specialized training needs, the UN Police Division has further built upon the process used to develop the PDT courses and has established the concept of "Curriculum Development Groups" (CDGs), whereby, all UN Member States – as well as other regional organizations and professional bodies – are invited to nominate an expert and/or their existing training materials to contribute to the joint development of a specialized course designed especially to meet the requirements of the UN Police.

The first such CDG began its work on creating a standardized course for UN Police on "Investigating and Preventing Sexual and Gender-based Violence" in the margins of the International Association of Women Police (IAWP) conference in Minneapolis in September 2010. The course will be completed at the CDG's second workshop in Entebbe, Uganda, in December 2010 and a series of five regional train-the-trainer sessions will be conducted during the course of 2011 to ensure the course's dissemination and implementation. Additional thematic CDGs will be launched by the UN Police Division in due course.

Furthermore, the UN Police Division has begun work on the development of an overarching strategic doctrinal framework for international police peacekeeping that will lead to development of standardized technical guidance in all areas of UN Police peacekeeping which will allow personnel coming from a domestic police service to be appropriately prepared to deal with the differences they will encounter when working in the internationally conflict-related environments.

These moves are designed to ensure effective mandate implementation by assuring that UN Police peacekeepers are well prepared, equipped, and enabled to deliver against reasonable, but standardized performance expectations, but this can only be achieved with the assistance of the policing agencies and their national authorities of 192 UN Member States. However, with their continued support, the UN Police will be able to deliver to societies recovering from conflict a more professional service with a lasting impact.

References

Ennals, D. (1959). *A United Nations police force?* London: Fabian International Bureau.

Le Roy, A. (2009). *Remarks of the Under-Secretary General for Peacekeeping Operations, To the Special Committee on Peacekeeping Operations*, 23 February.

UNAMID. (2011). *UNAMID Facts*. Retrieved April 20, 2011, from http://www.un.org/en/peace-keeping/missions/unamid/facts.shtml.

United Nations. (2005). *United Nations Police Handbook: Building Institutional Police capacity in Post-Conflict Environments*. New York: Department of Peacekeeping Operations.

United Nations. (2006). *Report of the UN Office of Internal Oversight Services: Effectiveness of Peacekeeping Training in Peacekeeping Operations (OUSG-06-751)*. New York: United Nations Secretariat.

United Nations. (2008). *Report on the Strategic Peacekeeping Training Needs Assessment. Integrated Training Service Policy, Evaluation and Training Division*. New York: Department of Peacekeeping Operations.

United Nations. (2009). *Core Business of UN Police and its Key Partners. UN Peacekeeping PDT Standards, Specialized Training Material for Police* (1st ed.). New York: Department of Peacekeeping Operations.

United Nations. (2010a). *General Assembly Resolution 1935*.

United Nations. (2010b). Report on the Progress of Training in Peacekeeping. *Report of the Secretary General*. New York.

Chapter 13
New Enforcement Challenges: Modern Piracy Faces Unprepared Local Law Enforcement

M.R. Haberfeld and Agostino von Hassell

Introduction

September 11th 2001 marked the beginning of a new era for police forces around the United States and the world based on the pressures, from local governments and the public, to provide an adequate response to the potential future attacks. While some police forces around the world had a long history of combating terrorism on a local level, like the Turkish National Police, Israel National Police or the Northern Ireland Police Services, local American policing, and most of its democratic counterparts were overwhelmingly unprepared and lacked the tools to address the new problem that appeared to be their new responsibility.

Since 2009, the United States started to wake up to the abundant threat to ships from small boats and the possibility of attacks coming from the sea and perpetrated on vessels and is considering appropriate counter-measures. The United States Navy and Marine Corps first dealt with such terrorist threats during the 1987–1988 tank war in the Persian Gulf where Operation Praying Mantis helped eliminate for some time the threat from small boast. These were state-sponsored terrorists coming from Iran.

How can United States and countries with an extended coast line and a national dependence on shipping counter-act such a threat? Terrorist can utilize the low cost method of attacking ships – move to steam slowly – in the congested waters, attack cruise ships and other commercial vessels, take hostages, use the vessels to create an environmental disaster or even a nuclear one.

M.R. Haberfeld (✉)
John Jay College of Criminal Justice, New York, NY, USA
e-mail: makih@sprynet.com

A. von Hassell
The Repton Group LLC, New York, NY, USA
e-mail: avonhassell@thereptongroup.com

M.R. Haberfeld et al. (eds.), *Police Organization and Training: Innovations in Research and Practice*, DOI 10.1007/978-1-4614-0745-4_13,
© Springer Science+Business Media, LLC 2012

This chapter discusses the roots and nature of the threat and recommends structural counter-measures, directly relevant for the local police forces who serve in cities with access to cost lines or other bodies of water and as such represent one of the first responding parties to any terrorist threat. Maritime threat, starts on land, evolves conceptually and then translates into action. Sometimes, the threat evolves miles away from the country against which it is perpetrated, sometimes it is home-grown. The focus of predictive policing is to identify the homegrown threat and prevent it from escalating, and at the same time detecting the foreign attempts that can and will evolve into action on land prior to proceeding into the waters. Creating new operational units to counter the evolving threat is the next step in countering maritime terrorism, one that no local police force can afford not to create.

Historical and Current Context of the Threat

To understand the need for a structural change and the organizational place of a new maritime counter terrorist unit within the police bureaucracy one need to understand the historical roots of the problem and the steps taken in the past to successfully eradicate this ancient threat. Since the terrorist attacks on September 11th, 2001, there have been drastic changes in the world of policing and law enforcement. Increased advancements in security procedures, strengthened investigation capabilities, as well as the development or expansion of counter-terrorism task forces, are just a few of the various different amendments that have emerged in order to fight terrorism. Constant efforts are being made in order to determine the most effective ways for preventing and deterring violent terrorist acts, including policing methods. The Lum, Kennedy, and Sherley (2006) study on the effectiveness of counter-terrorism strategies found that there was almost a complete absence of high quality scientific evaluation evidence on counter-terrorism strategies. Furthermore, across all the interventions studied, there was no consistent indication of positive effects of counter terrorism policy.

In so much as the agencies studied recognized the threat of terrorism as a real one, in the daily endeavors to create an effective set of counter –measures the one specific form of terrorism or a terrorist tactic, *maritime terrorism*, appears to be almost completely ignored by the overwhelming majority of law enforcement agencies. However, not only this threat is very real, as the following lines remind us, it is also a very old terrorist tactic, one we should be much better prepared to counter in the year 2011.

> Extraordinary commands would have to be created if Rome was to recover control of the sea from pirates. It was Pompey who benefitted most from the restoration of tribunician initiative. After his consulship, he waited in Rome while rival nobles undermined the position of Lucius Licinius Lucullus, who was campaigning against Mithradates in Anatolia, and made halfhearted attempts to deal with the pirates. Finally, in 67, the tribune Aulus Gabinius forced a bill through the popular assembly empowering Pompey to settle the pirate problem.[1]

---

[1] Encyclopedia Britannica: Pompey the Great (2009).

In the autumn of 68 BC, the world's infamous military power was subjected to a devastating attack by maritime terrorists. Ostia, a Roman port, was attacked, a consular war fleet was destroyed, and two prominent senators were kidnapped. The perpetrators of this daring attack were loosely organized pirates, the only ones who would dare to attack the Roman Empire at its time of glory.[2]

The events depicted above took place in the seventh century BC, today however, one needs to posit the question -is the threat posed by modern piracy real? Do we need to discuss it within the context of a real, and very much ignored terrorist threat or shall we continue to pretend that the days and times of maritime terrorism are long gone and buried together with the ruins of the ancient empires?

As history reminds us, the problem of piracy was a very real issue to tackle for the powerful Roman Empire. Pompey, one of its notorious generals, was charged with finding an adequate solution as early as 67 BC. United States (U.S.) is frequently compared to the Roman Empire – as a result of its military, political, social, and economic influence on the world – recent years' events, including Somali pirates hijacking a U.S. vessel, might have just have been the proverbial straw that broke the camel's back. The time has come to empower the U.S. military and its law enforcement, the contemporaries of the Roman popular assembly, to *respond to this growing threat. Yet, the question remains*: *Is piracy a serious and growing threat*, or an iconization of a number of incidents that, in the grand scheme of other threats, are just a peripheral menace to the world's security? As some contemporary authors posit, the latter might be the case and, as such, the reaction of the injured parties should not be exaggerated or taken out of proportion.

Piracy, in popular imagination, had been relegated to the world of fables and history, the cinema, and children's stories. Yet piracy is alive and well and now, in some regions, has connections to Islamic fundamentalism and its related terrorist tactics. Nowadays, pirates have recaptured the headlines, emerging from dusty pages of history into the crystallizing sharpness of CNN's "Breaking News" and the ledgers of maritime insurance companies. The English word *pirate* is an ancient term, whose origin can be found in the dawn of human history and navigation of the seas. The term is as common as the old saying, much quoted by German Grand-Admiral Alfred von Tirpitz: *"Navigare necessere est*; *vivere non est"* (Navigation is essential, life not so).

The original term is derived from the Latin term *pirata*, which developed from the Greek πειρατής (*peirates*) "brigand," and ultimately from πεῖρα (*peira*) "attempt, experience," implicitly "to find luck on the sea." The word is also cognate to *peril*. In the seventeenth and eighteenth centuries, sources often rendered the word as "pyrate." However, the term does not exclusively relate to robbery committed at sea, as other similar origins have a broader definition.[3]

Pirates have captured popular imagination and are seen as cult figures, such as Bonnie and Clyde – infamous robbers from the Great Depression period of the

---

[2] Harris (2006).

[3] http://www.etymonline.com/index.php?term=pirate.

United States. The popular glorification of groups of criminals, such as pirates, has led to children's games involving pirates and numerous movies, such as Disney's *Pirates of the Caribbean*, which has spawned two sequels to date. There is glorification of these bands of criminals long thought to be extinct even within major U.S. sports franchises. For example, Pittsburgh, PA has a professional baseball team named the Pirates; Tampa Bay, FL has a professional football team named the Buccaneers; and many high school and college sports teams use similar names that glorify this type of activity.[4]

Piracy, as a criminal enterprise, has occurred through the ages ever since the first ships were launched upon the waves. From the earliest days of maritime trade, criminals preyed on merchant shipping. Any commodity of value, either to the pirates or to those who would pay for their criminal ventures, was stolen or destroyed. Homer wrote about pirates; luminaries such as Julius Caesar were kidnapped by pirates. There is nothing truly new. Piracy is a fancy word for robbery – whether it be software "piracy" as practiced all over the world or capturing a ship and people for gain and ransom.

> The man who had seduced her asked her who she was and where she came from, and on this she told him her father's name. 'I come from Sidon,' said she, 'and am daughter to Arybas, a man rolling in wealth. One day as I was coming into the town from the country some Taphian pirates seized me and took me here over the sea, where they sold me to the man who owns this house, and he gave them their price for me.'[5]

Piracy is just one tool, within the arsenal of terrorist tactics, and the government-sponsored maritime terrorism was equally common throughout the ages. Drake – on behalf of the Virgin Queen Elizabeth – was instructed to use piracy to defeat the Spanish Empire. In its early years, the United States engaged in piracy against the superior naval forces of the United Kingdom. Despite the desire of the injured parties to pursue, throughout history, pirates escaped their hunters by seeking sanctuary in havens where they could ply their booty and relax without fear of prosecution. Nowadays, very much like the days past, such feral cities offer a similar lifeline to the contemporary pirates and this is precisely where law enforcement needs to develop an adequate response, on a local but also international levels.

Interestingly enough, some of the best-known pirate havens in existence during the Golden Age of Piracy (1690–1730), such as the Caribbean, have become "hot spots" for the today's maritime terrorists. What made these havens so appealing to pirates back then and equally appealing over 300 years later? Possibly the location, possibly the proximity of unstable governmental structure on land, or possibly the local population that was or may still be sympathetic to some of the causes espoused by these "freedom fighters."

Pirate activities virtually ceased in the nineteenth and twentieth centuries for a number of reasons:

---

[4] The official site of the Pittsburgh Pirates: http://pittsburgh.pirates.mlb.com/index.jsp?c_id=pit. The official website of the Tampa Bay Buccaneers: http://www.buccaneers.com/splashFL.aspx.

[5] http://homer.classicauthors.net/odyssey/odyssey15.html.

- The increase in size of merchant vessels; thus they became harder to attack
- Naval patrolling of most major waterways: major European naval powers, eager to protect colonies rich with natural resources, patrolled the seas
- Regular, mostly colonial, administration of most islands and land areas in the world
- General international recognition of piracy as an international offense[6]

However, recent years have brought about a resurgence in maritime terrorism, although some experts still express a dose of skepticism regarding the existence of a real threat. Prior to reaching any conclusion with regard to the scope, intensity, or possible duration of this new/old phenomenon one needs to understand the magnitude of the operational, legal, and policy challenges involved in responding to the semi-romanticized notion of piracy. Since 2001 and in particular in the years 2009–2011 maritime piracy has increased on a massive level and is now considered one of the major issues in the safety of global commerce and shipping.

Operational Hurdles

In order to respond with any degree of effectiveness to a threat posed on the high seas, the responding actor needs to be prepared for such a response. What seems to be evolving from the accounts of the incidents covered by various media outlets is a picture of a semi-coordinated, multinational effort that is accompanied by the individual response of a given country or a private owner of a specific vessel.

As of May 17, 2011 and for the first 4 month of 2011 the International Marine Time Bureau released these grim data:

Worldwide Incidents:

Total Attacks Worldwide: 173
Total Hijackings Worldwide: 23

Incidents Reported for Somalia:

Total Incidents: 117
Total Hijackings: 20
Total Hostages: 338
Total Killed: 7

Current vessels held by Somali pirates:

Vessels: 26
Hostages: 518 (http://www.icc-ccs.org/home/imb).

The above numbers of incidents, their scope and intensity, exemplify the operational hurdles that nations, governments, and private owners faced and will face in the

---

[6] Vallar: *Pirates and Privateers: The History of Maritime Piracy.* http://www.cindyvallar.com/pirates.html.

future with regard to adequate response to the maritime threats that, despite some academic dispute, pose a real problem to both private and public interests. Among the countries affected by these terrorist attacks are India, Iran, Pakistan, Oman, UAE, Greece, South Korea, China, Tanzania, Russia, Holland and many more. These countries were either directly involved, victimized or confronted by various acts of maritime terrorism. Undoubtedly, if these countries were subject to the same volume of terrorist attacks executed on land using other more conventional tactics, like hostage taking, bomb planting or suicide attacks, the world would have witnessed an unprecedented surge in legal, structural/administrative and operational counter response on the part of various law enforcement and criminal justice agencies. However, this is not the case with regard to a coordinated response to the maritime terrorism and the answer might be partially related to some of the following operational questions that need to be addressed but are still not:

1. What is the "right" response to a modern piracy phenomenon?
2. Is there the "right" response to a phenomenon of modern piracy?
3. Is there a difference between an effective response to an individual, stand-alone incident of piracy vs. an incident of maritime terrorism that has ties to structured terrorist groups on land?
4. Who should be charged with the decision-making process once the incident is in progress?
5. Is there a need to create a new operational unit within the current local and/or federal law enforcement structure?
6. Is there room for more involvement on an international law enforcement cooperation level?

From the operational hurdles to legal impediments, we might know what to do, but are we allowed from the legal standpoint to engage in such responses? Beyond the universally applicable answers to the aforementioned questions there is a need to look closer at each country's legal system to understand how any stand alone law enforcement or joint, military-law enforcement response, can be actually executed.

The Legal Impediments

Although our legal systems go back as far as our maritime security problems, it is not clear that we were ever in a position to enact all the laws necessary to counter the maritime terrorism. Similar to the case of 9/11, once an attack of a certain magnitude takes place, governments of many countries mobilize their legal systems to provide for an adequate response. In this speedy attempt to tackle a problem long in existence, governments and nations tend to overreact and, as Kraska (2009) refers to the problem, they tend to "miss the boat."

According to Kraska (2009) since 1994 the United States has considered joining the convention that outlines the legal rights and duties of the costal states and nations. Seventeen years later, we are still "considering." How many more incidents like the crisis with the *Maersk Alabama* at the Somali coastline in 2009 do we need to encounter before we stop considering and just join?

Right now from a legal standpoint, we are experiencing a mixed reaction to international treaties as well as our own inability to decide which laws would apply and which are relevant for the operational response to and prosecution of maritime attacks. Another issue is the public perception of governmental responses to the romanticized notion of piracy. Abdi Wali Abdulqadir Muse, the pirate captured subsequent to the hijacking of the *Maersk Alabama*, has been described as a misguided juvenile whose only crime, according to by civil rights lawyer Ron Kuby, was to enter the vessel "under a flag of truce to negotiate."[7]

Do we need an event equivalent to 9/11 and the following enactment of the Uniting and Strengthening America by Providing Appropriate Tools Required to Intercept and Obstruct Terrorism (USA PATRIOT) Act to determine what is the proper legal response and one that will, at minimum, deter and minimize the current increase in this particular form of terrorist tactic?[8] Law enforcement forces need to be empowered to think proactively about the real possibilities of terrorist attacks perpetrated by maritime terrorist and/or taking place on the territorial waters that surround their areas of jurisdictions. A clear legal definition that will enable operational deployment must be enacted and distributed to the agencies who appear to have the relevant geographic jurisdiction as first responders. For example, one critical target, an island of Manhattan, part of the city if New York, cannot afford not to be prepared, from the legal standpoint, for a maritime attack that will take place on one of the cruise ships that frequent its numerous piers. These elegant vessels are registered by foreign nations and as such constitute a legal hurdle in terms of possible access by the local law enforcement. Undoubtedly, many cities around the world face the same obstacles, cruise ships and other vessels, clearly visible to law enforcement personnel yet inaccessible from the operational standpoint, in the event of a terrorist attack due to their foreign registry status.

Finally, in addition to the operational and legal hurdles there are, first and foremost, the policy issues that, almost universally, impede any tactical response on the local law enforcement level.

The Policy Challenges

As one of the authors of this chapter experienced first hand over years of dealing with maritime security challenges, operationally sound practices that are legally justified do not always make for the acceptable policy recommendations. Historically, certain nations, like Japan for example, refuse to arm their crew members on board

---

[7] Guardian (2009).

[8] US DOJ: US PATRIOT Act. http://www.usdoj.gov/archive/ll/what_is_the_patriot_act.pdf; http://www.usdoj.gov/archive/ll/docs/text-of-paa.pdf.

their vessels. In this respect, despite the convincing and effective operational response by the Israeli security forces on the Italian cruise liner to the recent Somali attack, neither the Japanese government, nor the major Japanese shipping lines, would endorse contracting with the Israeli private security forces to provide for an adequate response to the threat.

Policies, especially those of governments, can be tricky and serve as the major impediment to operational effectiveness. Hacker (1977) provided a typology of terrorists and divided them into three categories: crusaders, criminals, and crazies.[9] The operational response to the different typologies should be very different. However, this operational wisdom has not translated to either legal or policy recommendations, as politics is often a major obstacle to effective operational response. We know, for over 30 years now, that different tactical responses would work better than others, depending on the motivational factors of the terrorist involved in the attacks, yet, the legal systems lag behind in affording the law enforcement tactical response with the lawful and authorized support.

In the similar venue, private industries are measuring their investments in maritime security in dollar signs that have to do with the purely mathematical equation of juxtaposing risk vs. liability. As Greenberg, Chalk, Willis, Khilko, and Ortiz (2006) clearly identify, it is all about risk and liability when policy issues are concerned.

This chapter offers some perspectives on an old problem that suddenly resurfaced as a phenomenon to be dealt with in an ad-hoc manner, despite its roots in history. What appears to be a very indicative thread of human behavior is our ability for self-deception and insistence that there is not much to be learned from the distant past, as our orientation is primarily rooted in a futuristic and almost hedonistic approach to life.

The measures passed by the Roman Senate in 67 BC have been compared by some as akin to the massive efforts to protect the United States against terrorism after September 11. It is worth mentioning that the entire grain supply to Rome – all carried by ship – was endangered by pirates and the sentiments of the public, after September 11, mirrored the Roman Empire's perception – the world was endangered and a drastic solution and response must follow. The Roman Republic was truly endangered, however, in the year 2011 there is a tendency to react swiftly to an evolving problem but once it is contained, for the moment, in an ad-hoc manner, the more thought through response appears to be very amorphous.

A rapid reaction, NOW, against piracy was called for, in 2009, but it is neither easy nor simple. Very much like the Roman Senate in seventh century BC, the U.S. Senate is reviewing this issue. In May of 2009, Democratic Senator Carl Levin[10] expressed his views regarding the recent surge in piracy off the coast of Somalia and in the Gulf of Aden, referring to the growing problem of piracy as moving away from the historical and entertainment arenas and onto the front pages on the world's newspapers. He recognized that although the naval forces of the world do have a

---

[9] Hacker (1977).
[10] Levin (2009).

critical role to play in deterring and combating pirates, the problem is more complex and requires a holistic approach combining military efforts with deterrence, collaboration with allies, and ongoing diplomatic outreach, very much along the lines of response in other volatile areas of conflict, like Afghanistan, for example.[11] What Levin failed to recognize was the need for a holistic approach that must include the local law enforcement forces that will be the first responders at the time the maritime terror strikes not just at the Gulf of Eden or Mumbai but amidst the seemingly peaceful and totally unsuspecting atmosphere of the megapolis of our times like the cities of Manhattan, London, Stockholm, Paris or Amsterdam.

Kraska and Wilson (2009) outlined and summarized some of the ideas that can be of value, with proper customization, for each and every country that faces the current or potential maritime terrorist threat. The two identify the operational and legal hurdles that need to be analyzed in order to determine the most viable solution.

Operational Hurdles

1. Combined Maritime Forces (CMF) in Bahrain created Combined Task Force 151, a multinational counter-piracy naval force of more than 20 nations. Previously, coalition efforts against piracy included ships and aircraft from CTF-150, which was established at the outset of Operation Enduring Freedom to conduct Maritime Security Operations (MSO) in the Gulf of Aden, the Gulf of Oman, the Arabian Sea, the Red Sea, and the Indian Ocean. However, their geographic presence does not provide an adequate local answer to a problem that might evolve, at any given moment, in Europe or North America or any other distant country.
2. Merchant ships taking additional steps by avoiding the problematic areas all together and taking a longer and more costly trip instead. Many ship owners decided to avoid Aden and would send ships around the Horn of Africa, adding 11–12 days of sailing time. However as piracy is emerging off the cost of western Africa (Nigeria, Sierra Leone, Angola) this may defeat this operational change.
3. Some vessels increase the passive and nonlethal security measures, like ringing lifelines with concertina wires, fire hoses to repel boarder, bright lights, or the Long-Range Acoustic Device, but all are limited in their deterrent value.
4. Piracy is a battle not restricted to the high seas. "Pirates don't live at sea. They live ashore. They move their money ashore. You can't have a discussion about eradicating piracy without having a discussion about the shore dimension."[12]

Although Kraska and Wilson identify the concepts as they relate to the military/navy response, the authors of this chapter posit that a careful examination of each concept offers a possible customized solution for a local law enforcement force.

---

[11] http://www.isria.info/en/5_May_2009_118.html.

[12] Washington Post, 2009, May 4. Fight against pirates also needed ashore. Statement by Chief of Naval Operations Admiral Gary Roughead; Shelal-Esa (2009).

Such an examination would render the following recommendations for the law enforcement use:

1. Creation of a new operational/tactical Joint Maritime Terrorist Task Force – JMTTF – composed of law enforcement agencies subject to the maritime threat due to their geographic locations, in cooperation and consultation with the military and the navy, to be not just restricted to the resources of one country but rather be composed of a number of member nations.
2. JMTTF in consultation with the proper maritime authorities local law enforcement authorities should advise merchant and cruise ships to change their routes on a regular basis, and keep the routes rotating in a way that will make planning a maritime attack much more difficult.
3. JMTTF in consultation with the proper maritime authorities and local law enforcement authorities should advise merchant and cruise ships to increase their security measures, and make them aligned and supplementary to the capabilities of the local law enforcement, in any given jurisdiction.
4. JMTTF in consultation with the appropriate law enforcement units, on a local, federal and international level should monitor maritime terrorists ties and their support networks ashore.

Kraska and Wilson address the global legal hurdles of the response that need to be customized by the local law enforcement, since no operational response is possible without the proper legal framework that enables its valid execution. Such hurdles need to be addressed and answered by the federal and local legislation within the framework of international cooperation. Not much has been done, so far, to address the following issues:

1. What to do with the caught criminals or the "persons under control" (PUC)?
2. What should be done with the victims?
3. What should be done with the injured?
4. Who will prosecute the pirates?

If the PUC, the victims, the injured, and the pirates, are all subjects of foreign countries, a very realistic scenario that can evolve in the event of a cruise ship hijacking by any maritime terrorist group, then clearly defined answers to the above mentioned obstacles need to be provided to the local first responders. Without such a framework the effectiveness of their operational response is severely impeded if not all together impossible.

Evaluating Kraska and Wilson's possible solutions can provide the most valid template for a legal response on a local level. If the lawmakers of the United States or any other country concerned with the implications and consequences of maritime terrorism will adopt the template of "possible solutions" listed below, it will afford its local law enforcement a solid ground to execute its operational capabilities. The italicized portion of each solution is the recommended change and/amendment to the existing policies recommended by the authors of this chapter.

Possible Solutions

1. During armed conflict, merchant vessels may be boarded under the right of visit and searched to determine the neutral character of the goods on board, but that rule of naval warfare does not apply to maritime piracy. *This policy needs to be amended to be applied during maritime attack and extended to local law enforcement forces.*
2. In peacetime, a vessel may be boarded by the naval forces of a state other than the state of registry with the consent of the flag state under articles 92 and 94 of the Law of the Sea Convention. *This policy needs to have an elevated dissemination level and be extended to local law enforcement forces.*
3. The United States recognizes that the master of the vessel also may provide consent to a boarding of his vessel. *This policy needs to have an elevated dissemination level and be extended to local law enforcement forces.*
4. Under article 51 of the UN charter and customary international law, all nations may exercise the right of individual or collective self-defense against a vessel committing a hostile act or demonstrating hostile intent. *This policy needs to have an elevated dissemination level and be extended to local law enforcement forces.*
5. Naval forces also may board merchant vessels under the right of approach and visit pursuant to article 110 of the Law of the Sea if there are reasonable grounds to suspect the vessel is engaged in piracy. *This policy needs to have an elevated dissemination level and be extended to local law enforcement forces.*
6. The extension of port state control measures may be used by the port state authorities to board a vessel that has declared a nearby port. *This policy needs to have an elevated dissemination level and be extended to local law enforcement forces.*
7. The UN Security Council may authorize all states to take action against piracy under chapter VII of the UN charter, providing yet another potential authority for boarding pirate vessels.[13] *This policy needs to have an elevated dissemination level and be extended to local law enforcement forces.*

According to Meade (2009), the European Union (EU) is close to creating a legal framework that will allow naval forces operating in the Gulf of Aden to prosecute the perpetrators of maritime attacks. Some of the potential jurisdictions that have been identified are Kenya, Tanzania, Ethiopia, and Egypt. However, no overarching legal framework has yet been established. This solution would be especially welcomed by the International Chamber of Commerce Shipping told *Lloyd's List*, which is obviously a major stakeholder in these legal developments. In May 2009, Russian President Dmitry Medvedev instructed Prosecutor-General Yuri Chaika to contact his foreign counterparts to devise a mechanism of bringing to justice those responsible for piracy, including creation of an international criminal tribunal.[14]

---

[13] Kraska and Wilson (2009).

[14] http://www.itar-tass.com/eng/level2.html?NewsID=13903497&PageNum=0.

Owens (2009) suggests that one school of thought argues that we should do little or nothing because the cost of stamping out piracy again is too high. The critics of a more concentrated effort to combat maritime terrorism point out that some 21,000 ships transit the Gulf of Aden every year and maintain that 50 successful pirate attacks doesn't really constitute much of a threat, certainly not one worth expending the resources necessary to eliminate it. Finally, piracy in this part of the world does not appear to be a U.S. problem; it might create an annoyance, but it doesn't, for the most part, affect U.S. shipping. Thus focusing on piracy is an example of overreaction to a series of events that should not even be defined as a problem. However, these authors posit that that piracy is a threat to a peaceful, commercial "liberal world order," especially during the economic crisis of the early twenty-first century and the respective law enforcement agencies should pay much attention to the very possible transplant of the maritime terrorism tactics to the shores of United States and other democratic countries around the world.

The capture of 11 Somali pirates by a French naval ship adds yet another layer of considerations to the debate between those who perceive maritime terrorism as a real threat and the ones who prefer to treat it as a mere nuisance.[15]

When the pirates mistake the French naval ship for a commercial vessel the nuisance has the potential for far-reaching consequences with much deeper political ramifications. There is no guarantee that the military response of a naval ship under attack will always end with the given incident, without using it as a precedent for a much more complex action-response. Dunnigan (2009) points to the fact that the Somali pirates are now operating as far 1,500 km from the African coast. Their sophistication extends to the use of the media as a force multiplier when they attempt to portray themselves as patriots who are getting a payback from the foreigners who are illegally exploiting the Somali waters. If this label catches the minds and the hearts of the local populations in the feral cities and the larger audience around the world, we will truly find ourselves in a bind in terms of acceptable and accepted operational and legal responses.

Conclusions

The very cliché notion of freedom fighters vs. terrorists has a real potential of impeding the efforts of many nations in their attempt to curb maritime terrorism. It is almost a compulsory obligation to look at the developments of modern piracy and maritime terrorism in the twenty-first century as a paradigm and extension of the problems that plagued the Roman Empire and learn from their response – especially the combination of the legal and the military that draws some parallels for our times when addressed within the context of a domestic maritime terrorism threat when the function of the ancient military is replaced or supplemented by the local law enforcement.

---

[15] Reuters (2009).

While building upon the criminological theories of crime prevention, the response of the Roman Empire appears to tackle the hurdles identified at the onset of this chapter. The democratic foundation for the nations involved in the response to maritime terrorism problems, the mandates that the legal framework should be the one addressed first, before any tactical and operational response is examined and institutionalized within the local law enforcement structure. The Roman General Pompey should be credited with providing a template for a response in the twenty-first century. His multipronged approach to the maritime problem can and should be replicated today.

In 67 BC, the tribune, A. Gabinus, proposed to pass a law (lex Gabina) that would require the Senate to appoint a commander of consular rank with some extraordinary powers, for 3 years by land and by sea, to suppress the piracy that, at that time, infested every part of the Mediterranean. Pompey managed to take the proper advantage of this law and in merely 3 months had the seas completely cleared from the piracy threat.[16] His second prong must be supplemented, nowadays, with the law enforcement response, as a combine effort between the military, more specifically the various naval services, and the federal and local law enforcement agencies. It is impossible to create an adequate counter-action to a threat coming from the water and evolving on the water by deploying military or law enforcement forces only. It is only this holistic approach that will involve a combination of the two that can provide the needed proactive and reactive response.

As terror is increasingly becoming a global issue dealing with terror also requires global efforts. Efforts shown by individual countries will not be effective unless they receive some global involvement and cooperation from all the countries. Interpol and Europol are leading the way in this approach and have recently entered the picture with calling on all 192 members of the United Nations countries to work with Interpol and Europol to fight criminal networks involved in maritime piracy off the coast of Somalia. Such cooperation between Interpol and Europol in information exchange and analysis of piracy related material has already resulted in the identification of links between a number of cases and individuals based on DNA, fingerprint and telephone analysis. Furthermore, The EU Council has adopted a decision which will see the EU's on-going military mission against maritime piracy off the coast of Somalia use the Interpol's global network and tools to fight the criminal networks behind piracy in the Gulf of Aden. These initial steps however, should provide a baseline for creation of the JMTTFs on a local law enforcement level. In the short term, there is an urgent need to improve close ties with the law enforcement agencies of the countries in question. There needs to be a parallel and mutual familiarity between the concepts of maritime terror and its impact on the world peace. In order to gain the support of the law enforcement personal there must be a common language and understanding of maritime terrorism, which threatens not only the west, but also the future of the entire world. To achieve this goal there is a need to gain the support of the people in countries that harbor maritime terrorists and isolate the terrorist organization at their

---

[16] http://www.uah.edu/society/texts/latin/classical/cicero/promanilai.html.

own homeland. This is particularly important in fighting maritime terror in the long term. There is an urgent need to develop a common language and concepts in terms of who is a maritime terrorist and what is international maritime terrorism phenomenon. This can only be achieved by the creation of a cooperation between the social scientists who research and study this field and practitioners who actually work in the field as military and law enforcement officers and creating the JMTTFs.

Since there is no single cause and explanations for the phenomenon of maritime terrorism, but there is plenty of history and current opportunities, every case and terrorist organization needs special focus of attention from the researchers and practitioners alike, with a starting point rooted in a base-line template, provide in this chapter, that will serve as a springboard for customization, be it the heavily decentralized American law enforcement or any other police force, worldwide, confronted with the much ignored maritime terrorism threat.

Modern Piracy will flourish and affect the economic balance of the world, if local law enforcement agencies will refuse to swiftly reorganize its administrative structures and create a proactive response to this evolving terrorist tactic.

References

Dunnigan, J. (2009). Why the pirates are immune from attack. *Strategypage*, May 5, 2009. Retrieved May 8, 2009, from http://www.strategypage.com/

Encyclopedia Britannica: Pompey the Great. (2009). Retrieved May 1, 2009, from http://www.britannica.com/EBchecked/topic/469463/Pompey-the-Great

Greenberg, M. D., Chalk, H. H., Willis, I., Khilko, & Ortiz, D. S. (2006). *Maritime Terrorism: Risk and Liability. Rand Center for Terrorism Risk Management Policy. RAND Corporation*, Santa Monica, CA. Retrieved May 1, 2009, from http://www.rand.org/pubs/monographs/2006/RAND_MG520.pdf

Guardian, S. (2009). Teenage Somali pirate arrives in US facing trial over Maersk Alabama attack. April 21, 2009. Retrieved May 1, 2009, from http://www.guardian.co.uk/world/2009/apr/22/somali-pirate-trial-maersk-alabama

Hacker, F. J. (1977). *Crusaders, Criminals, Crazies: Terror and Terrorism in our Time*. New York: W. W. Norton & Co

Harris, R. (2006). Pirates of the Mediterranean. *New York Times,* September 30, 2009. Retrieved May 1, 2009, from http://www.nytimes.com/2006/09/30/opinion/30harris.html

Kraska, J., & Wilson, B. (2009). Fighting piracy: International coordination is key to countering modern-day freebooters. *Armed Forces Journal*. 24. Retrieved May 16, 2009, from http://www.armedforcesjournal.com/

Levin, C. (2009). *Opening Statement of Senator Carl Levin, Senate Armed Services Committee Hearing on Ongoing Efforts to Combat Piracy on the High Seas*. May 5, 2009. Retrieved May 16, 2009, from http://levin.senate.gov/newsroom/release.cfm?id=312458

Lum, C., Kennedy, L. W., & Sherley, A. (2006). Are counter-terrorism strategies effective? The results of the Campbell systematic review on counter-terrorism evaluation. *Journal of Experimental Criminology, 2*, 489–516

Meade, R. (2009). EU close to legal framework on piracy prosecutions. *Lloyd's List*, February 27, 2009. May 3, 2009. Retrieved May 16, from http://www.lloydslist.com/ll/news/viewArticle.htm?articleId=20017622826&src=rss

Owens, M. T. (2009). What to Do about Piracy? *Foreign Policy Research Institute*. April 2009. Retrieved May 16, 2009, from http://www.fpri.org

Reuters. (2009). *France captures 11 suspected Somali pirates*. May 3, 2009. Retrieved May 16, 2009, from http://www.reuters.com/article/worldNews/idUSTRE5421QE20090503

Shelal-Esa, A. (2009). Fight against pirates also needed ashore. *Reuters*. May 4, 2009. Retrieved May 16, 2009, from http://www.reuters.com/article/worldNews/idUSN0440838820090504?sp=true

Index

M.R. Haberfeld et al. (eds.), *Police Organization and Training: Innovations in Research and Practice*, DOI 10.1007/978-1-4614-0745-4,
© Springer Science+Business Media, LLC 2012

Printed by Publishers' Graphics LLC
MO20120921-182-086

LUCAN LIBRARY
TEL. 6216422

LUCAN LIBRARY
TEL. 6216422